BURNIN' DAYLIGHT

Burnin' Daylight

Building a Principle-Driven Writing Program

RYAN J. DIPPRE

UTAH STATE UNIVERSITY PRESS
Logan

© 2024 by University Press of Colorado

Published by Utah State University Press
An imprint of University Press of Colorado
1580 North Logan Street, Suite 660
PMB 39883
Denver, Colorado 80203-1942

All rights reserved

 The University Press of Colorado is a proud member of
Association of University Presses.

The University Press of Colorado is a cooperative publishing enterprise supported, in part, by Adams State University, Colorado State University, Fort Lewis College, Metropolitan State University of Denver, University of Alaska Fairbanks, University of Colorado, University of Denver, University of Northern Colorado, University of Wyoming, Utah State University, and Western Colorado University.

ISBN: 978-1-64642-639-3 (hardcover)
ISBN: 978-1-64642-640-9 (paperback)
ISBN: 978-1-64642-641-6 (ebook)
https://doi.org/10.7330/9781646426416

Library of Congress Cataloging-in-Publication Data

Names: Dippre, Ryan J., author.
Title: Burnin' daylight : building a principle-driven writing program / Ryan J. Dippre.
Description: Logan : Utah State University Press, [2024] | Includes bibliographical references and index.
Identifiers: LCCN 2024002491 (print) | LCCN 2024002492 (ebook) | ISBN 9781646426393 (hardcover) | ISBN 9781646426409 (paperback) | ISBN 9781646426416 (ebook)
Subjects: LCSH: Writing centers—Administration. | Writing centers—Research. | English language—Rhetoric—Study and teaching (Higher) | College administrators—Vocational guidance.
Classification: LCC PE1404 .D555 2024 (print) | LCC PE1404 (ebook) | DDC 808.0420711—dc23/eng/20240311
LC record available at https://lccn.loc.gov/2024002491
LC ebook record available at https://lccn.loc.gov/2024002492

Cover photograph by Annie Vo / Unsplash.com

To Bob Barbieri, a long-serving football coach and mentor at Pittston Area High School and Wilkes University

Contents

List of Illustrations ix

Acknowledgments xi

Introduction: Small, Stubborn Facts and Principled Practice 3

Part I: From the Ground Up 27

1. The Lay of the Land 31
2. Identifying Facts and Rendering Accounts 47
3. Articulating Principles, Principled Practices, and Stories of Writers and Writing 62

Part II: The Little Picture 79

4. Developing Strategies and Tactics 83
5. Identifying and Working through Problems 101
6. Overcoming Clashes of Principle 119

Part III: The Long View 135

7. Growing a Program via Grand Strategies 139
8. Purposeful Innovation 154
9. Building Sustainable Structures and Practices 168

   Conclusion: Writing Programs for Human Beings 180

References 189
Index 209
About the Author 211

Illustrations

Figures

0.1. Small, stubborn facts   10
0.2. Map of this text   19
1.0. Part I's role in the work of this text   28
4.0. Part II's role in the work of this text   80
7.0. Part III's role in the work of this text   136
10.1. The work of this text   181

Tables

4.1. Enacting a strategy   92
5.1. A process of resolving problems   115
6.1. Addressing clashes of principle   131
7.1. A process for generating ideas for grand strategies   146
7.2. A process for articulating grand strategies   149
7.3. A progression for recruiting interested parties   151

Acknowledgments

A brief note: the author proceeds for this book will be going to the Bo Tkach Memorial Foundation. Serving Carbon, Lehigh, and Northampton Counties in Pennsylvania, the foundation both raises awareness of and provides resources for mental health issues such as Obsessive Compulsive Disorder. The foundation funds a variety of youth programs and scholarships throughout the year. To learn more, visit botkach.com.

When my first book, *Talk, Tools, and Texts* (WAC Clearinghouse, 2019) came out, my mother pointed out that I just gave a thank you to general groups in my acknowledgments, like "my family," rather than naming names. That was on purpose: I was worried about leaving people out. I was planning to do the same thing for this book. But then my cousin paged through *Talk, Tools, and Texts* and asked, "Is this English?" And I thought, hey, Mom's got a point. So I'm about to get pretty specific.

It is only appropriate that I begin by thanking Rachael Levay, the excellent editor I worked with on this book. She was supportive, thoughtful, and incredibly forgiving as I blew by due dates at a dead sprint. This book is what it is because of her outstanding guidance and support throughout. Thanks, Rachael. And thanks to Laura Furney, Beth Svinarich, Dan Pratt, Darrin Pratt, and Cheryl Carnahan for their efforts to carry this book (and, at times, me) over the finish line.

Burnin' Daylight was something I had been thinking of since I started working as a writing program administrator (WPA). It had many different early iterations, but it really came together thanks to a fellowship I received in spring 2021 from the University of Maine's College of Liberal Arts and Sciences. Thanks to Dean Emily Haddad and English department chair Steve Evans for their support on that fellowship.

I was able to follow up this early work with a sabbatical in fall 2021. If Assistant Director of Composition Mary Plymale Larlee had not been willing to step in as director for that term, this book still wouldn't be finished. But Mary did more than just step in on a sabbatical: her collegiality, brilliance, and considerable administrative and teaching skills helped me figure out the kind of WPA I want to be. Thanks, Mary.

Mary isn't the only one I had the pleasure of working with on WPA matters. Upon arrival at UMaine, I enjoyed the support of then-chair Laura Cowan, the deep experience of Director of Composition Pat Burnes, the assessment and teacher training insights of Dylan Dryer, and the thoughtful ideas of Writing Center Director Paige Mitchell to make a productive and (I hope) smooth transition into the role of director. A long list of capable mentors to first-year teaching assistants also helped me with this work during the years 2015–2023: Ryan Ware, Kayla Ouellette, Charlotte Asmuth, Kelly Hartwell, Peter Lowe, Paul Eaton, Morghen Tidd, Ben Markey, Tori Hood, and Lydia Balestra have been excellent members of what we at UMaine call the "WPA Team," and I deeply appreciate their work these past years. Some of my writing on grounded theory in chapter 2 is tied to collaborative work I did with Kelly Hartwell, August Adent, and Elizabeth Zavodny in 2018. Thanks to all of you for our productive conversations.

Erin Workman, David Stock, and Lesley Bartlett have offered helpful feedback on my work. Zack De Piero reviewed early drafts of my book proposal. Fellow WPA Lauren Bowen has always been willing to commiserate with me when things go sideways (as things do). Several Dartmouth Summer Seminar visits have quietly influenced many parts of this text—thanks to Christiane Donahue for her ongoing work to offer such an excellent program. I also thank Talinn Phillips, my collaborator on all things lifespan. Without such a capable collaborator, I would have thrown my laptop into the sea by now. Or maybe the sun.

Throughout this book, you can see the threads of influence by five people: Linda Adler-Kassner, Charles Bazerman, Jason Duque Raley, Judith Green, and Tim Dewar. They have been a constant influence on my work since graduate school, and that's not going to change, ever, probably. A heartfelt thanks to them and the lasting influence of their mentorship.

Thanks to those I worked with in my early teaching years at Delaware Valley High School for shaping my teaching values. Sue Curtin was a particularly helpful mentor. She's under the mistaken impression that she set me up with my wife. But other than living that lie, she's great. Thanks also to Crystal Wummer, Deanna Zarzecki, Jackie Weston, Bryan Pol, and many others for their collegiality.

This book is dedicated to Coach B., so I need to thank the various coaches I've had and have worked with throughout my time in football, from Delaware Valley High School to Wilkes University: Coach B., Keith Olsommer, Frank Sheptock, Nick Barbieri, Al McElroy, Nick Quaglia, Jim Donnelly, Joe Raniero, Joe Spinetta, Tony Bajor, Keith Klahold, and many others. What I learned working with all of you continues to shape the work I do today, and I hope you can see that in these pages.

The people I've leaned on since before starting graduate school continue to come through: Josh, Jason, Jeff, Kristen, Jessie—I couldn't have done this (or anything leading up to it) without you. A special thanks to Josh and Kristen and their families for their recent support as this project crossed the finish line. A brief vacation with my family and Josh, Sina, and Ava allowed me to scream at the sea and shake the tension of getting this book to reviewers. And attending a Wilkes homecoming game with Josh, Sina, and Ava, as well as Kristen and her family—Ryan, Hannah, and Brooke—helped me stay distracted while I waited for feedback to come in.

So I'll start thanking family by thanking my mother, and not just for the idea about the acknowledgments. Thanks to her and my stepfather, Keith, for their continued support of my work and their willingness to put up with the fact that their grandchild is several hundred miles away from them. Thanks also to my father and my stepmother, Kate, for their visits and support while I undertook this work. I know that academia works in weird ways, and it's probably difficult to understand what progress looks like. Is it a good thing that I'm working on a book for years at a time? You probably weren't sure but were supportive anyway. Thanks to my in-laws, Hal and Paula Baillie, for their continued support of my work. I know we're a long way from Scranton, and the Wilkes-Barre to Bangor flights are not exactly direct, but you've always been supportive. And thanks to my nephew, Graeme, for the entertaining FaceTime calls and positive energy.

My sister, Lauren, has been a steady source of support ever since I was in graduate school, and I appreciate her willingness to listen to my various complaints and celebrate the wins. Her visits, penchant for showering my son with gifts, and helpful insights have made the work I do easier. I also have two brothers, Danny and Quinn. Hi guys. How's it going?

I close with a heartfelt thanks to my wife, Lindsey, and my son, Joe. It's with their continued and unfailing support that I was able to get this work over the finish line. Lindsey, thank you for being willing to let me sit in front of a laptop and mutter to myself. I know it looks like I'm not doing a thing, and I appreciate the faith you have in me that it will, in fact, turn into something eventually. Joe, thank you for not letting me sit at the laptop and mutter to myself for too long. You seem to know when the words on the page (or the words not on the page) are getting me frustrated, and you're always there to ask me to play a game, or sing a song, or have a snack, or otherwise get away from the work for a bit. And it always helps. I love getting to spend every day with both of you, and I love you both so much.

BURNIN' DAYLIGHT

INTRODUCTION

Small, Stubborn Facts and Principled Practice

This book is dedicated to Bob Barbieri—better known to those who played under him as "Coach B."—whom I first met when I arrived at Wilkes University in the summer of 2002. I was an undersized lineman from a school not yet heralded in northeastern Pennsylvania for its football prowess. Coach B., in contrast, had been at Wilkes for about a decade and was something of a legend. A highly successful student-athlete in high school and college and later an even more successful head coach at Pittston Area High School, Coach B. had, in the early 1990s, jumped in as an assistant on a new coaching staff that was attempting to return Wilkes football to its former glory, which it did by claiming a conference crown in 1993.

In 2002, Coach B. was working the offensive line and focusing particularly on guards and centers, the positions I played. Aside from our overlap in positions, though, Coach B. and I couldn't have been further apart. He was an established expert in the area, and I was an underweight freshman at the bottom of the depth chart who had been run over (twice) during "walk-through" drills in the first few practices. (For those not familiar with football: "walk through" implies that no one was running. I got run over anyway.)

The heat was brutal in August 2002, so our double-session practices were also brutal. It was two weeks of nonstop work: meeting, practice, meeting,

https://doi.org/10.7330/9781646426416.c000

practice, meeting, bed. Somewhere in there, I assume that we also ate. It would have been easy for me—the guy on the bottom of the depth chart trying to memorize a playbook, stay awake in film sessions, eat enough to keep my weight up in the heat, and maybe get to know some of the other people on the team—to pack it in and head home, or at least to fall behind on any of the many things we had to do throughout those two weeks.

Thankfully, Coach B. was there. He paid particular attention to folks like me—those trying to find their way through this, trying to make sense of what was going on. He would call our attention to particular parts of plays when the starters were on the field, to help us get a sense of how to do our jobs. He would note, while we were reviewing film of practice, when one of us on scout team did a good job—"gave a good look"—mimicking the opponent for the starters during practice. Since "giving a good look" regularly meant "doing what the opponent would do and being hit for it," it was nice to get the praise, even if we were too exhausted to process it that much.

It's not difficult, looking back on how that season (and later seasons) unfolded, to see how Coach B.'s work in those moments helped all of us—newcomer and veteran alike—understand how we needed each other, how we all had to be responsible to one another, if we were going to be successful as a team. By pointing out and celebrating the necessary work of a scout team player, Coach B. was helping us recognize how each small part contributed to a complex whole. Coach B. was aware not only of who he was talking to but of who was *around* when he was talking to them: the pat on the back to a freshman that was done in sight of a veteran or the chewing out of veteran that was done in sight of a freshman shaped what we all would take for granted about what would and would not make us successful as a team.

Coach B.'s attention to the small details and their social consequences is at the heart of this book and at the core of what I see myself doing as a writing program administrator (WPA). The events, language, and objects people are creating and sharing in all corners of our programs—and the stories that emerge across institutions and regions as those things coalesce into broader narratives—are our ways into articulating and enacting more enduring, sustainable, and principle-driven writing programs over time. I've designed this book to guide WPAs through that work.

Of course, WPA work is wide and varied, and different institutions have different kinds of needs (as do the WPAs in them). Even writing programs that might be broadly similar categorically (say, first-year programs in regional-comprehensive universities) might be dissimilar in a range of other, more specific aspects. Toward that end, I have aimed to articulate, in the next section, my own positionality and the assumptions I have made to create a more widely applicable approach to taking on WPA work and building principle-driven, sustainable writing programs with it. The core assumption I work from, however—that is, the one I think is most widely shared across WPA positions—is that WPA work varies in scale, from creating new course offerings to a single communicative act between a student and a teacher. The varieties of scale WPAs work with can be overwhelming and can easily lead us to lose the forest of our programmatic and career goals for the individual trees of the next problem that needs to be solved, the next email that needs to be answered, or the next phone call that needs to be returned. This text aims to enable WPAs to work through those varieties of scale and create the kinds of principle-driven programs that can be sustained over time.

My Positionality

I am a cisgender, white male WPA of a first-year composition program at a research university in northern New England. At the time of this publication, I am tenured, although the work of this book in the early stages occurred at the end of my pre-tenure period. As a WPA, I have some resources at my disposal: I work with a team of teachers in writing studies to run the program, and I enjoy the support of my department, chair, and dean for the work I and my program do.

I bring up my positionality here to anticipate, for both the reader and myself, the blank spots that emerge when I bring my own experience to bear in designing this text. The experience I have as a WPA at a research university is not the same as that of someone at a small, liberal arts college, a historically Black college or university (HBCU), a regional-comprehensive university, and so on; my awareness of these differences has helped me broaden the discussion throughout this text by linking to WPA work going on at a range of other institutions.

But articulating my own positionality is just part of a multi-pronged approach I use to make this text as accessible as possible for a wide range of WPAs. I also draw on an interactional framework, as articulated in chapter 1, to help WPAs look at issues at a range of levels, from the organization of a meeting or a class to the ongoing assessment of the program. This framework also allows me to further connect my work in this book to the many resources WPAs have developed over the past several decades in both particular program sites (e.g., Jackson 2021) and particular positionalities (e.g., Phelps et al. 2019; Wenger 2014).

In addition to guiding my revisions of this text and shaping my theoretical commitments, articulating my positionality has encouraged me to detail, as much as possible, the assumptions I am making about WPA work and the needs, desires, and motives of the WPAs (and future WPAs) who are reading this book. I begin this work in the following paragraphs. Of course, just as we'll discuss when developing principles at the conclusion of this introduction, what we can *say* about what we are assuming (and valuing) is just the tip of the iceberg: readers will note a good deal many more assumptions than I list here. It is my hope that what I've articulated below will help readers identify, understand, and work with / push against those assumptions they see cropping up.

Assumptions I Am Making in This Text

As I wrote this text, I imagined an audience of people in particular WPA circumstances. Specifically, I have crafted this text for three separate audiences:

- Graduate students in a WPA course, who have "adopted" a writing program as part of that course
- New WPAs in tenure-track or non-tenure-track positions during their first few years at a new institution
- People returning to a WPA role after a considerable absence (perhaps to step into other, unrelated administrative roles).

These people have a range of different circumstances they are working in, but there are a few common elements about those circumstances that I used as building blocks to frame this text.

I'll begin with the obvious, which is that I am assuming a wide range of personnel that people have to work with. Some new WPAs might be the only writing studies person on their campus; others might work as part of a large (and rotating) committee. The graduate students in a WPA course might be adopting a writing program on their own or with fellow graduate students. And some people might have varying kinds of committees they work with and through as they pursue WPA work, in which case they would be doing fewer of these things individually and more of them as part of (or with) some kind of team. I make some assumptions about who people are working with—that there are chairs and deans to report to, for instance—but overall I aim for a flexible document, something that can be used by a solo WPA or a large administrative team.

Second, these WPAs are in positions of considerable *responsibility* but not that much actual *authority*. They might be in charge of staffing, say, a first-year writing course each semester, but they are not able to hire particular faculty; they have to work with those approved (in part or in full) by others. To get things done, these people have to build alliances on campus, make persuasive arguments, and so on. This text imagines ways for people to make decisions about how to build arguments, alliances, and the like without necessarily having the power to demand certain kinds of changes to teaching or the program.

Third, the people I'm imagining for this text are strapped for resources, to a greater or lesser extent. The streets of the many institutions we work in are hardly paved with gold; we have to make do without some things, drive hard bargains to get others, and otherwise make a lot with a little, somehow. One of the most important, and most limited, resources for these people is *time*. They lack time to get things done, although the time they have (and lack) varies with the academic calendar. Readers will note, throughout this text but particularly in part I, a range of options for readers: people can (if they have the time reassigned to it) dive into the deep, nuanced details of particular aspects of campus life, or they can make do with easily accessed information that can give them a general picture of campus life to work with. And anything in between. This flexibility is designed to let people make use of this text as their time commitments allow.

Fourth, those reading this text will, because of their newness in the role or the institution or both, be navigating new and murky waters. I can imagine someone who has spent their professional life at a single institution needing less of this structure than someone who was in the position I was: fresh off of a cross-country move, trying to remember the names of the buildings, and frequently (though, I hope, not noticeably) getting the names of people confused.

Those are the assumptions I am making about the readers of this text in terms of their relationship with the institution they are part of and the circumstances of those institutions. But I am also making assumptions about the motivations of the readers of this text. These descriptions act like the descriptions above: the further away you are from them, the more work you might have to do to make this text useful for you.

I am assuming that you, the reader, want to improve your program *structurally* rather than individually. That is, you don't want your program to improve just because you're there, day in and day out (although that's nice). Rather, you want your program to improve in ways it can continue to build on *after you're no longer part of it*. I want to imagine how we can *structurally transform our corner of higher education* so we might leave our programs and our institutions a little better than we found them, which later folks can build upon.

Toward that end, I assume also that you are a WPA (or future WPA) interested in *community*: in our field, in your institution, in your department, and in your local area. If we've learned nothing else during the Covid pandemic—and ample evidence suggests that we have not—we've learned the vital importance of community, of what we owe one another, of how we're responsible to those around us in our thoughts and deeds. Being a WPA is one way to participate in, shape, and build a range of communities; it is my assumption that this work is not only important but central to your understanding of the roles you inhabit.

Now, you might be looking through these assumptions and seeing yourself in some of those I mentioned and not others. Or you might be of two minds about a few things. I will freely admit that I came to UMaine expecting to be here for a few decades and running a writing program throughout that time. And yet, as I was working on this text, I frequently found myself wondering why I was several hundred miles from the friends and family who needed me in the midst of the greatest health crisis in living memory. Rather than marking that as an issue to ignore or push past, I suggest keeping such tensions in mind, letting them help you make sense of this text and the options it presents you with. I'm recalling a quote from Lou Holtz, who, when asked why his team played so well in the third quarter, mused, "I guess after the half our players forget the game plan and do what they think is best" (quoted in Liebman 1997, 97). Take this text in a similar way: let it give you a sense of what you can do, and then do what you think is best.

One more note of assumptions that shaped this book before I move on. This is best highlighted by my work with Heather Buzbee. Heather was a graduate student at the University of South Carolina, taking an excellent WPA course with Kevin Brock. In one of our meetings during the semester, Heather noted that a lot of the literature on being a WPA (particularly a pre-tenure WPA) was a bit of a bummer. I found myself agreeing with her (and with Lynn Z. Bloom [2002], who explores the issues of fun and the WPA position). After all, the general advice I tended to get about being a pre-tenure WPA was, well, to *not* be a pre-tenure WPA.

Looking back over my years of work, however, I realized that I wanted to emphasize—as I hope I did for Heather, as well as others who "adopted" our writing program in WPA courses—that WPA work is *fun*. It has its down sides, sure, but it's also exciting and meaningful. It's far more fun than we often see at a casual glance through research or what we might think when we hear a WPA vent about a tough day (or semester) at the office. It's a chance to help people live the lives they want to live and on a large scale: what we do impacts some of the most vulnerable populations in the university, and it impacts a part of their lives (writing) where that vulnerability may be keenly felt. The final assumption of this book, then, is that it can be a lot of fun to run and build a program; to show that there's a joy in this work and a chance to simultaneously develop a meaningful career, a productive program, and an exciting and engaging work life.

The remainder of this introduction provides a framework and a set of key terms for the rest of this book. I start by defining the *small, stubborn facts* that will serve as the bedrock on which this book is built. This gives way to *principled practices*, which will be the "way in" to this text for the reader—from the work done to identify values and valued practices, we'll establish how to build a meaningful, sustainable writing program. And, of course, have fun while doing it.

Starting with Small, Stubborn Facts

Small, stubborn facts are at the heart of how I imagine my work as a WPA. I think that looking through records, constructing facts from those records, and using those facts to tell stories about writers and writing is the most important thing I do as a WPA. Higher education teachers and administrators are working in a neoliberal nightmare that is, as of 2024, quickly shifting to a dystopian hellscape: people are doing more work for less pay and working with fewer resources and without a sense of a brighter future for the industry and the world. In these circumstances, it's no surprise that people work from small bits of information to make assumptions about students and their writing. The conclusion that "students can't write" or "student writing is getting worse" is often dismissed as cruelty to students. And it is, but there's a bigger picture to consider: that those saying it are trying to survive in unfavorable circumstances, and the conclusions they come to are the result not necessarily of intentional meanness but of theorizing with insufficient data.

My response to these negative stories about student writers and writing is to provide small, stubborn facts. I call these facts *small* because I search for

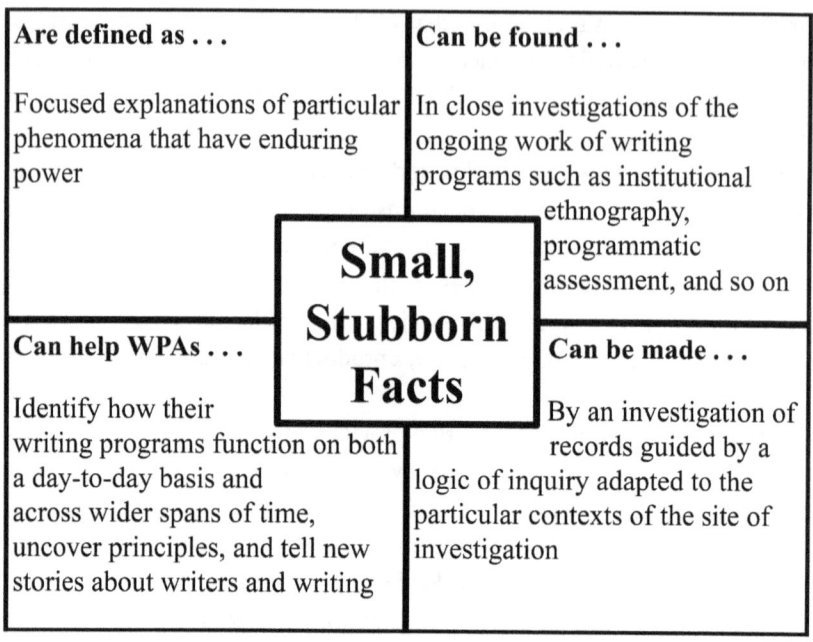

FIGURE 0.1. Small, stubborn facts

facts that require little by way of explanation: the number of students passing an end-of-term portfolio review in any given semester, for instance. This fact explains little but explains well.

In addition to being small, I also want the facts I look for to be *stubborn*. I want facts that are an aggravating and enduring presence to someone trying to claim that students can't write, that students are plagiarizers, that students "don't know how to write a sentence." If someone tells me that students are incapable of doing the work of English 101, for instance, I can provide a ten-year average of passing rates that indicate this isn't the case. Now, to be sure, someone dedicated to not liking the way the program operates will start doing the work to get around that fact. It isn't impossible, but it isn't easy because the fact is *stubborn*. It's hanging in there, daring the critic to find new ways to work against it.

Of course, stubborn facts can work against me as well as for me, particularly when they are part of a broader story about student writers and writing. So, in addition to trying to find small, stubborn facts to create new stories about writers and writing, we'll also be looking at how others around us—students, teachers, and administrators in the program, as well as those outside the program, and members of the community—go about establishing facts (stubborn and otherwise) that shape how student writers and student writing are understood (figure 0.1).

My interest in small, stubborn facts emerges from my work in graduate school. In one of my first meetings with my adviser, he encouraged a passion for what he called "really cool facts." "One good fact," he said, "can take care of a lot of theories." Paying close attention to little, seemingly insignificant aspects of the act of writing, or classroom interaction, or a response to feedback on writing came to shape the trajectory of my research through graduate school and into my appointment at the University of Maine.

It was this interest in small, stubborn facts that shaped my views of administrative work and what a WPA might do and could do to build alliances, expand and innovate in the program, and shape instructional choices. This interest, by extension, shaped the questions I asked, such as "how do new TAs adapt to a writing about writing curriculum," "how do accommodations from Student Accessibility Services align with the needs of those students as they enter English 101," and "how are we communicating with students about their grades throughout the term." These kinds of questions were tightly focused and gave me information I could use to build some small, stubborn facts on.

Note that I consistently discuss facts as "constructed" or "built" throughout this section. My use of the word *facts* might suggest to readers something of a positivist orientation. But my notion of "facts" is contingent on a phenomenological and ethnomethodological notion of rationality and sees a "fact" not as something entirely indisputable, existing outside of human language in any way. Instead, I see facts as socially agreed-upon understandings that while not indisput*able*, are *difficult* to dispute in particular circumstances and, if situated in the appropriate story, *become* frequently undisputed. Facts are, in my framing here, a social accomplishment, a way to influence how people in particular institutions talk about student writers and writing.

I will develop my notion of facts as part of the intersubjective accomplishment of rationality further in chapters 1 and 2. For now, I can provide an example of how a fact, as part of a broader story, can be used to shift the way particular interested parties talk about student writers and writing. Consider, as a hypothetical example, a department on a university campus that is unhappy with the term papers being shared in the core courses of the major. The chair of that department contacts the director of first-year writing to demand to know why students are arriving at the core courses unprepared to do the work assigned.

The director might respond by introducing a small, stubborn fact: student success rates on the end-of-semester portfolio review. Students are, on average, learning to do difficult kinds of writing in their semester of English 101 that they did not know prior to entering the course. This writing has some of the characteristics the department is looking for. So it would seem, then, that the students are not *unprepared* to do this kind of writing—they have demonstrated that they can, in fact, do it. There seems instead to be some kind of problem translating what they know to the new circumstances of their core courses. What, the director might ask the department chair, could be some of the reasons for this disconnect? Further, what data might we gather to find out?

Note the shift in attention. The department chair's initial outreach was about *student knowledge and ability deficits*. The director's response is about a *structural problem* that has caused students to be unable to demonstrate their best work. The story is no longer about what students can't do and has become instead about how two different programs might work together better.

Of course, the beauty of hypothetical examples is that they can easily have simple resolutions and happy endings. This is not always the case, though, and I'm sure the reader can easily imagine a department chair not replying kindly to the director's attempted reframing of the problem. But the example does demonstrate what a small, stubborn fact can do: it can serve as a starting point for developing and advancing new stories about writers and writing. Furthermore, the stubbornness of those facts can make these stories durable, longer lasting in the face of changing circumstances on campus.

This general idea of constructing and accumulating small, stubborn facts as the basis of telling new stories about writers and writing will inform the chapters that follow. We'll also be looking at how other people—in the program, in the university, in the community—go about creating facts that shape the stories about writers and writing that are being told. But as I've identified them above (and will develop further in chapter 1), you might get the sense that facts are everywhere. We are always talking and acting (and interacting) them into being, always making them real again with each passing moment. So, if that's the case, how can we possibly decide what facts to study, to follow, to try to understand, to try to put into the world? I answer this question with the concept of *principled practices*, which I describe in the following two sections. Just as searching for small, stubborn facts helps me see how a program is operating and how I might further develop the work of that program, principled practices direct my attention to facts that need attending to.

What Is Principled Practice?

My notion of *principled practice* draws on its use by Arthur N. Applebee (1986) and Peter Smagorinsky (2002, 2009) but is informed heavily by Linda Adler-Kassner's (2008, 2016) use of *principle*. Principles, according to Alder-Kassner (2016, 461), are "the beliefs and values that lie at the core of what we do." Principles help us make decisions about what we value and how we value it, help us prioritize some things over others in the limited time we have to do the complex work of running a writing program. As Ruth Benander and Brenda Refaei (2021) demonstrate in their study of equity at Blue Ash College, what we value shapes our programs in concrete and tangible ways.

I blend this notion of *principle* with the Applebee (1986) and Smagorinsky (2009) notion of *principled practice*. The concepts were developed to address different issues but have considerable overlap. Adler-Kassner is discussing the principles that shape our WPA decisions. Applebee and Smagorinsky, in contrast, are discussing teaching decisions for and in the classroom. Applebee (1986, 5), writing nearly four decades ago, was responding to the tensions between research and practice and considering why so many efforts to develop widely applicable model approaches to teaching "fail to achieve widespread reform of educational practice." Applebee identifies the root of these failures as researchers and teachers having focused on the wrong things: "We have allowed our understanding of teaching and learning to focus on *what* we do when we teach—the activities and curriculum—rather than on *why* we do it—the principles underlying instruction in general and our subject in particular" (5–6, original emphases). By focusing on *what* people do in successful programs and providing detail about these programs, practitioners attempting to implement these programs are unable to adapt the detail to the needs and circumstances of their students; thus, they unintentionally diminish the chances of the program succeeding.

Applebee's solution to this problem was to draw on *principled practices*. With principled practice, researchers rely on the skills of practicing teachers, not to implement step-by-step curricula but to identify the principles underpinning curricular initiatives and use those principles to guide the implementation of said initiatives in new locations. Applebee (1986, 6–7) develops this concept further by arguing that this researcher-practitioner relationship would be the launching point for developing new principles and activities: "Rather than the 'teacher proof' models of good instruction that have dominated previous reforms, models of principled practice would rely on the expertise of the practicing teacher to transform those principles into realistic approaches for particular contexts of schooling. Rather than new activities, such reforms would lead to new principles for orchestrating activities, for choosing what should happen next and why." Applebee's notion of thinking through teaching choices based on principles rather than particular classroom activities demands the *articulation* of such principles: that we be able to say what we value, just as Adler-Kassner (2008, 2016) suggests.

Smagorinsky takes up Applebee's call for principled practice, but he does so to critique the emerging notion of *best practice* in teaching English language arts (ELA). Like Applebee, Smagorinsky argues that context matters in teaching and that what seems to be a "best practice" in one setting might be problematic in another. Smagorinsky (2009, 20) instead urges a return to principles: "Teaching through principled practice challenges teachers to think about what is appropriate given the unique intersection that their classroom provides for their many and varied students; their beliefs about teaching and learning; the materials available for them to use; and the public, professional, and policy contexts in which they teach." For Smagorinsky, as for Applebee, the context has an influence on how research is used in a particular classroom; it is up to a trained and dedicated teacher to draw on principle, engage in disciplined reflection, and make teaching choices that are responsive to what research shows and what students need.

Applebee and Smagorinsky are useful in outlining the role principle plays: how it builds connections between research and practice, how it positions the teacher as expert, and how it empowers teachers to use their expertise to make informed choices. When we align this with Adler-Kassner's (2008, 2016) notion of principle, we can see the ways principle might shape anything from programmatic direction—such as aligning with a particular interested party on campus to launch a new initiative—to the relationship between teachers and a WPA in a writing program.

Adler-Kassner (2008, 2016) offers the language of *strategies* (long-term plans informed by and supporting principles) and *tactics* (day-to-day work that moves long-term plans along) to explain how a WPA might enact a principle across a range of time spans. We will be addressing strategies and tactics further throughout this text, but I want to highlight for the moment the connections between strategies and tactics and the informed choice making of teachers that Applebee and Smagorinsky imagine. Just as they imagined teachers as skilled experts capable of making informed decisions about their classrooms, this text positions the WPA as an expert in the work of running a writing program, as someone capable of wielding disciplinary knowledge and the particulars of a given writing program to map out a path forward, address problems, and communicate with interested parties. Defining principles and the ways they are enacted is a useful way to take on that work.

So, what *is* principled practice for a WPA? It is decision making that is informed by values, by expertise in the field, and by the particular needs of the contexts in which the WPA is working (see Buyserie et al. 2021 as an example of a similar approach). Throughout this book, I will be drawing on *principled practice* as a tool to focus on, analyze, and develop *small, stubborn facts* that can help us tell new stories about student writers and writing, as well as understand the facts already in operation in a particular program. In the next section, I lead the reader through a set of questions that can help identify some principles and possible ways they can be enacted. This work will be an important starting point for taking on the challenges of part I of this text.

Before moving on, however, I want to underscore how difficult it is to identify our values. While we can always think of a few things we stand by, a few hills we might be ready to die on, there is a range of values that we often hold so closely, act on so instinctively, that we do not realize they are there. For each principle we articulate, there are many more that we have not (and perhaps *cannot*) articulated. Furthermore, when we think about the principled practices of an entire writing program, we can imagine them happening in a range of ways: you might have principled *administrative* practices, principled *teaching* practices, and perhaps more.

The principles readers establish below will change. The list will be added to. The list will be subtracted from. And that is as it should be. As we live our lives, we find new ways to articulate what we value. We also come to new understandings about those values. And, finally, we develop new values. The articulation of a value as a principle isn't the end of the journey. It's the beginning of realizing the kinds of WPAs we want to be and the kinds of programs we want to build.

Tracing Principled Practice

Principles and practices do not always intertwine. Sometimes we have practices that are informed by our principles only at a distance or perhaps not at all. We carry some administrative, research, and teaching practices with us from one program, study, and class to the next—not because they support what we value but because (1) we are comfortable with them and (2) we have not reflected on a practice to realize that it is disconnected from (and maybe contrary to) what we value. What we need to think about are practices that bring, front and center, our values into focus in ways that are not distanced or contradicted. It's here that we can begin to learn the most about what we value, so that we can later trace out the distance between our values and our actions in other choices we make.

A principled administrative practice that highlights this is my decision to underscore the importance of learning management systems (LMS) use in my writing program. This might seem like a rather straightforward issue—or perhaps no issue at all, if your institution requires a particular LMS—but upon my arrival at UMaine, there was no widespread use of LMS in English 101. Teachers occasionally *did* use them, of course, but people also did things simply on paper, with materially submitted assignments and printed assignments. And some people found a middle ground with email and Google Drive.

Emphasizing the use of an LMS came with my growing awareness of the importance of creating accessible classrooms for students. Students cannot always be in class, and for good reason: they might have to pick up an extra shift at work, or they might have a medical condition that prevents them from attending. Having a single place for them to go so they can see copies of board notes, summaries of class meetings, assignment prompts, and assignment prompt submission portals allows students to more easily and effectively access materials from classes they could not attend.

Now, there are other reasons to support an LMS, but this highlights a value (creating accessible classes) and a practice (using an LMS) coming together to demonstrate the program operating with its priorities in order. Furthermore, the principle can guide the particular ways we go about using an LMS. After all, an LMS *on its own* does not make a course more accessible: we need to use the space deliberately to make it so. There is a productive back-and-forth between a principle and its enacted practice that allows, over time, for a deeper understanding of each.

The exercise below is a way to build on the ideas I highlighted above to guide readers to some principled practices—and, from those principled practices, to a tentative articulation of (some of) their principles. This is important work to do before starting to look at the nuts and bolts of a writing program. Understanding how a program is working is certainly important, but a new WPA's entry into a program means that what *they* value will come to shape the program too, and articulating (some of) those values at the start is a useful way to notice the distinctions between those values and what the program values in its claims and actions.

I keep saying that readers will articulate "(some of)" their values: WPAs and teachers aren't ever finished realizing what they value and how they value it. Often, some of the most important, closely held values people have are not articulated until there's a clash of some kind. So, readers will be learning more and more about what they value throughout this text. What the guide below provides is merely a starting point.

Articulating (Some of) What You Value: A Starting Point

The list of questions below will help you get started by pinning down some principles, some practices, and some principled practices. Like all aspects of this book, this can be done individually (if you are, say, the lone compositionist in a department) or collaboratively (if you are working with a team of WPAs). See the questions as a point of departure; you may find yourself running with some and not others, using them to lead you down new avenues of thought, and so on. The goal is to end the activity with a sense of some principled practices, which you'll build on in part I. As long as you did that when you finish the activity, congratulations. You did it right.

1. Start with some values about administration and teaching that are obvious to you: principles you've noted before, that perhaps even close friends or colleagues might be aware of.
2. Identify some administrative or teaching practices you've valued in the past or that seem important to you in some way. At this step, the distance between the principle and practice isn't important; we'll address that in a bit. Just write them down in as much detail as is useful to you.
3. Write down some moments you've experienced, read about, or heard about (from professors, colleagues, listservs, and others) that have sparked an emotional reaction from you. Include some detail about *why* you think these moments caused the emotion you experienced. What was it that gave each moment that memorable spark?
4. Look across what you did in steps 1–3 and try to see the overlap. Where the overlap among what you value, what you practice, and what you react to emotionally? What relationships do you see? It's at these intersections of acknowledged principle, valued practice, and emotional response that we can see values and actions feeding off of one another. It's here that we can identify that which we hold most dear. Most likely,

these intersections will give you more than one value. That's fine—write them all out for this step. You may find yourself blending them together later.

5. Write out the principles that emerged for you. Try to provide two parts: a word, phrase, or sentence that encapsulates what you value (the principle), and a short text that elaborates that value with description, examples, and perhaps connections to other values (the practice).
6. Finally, write down any questions you have about what you've valued. Identify anything you might be unsure about, some notes toward principles you can't quite articulate, and any lingering experiences from steps 3 and 4 that you'd be interested in circling back to.

Once you've finished with these steps, you'll have a set of principled practices to set you up for taking on the work of part I. Again, these principled practices are just a starting point for you; you'll likely uncover more things you value as you move along in this book. But having an idea of what you value before you dive into the site of a writing program will become more and more useful as you progress through the book and start to make plans for a future program that intertwines your values and the program you are part of.

Where We're Heading: An Outline of This Book, and Its Role on Your Bookshelf

This book is divided into three parts, each of which is designed to build on those that came before it. A fair amount of recursivity is built in, so readers can return to this text again and again in future years and work toward useful programmatic insights from various starting points. Figure 0.2 provides a representation of how the entire text fits together.

In part I, I provide a road map for examining a writing program "from the ground up"—that is, to see how the program works, what problems it solves, and what issues it creates. In chapter 1, I create a framework and general approach for taking on this work. I also provide guidance on collecting artifacts for analysis. In chapter 2, I lead the reader through the ways these artifacts can be examined to assemble facts—explanations of how the program operates, both on a day-to-day basis and across longer stretches of time (the quarter/semester, the year). Chapter 3 leads the reader through identifying how these facts coalesce into particular principles, principled practices, and broader narratives that are being told by the program about student writers and student writing. Through careful reflective work, WPAs can be sure that

Small, Stubborn Facts and Principled Practice : 19

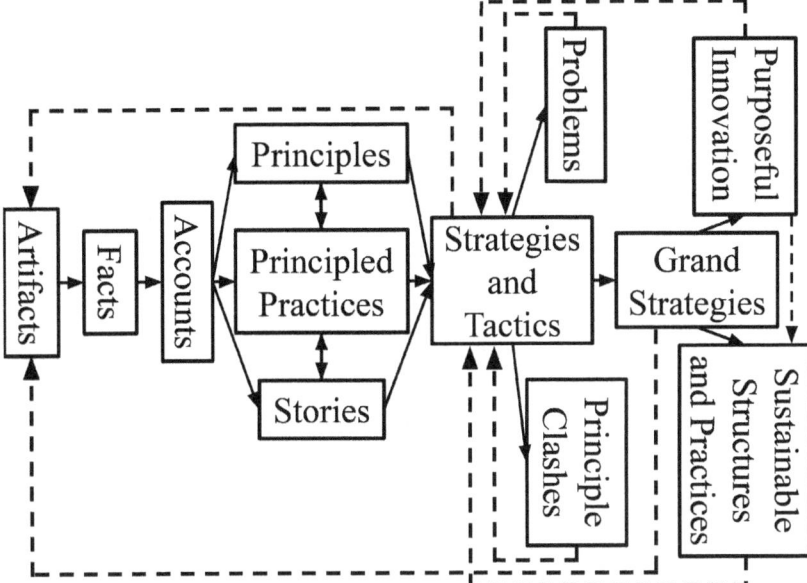

FIGURE 0.2. Map of this text

the facts they have assembled and mobilized are and remain grounded and that innovations that emerge remain tightly aligned with the problems the WPA notices "on the ground."

In part II, I turn attention to the "little picture" of the next one to three years of the program, drawing on the facts WPAs have identified as being constructed, the principles underpinning those facts, and the principled practices and stories those facts coalesce into. In chapter 4, I lead the reader through an identification of, in Adler-Kassner's (2008) language, the *strategies* and *tactics* they can plan for the next few years. In chapter 5, I home in on strategies and tactics to solve agreed-upon issues: long-standing concerns the program's constituents agree need to be addressed but that have not been successfully addressed. In chapter 6, I lead the reader through the strategies and tactics that are aimed at clashes of principle between the WPA and the program constituents. At the conclusion of part II, readers will have a good sense of how to use part I's results to plan programmatic change for the next few years.

In part III, I take the "long view" of decades and help readers develop "grand strategies" for their writing programs. In chapter 7, I lead WPAs through the development of "grand strategies," or extremely long-term, always unfinished goals. In chapter 8, readers will mobilize their grand strategies by planning out purposeful, targeted programmatic innovation. Through purposeful innovation, WPAs can continue the growth of the program without undermining successful aspects of it. The ongoing tinkering offered by purposeful innovation also provides a chance for WPAs to see what they and their program value in new ways, in new circumstances. In chapter 9, I lead readers from targeted (and successful) innovations to the creation of *sustainable structures and practices*, or transformations of the program that come to be seen as unquestioned, constitutive elements of the program by those in it. It is through the development of such sustainable structures and practices that program growth and change can perpetuate across years and decades.

I close the book by attempting to frame the work of WPAs in a broader context, with a bigger mission than simply operating a writing program successfully (not that that isn't, in and of itself, a significant accomplishment). WPAs are not simply cogs in a higher education machine: they are in a position to make the bureaucracy of higher education more human, more geared toward the needs of students attempting to find growth, meaning, and success in their lives in and beyond school. After all, what is the point of leading, being in, or even having a writing program if you can't use it to help someone live the life they want to live?

The above outline provides a sense of what is going to happen in this book. But I also wrote this book with an idea of what it might do on a WPA's bookshelf. When I am in the library hunting for a book, I always end up walking out with a few more than I intended to. It's the experience of most academics in a library, I think: we see the book we want and right next to it is another book on a similar topic that might be helpful. And another one next to that. And they're all free. So, I succumb to temptation and end up dragging a few more to the kiosk than I originally intended. Perhaps even more than a few.

When I was writing this book, I tried to imagine what that bookshelf might look like around it. Not in a university library but in a WPA's library. What does this book need to work in concert with? What set of texts would be helpful for WPAs as they take on the work of building a sustainable writing program? My imagined bookshelf of texts around this book is as follows, in no particular order:

- *The Activist WPA*, by Linda Adler-Kassner (2008): This book can help readers figure out how to promote positive change from the WPA position.

- *A Rhetoric for Writing Program Administrators*, edited by Rita Malenczyk (2013): This book is a helpful compendium of terms, ideas, and resources for WPAs.
- *Institutional Ethnography: A Theory of Practice for Writing Studies Researchers*, by Michelle LaFrance: This book complements the close-to-the-ground study of writing programs the first part of this book guides readers through.
- *Making Administrative Work Visible: Data-Driven Advocacy for Understanding the Labor of Writing Program Administration*, edited by Leigh Graziano, Kay Halasek, Remi Hudgins, Susan Miller-Cochran, Frank Napolitano, and Natalie Szymanski (2023b): This book provides a range of approaches that will help readers not only make their WPA work visible but also gain a better sense of what that work is and how to do it.
- *Toward More Sustainable Metaphors of Writing Program Administration*, edited by Lydia Wilkes, Lilian Mina, and Patti Poblete (2023): This volume will help readers get a sense of how they can make their work and that of their program more sustainable over time.
- *The Things We Carry: Strategies for Recognizing and Negotiating Emotional Labor in Writing Program Administration*, edited by Courtney Adams Wooten, Jacob Babb, Kristi Murray Costello, Kate Navickas, and Laura Micciche (2020): This book will guide readers through the affective complexity that comes with being a WPA.
- *A Working Model for Contingent Faculty*, by Robert Samuels (2023): If WPAs are working with contingent faculty (and most are), this book will be a useful guide to making things as equitable as possible, given available resources, responsibility, and authority.

These books are certainly not the only available texts on WPA work (I have more in each chapter, which I explain in the next section), and they are not required for readers to take up the work of the book. But for those familiar with WPA research, this text and its purposes can best be understood in the context of this "bookshelf." And for those new to WPA work who might like a small selection of widely varied but resonant resources, this list would be a good place to start.

A Note on Resources in Each Chapter

At the end of each chapter, I identify a handful of resources that might help readers address the concerns of the chapter. I am not aiming for a comprehensive list of resources but rather for a collection that is suggestive of the wide span of resources available to WPAs as they take on the work of building sustainable writing programs. It was a difficult balance to strike: I wanted to give readers enough resources to help them take up the work of each chapter in greater detail but not so much that they are engulfed in citations.

My decisions about what to and not to include in each set of resources were guided by several sets of criteria. First, I wanted each chapter to have a mix of *germinal* and *recent* research. "Germinal" in this case means that the research is long-standing in our field and continues to be pertinent to the work we as WPAs have to do today. Susan H. McLeod's *Writing Program Administration* (2007) stands out as a good example; it provides useful insights into WPA life, even almost twenty years after publication. By "recent" research, I mean research in the last five or so years of my writing this book that resonates with the topics of the chapters in some way. Five years is not a hard deadline, as readers will see when reading the resource lists.

I also wanted texts that could help people do different kinds of things with the topics in each chapter. Toward that end, I identified texts that acted in three different ways in relation to the topics of each chapter. In my notes, I referred to these texts as *sensitizers, contextualizers,* and *methodologizers*. (I never intended to share these names with others—I thought the references might be helpful only much later, and I regret that I did not think of better names.) *Sensitizing* texts help the reader develop sensitivity toward particular aspects of a writing program: the impact of race on assessment, for instance, or the role of gender in student evaluations of teaching. *Contextualizers* are texts that provide a wider context of the WPA experience, such as the Program Profiles in *Composition Forum*. Finally, *methodologizers* are texts that can help WPAs take up the work of the chapter in particular aspects of the program, in the way Michelle LaFrance's *Institutional Ethnography* (or any of the texts in the recent explosion of IE work—see Odasso [2022]) can help WPAs trace out the facts at work in their programs.

These two sets of criteria gave me plenty to work with. But, as I put the resources together for each chapter, I noticed that they were clumping together on certain topics, like assessment. To resolve this concern, I identified five common topics in WPA work to address in resources throughout the book: assessment, curriculum, labor, placement, and professional development. I wasn't able to cover each of these topics in every chapter, but working with that intention provides the entirety of the book with a range of topics WPAs can engage with. I also aimed to have these resources work across a range of sites—community colleges, small liberal arts colleges, regional-comprehensive universities, and so on. This should help WPAs working in different settings adapt their use of this text to the demands of their context.

My final set of criteria was a mix of material that was and was not open access. Not everyone has the kind of library access they need to get behind certain paywalls, and not everyone can afford to go on a shopping spree at Utah State University Press. But the inclusion of some texts in this book might help some of you make the case that you need to purchase them, either for the university library or through departmental budgets.

There is a lot of exciting and groundbreaking work in WPA research today, and it was not easy to make decisions about what to include and what to exclude. Even some older texts that the field has developed beyond (e.g., Potts and Schwalm 1983) seem as though they may be useful to illustrate the histories informing the writing programs we work in today. To alleviate some of my anxiety over these choices (in addition to writing this perhaps overly long explanation), I separated, whenever it seemed appropriate, the in-text citations from the resource list. So, if I mention something in a chapter, I usually do not add it as a resource at the end of that chapter—not because it isn't important but because you already read it, and you can find the citation at the end of the book. I encourage you to think of each set of resources as a starting point for diving further into the research on writing program administration as you take up the work of each chapter, using not only the readings but the places those readings can be found (books, journals, edited collections) as a wider space to explore.

A Closer Look at Principles and Principled Practices

Readers interested in learning more about principles and principled practices might benefit from the texts below. The discussion of principles I draw on is firmly rooted in WPA work and emerges primarily from the work of Linda Adler-Kassner. The discussion of principled practices has its roots in ELA instruction and is a conversation that stretches back to Arthur Applebee's time as editor of *Research in the Teaching of English* in the 1980s. "Context and Positionality" resources can help WPAs think through the complex specificities of their programs and interactions with them. Finally, "WPA Histories" offers broader, historical contexts that can help WPAs make sense of their programs within the context of a wider history.

BACKGROUND ON PRINCIPLES

Adler-Kassner, Linda. 2008. *The Activist WPA: Changing Stories about Writing and Writers.* Logan: Utah State University Press.

Adler-Kassner, Linda. 2016. "What Is Principle?" In *A Rhetoric for Writing Program Administrators*, second edition, edited by Rita Malenczyk, 460–474. West Lafayette, IN: Parlor Press.

Isabella, Marcy, and Heather McGovern. 2018. "Identity, Values, and Reflection: Shaping (and Being Shaped) through Assessment." *New Directions for Teaching and Learning* 155: 89–96.

Jensen, Darin, and Emily Suh. 2020. "Introducing Lived Interventions: Located Agency and Teacher-Scholar Activism as Responses to Neoliberalism." *Basic Writing e-Journal* 16 (1): 1–11.

BACKGROUND ON PRINCIPLED PRACTICES

Applebee, Arthur N. 1986. "Musings . . . Principled Practice." *Research in the Teaching of English* 20: 5–7.

Hillocks, George. 2009. "A Response to Peter Smagorinsky: Some Practices and Approaches Are Clearly Better than Others and We Had Better Not Ignore the Differences." *English Journal* 98 (6): 23–29.

Smagorinsky, Peter. 2002. *Teaching English through Principled Practice.* Upper Saddle River, NJ: Merrill Prentice-Hall.

Smagorinsky, Peter. 2009. "EJ Extra: Is It Time to Abandon the Idea of 'Best Practices' in the Teaching of English?" *English Journal* 98 (6): 15–22.

Smith, Nicole Boudreau. 2017. "A Principled Revolution in the Teaching of Writing." *English Journal* 106 (5): 70–75.

CONTEXT AND POSITIONALITY

Franklin, Joseph. 2021. "Transnational Writing Program Administration: Mobility, Entanglement, Work." PhD dissertation, University of Louisville, Louisville, KY.

Greer, Murphy, and Troy Mikanovich. 2023. "Labor and Loneliness of the Multilingual WPA." In *Making Administrative Work Visible: Data-Driven Advocacy for Understanding the Labor of Writing Program Administration*, edited by Leigh Graziano, Kay Halasek, Remi Hudgins, Susan Miller-Cochran, Frank Napolitano, and Natalie Szymanski, 203–216. Logan: Utah State University Press.

Kynard, Carmen. 2023. "Administering While Black: Black Women's Labor in the Academy and the 'Position of the Unthought.'" In *Black Perspectives in Writing Program Administration*, edited by Staci Perryman-Clark and Collin Lamont Craig, 28–50. Urbana, IL: National Council of Teachers of English Books.

McClure, Randall. 2008. "An Army of One: The Possibilities and Pitfalls of WPA Work for the Lone Compositionist." In *The Promise and Perils of Writing Program Administration*, edited by Theresa Enos and Shane Borrowman, 102–108. West Lafayette, IN: Parlor Press.

McGlaun, Sandee K. 2007. "Administering Writing Programs in the 'Betweens': A jWPA Narrative." In *Untenured Faculty as Writing Program Administrators: Institutional Practices and Politics*, edited by Debra Frank Dew and Alice Horning, 219–248. West Lafayette, IN: Parlor Press.

Phillips, Talinn, Paul Shovlin, and Megan L. Titus. 2016. "(Re)identifying the gWPA Experience." *WPA: Writing Program Administration* 40 (1): 67–89.

WPA HISTORIES

Heckathorn, Amy. 2004. "Moving Toward a Group Identity: WPA Professionalization from the 1940s to the 1970s." In *Historical Studies of Writing Program Administration: Individuals, Communities, and the Formation of a Discipline*, edited by Barbara L'Eplattenier and Lisa Mastrangelo, 191–220. West Lafayette, IN: Parlor Press.

McLeod, Susan H. 2007. *Writing Program Administration*. West Lafayette, IN: Parlor Press.

McLeod, Susan H., David Stock, and Bradley T. Hughes, eds. 2017. *Two WPA Pioneers: Ednah Shepherd Thomas and Joyce Steward*. Fort Collins and Boulder: WAC Clearinghouse and University Press of Colorado.

Ritter, Kelly. 2018. "Making (Collective) Memory Public: WPA Histories in Dialogue." *WPA: Writing Program Administration* 41 (2): 35–64.

Rudy, Jill Terry. 2004. "Building a Career by Directing Composition: Harvard, Professionalism, and Stith Thompson at Indiana University." In *Historical Studies of Writing Program Administration: Individuals, Communities, and the Formation of a Discipline*, edited by Barbara L'Eplattenier and Lisa Mastrangelo, 71–88. West Lafayette, IN: Parlor Press.

PART I

From the Ground Up

Like all great coaches, Coach B. was relentless in his attention to detail. Footwork, hand placement, communication—you name it, we spent an inordinate amount of time on it in practice. And then we watched film of the practice, to see where things broke down, what needed changing, what needed even more attention to detail. It was in these brief moments—the first step after the snap, the height of our shoulders on a play-action pass, the spacing of ourselves from one another on a given run play—that we developed a shared understanding, a shared set of values, and a shared sense of rationality that would inform the work the team did together. In seeing and doing certain things, we named them, discussed them, tried to unpack how they should work, and got better at doing them. In part I, you'll be attending carefully to the details of how the program you are now directing works: what the parts are, what people do and name, and how those doings and namings form a shared set of understandings of how the program operates and why.

In the introduction to this book, readers ironed out some principles, practices, and principled practices they are bringing to the writing program that they will study through the chapters of this text. Identifying these values (and the ways you enact them) is important for a couple of reasons. The chapters of part I guide readers through a careful study of the on-the-ground reasoning,

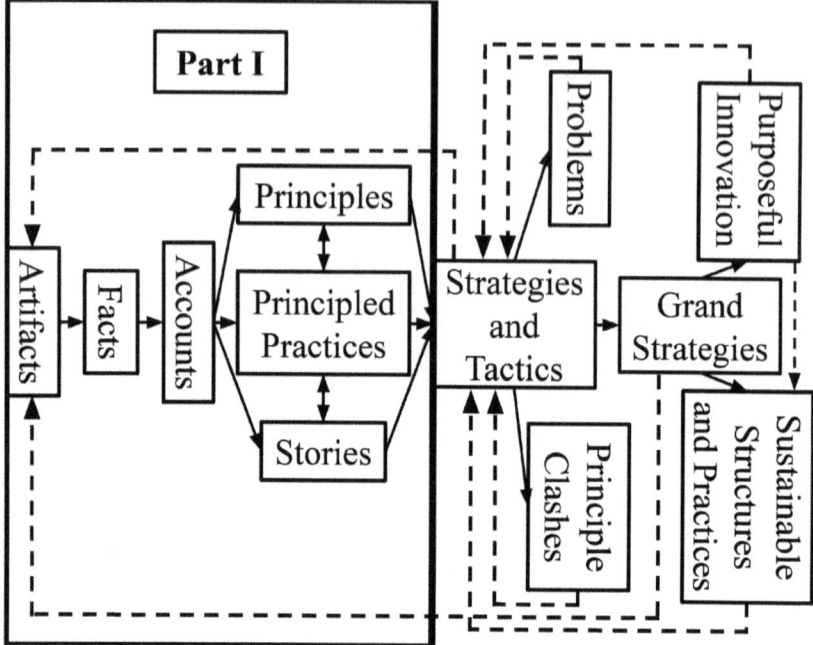

FIGURE 1.0. Part I's role in the work of this text

decision making, and values of a writing program. Having already outlined (in the introduction) what they value and how they value it ahead of time, readers will be better able to notice when they are making assumptions with their own values and practices in mind. Doing so can obscure the work a program is actually doing and lead to misunderstandings that can create problems as we generate innovations in parts II and III (figure 1.0).

Identifying principled practices also sets the stage for transforming, refining, and revising them in response to what you see in your writing program. The frame clash that can occur between the program and what the writing program administrator (WPA) values can lead them to more carefully examine what it is they value, why they value it, and how they enact it. Realizing what we value, after all, isn't a once-and-for-all act: it's a part of being human, a part of understanding who we are and what our place is in the world. The work readers have already done will help make their study of the writing program also, and at the same time, a deep and considered investigation of what it is they value. This work is going to be running in the background of chapters 1 and 2 and will move to the foreground in chapter 3.

Extending the "grounded" metaphor of some earlier work (Dippre 2023a), the central focus of part I is getting a sense of the program "from the ground up": what makes the program run, how it runs, what it values, and how it values it. Part I will build on the notion of "facts" I outlined in the introduction. Rather than using that notion to build new stories of writers and writing (something focused on in parts II and III), however, part I will instead use it to understand what's happening in the writing program: what facts are getting constructed in it? What stories are those facts used to tell?

Throughout part I, I will continually encourage the reader to make haste slowly. Part I is not about planning for change, innovations, or solutions. It is aiming for an insider's perspective on the operation of a writing program. In chapter 1, I will provide a framing for studying a writing program and guide the reader through a collection of various artifacts. In chapter 2, readers will draw on these artifacts to assemble small facts about the program—ones they can use to generate a sense of the stories about writers and writing that are told in their program, as well as how those stories are told. It is in this chapter that the groundwork for programmatic innovation—the focus of part II—is laid. Finally, in chapter 3, readers will engage in a careful reflection of the facts and stories they have assembled, attain external feedback, and make any revisions that might be needed.

At the end of part I, then, readers should have an empirically grounded understanding of the facts this program builds, the stories the program tells with those facts, and the values underpinning both. It is off of this understanding that they can begin to plan, introduce, and execute programmatic change at both a small and a large scale (which we'll get to in parts II and III).

1
The Lay of the Land

Coach B. had several phrases that he returned to again and again throughout a season, and one of them was *burnin' daylight*. As in "let's go let's go let's go. We're burnin' daylight out here." We'd hear that refrain as we ran from one drill to another during a practice. Even if it was a 6 a.m. practice and we linemen were perfectly fine with burning some daylight, we hustled anyway. No one wanted to let Coach B. down. And no one sure as hell wanted to find out what would happen if we did, in fact, burn too much daylight.

In addition to the sense of hustle that *burnin' daylight* inspired in those who heard it, there was also an air of something else: excitement. Great things loomed on the horizon, and we were hustling not just to avoid burning daylight but to make sure that we met those great things prepared, ready to go. It's that excitement—the fun I mentioned in the introduction—that I hope carries across in this work. Being a writing program administrator (WPA) can be exciting and fun, and the work of a new WPA to understand how a program operates (the focus of this chapter) is particularly enjoyable. It's a chance to hear from competent, passionate people about the things they are competent and passionate about. You get to hear about the broad values guiding what they do in the classroom, what they love about their jobs, and how they live their lives. You get to hear the living, breathing writing program at work.

https://doi.org/10.7330/9781646426416.c001

You can also get useful insight into the nuts and bolts of everyday life in the program: who makes the coffee really strong when they put on a new pot in the office; where to find an open copier if the one in the program office jams; and who to talk to in the offices of different departments, programs, and university services when problems arise. These seem like small things until the copier breaks, or you need a helping hand from Student Services, or you're awake at 2 a.m. because whoever put a new pot of coffee on in the mid-afternoon clearly has a much higher caffeine tolerance than you do.

What I'm saying is, you learn a lot of things. Some of them are helpful to you on a day-to-day basis, and some are helpful in understanding the long-term trajectory of the program. But it is all potentially helpful. This chapter focuses on planning out a collection of artifacts—from notes about how the copier works to the lore of the history of the program and anything in between. That work involves having meetings, looking through history, and checking out different kinds of genres in use. There is no need, at the moment, to be concerned with turning those artifacts into facts (which is a job for chapter 2). There is no need to judge any of what is collected, other than to use it to guide the collection of additional artifacts.

The Case for Facts: Responsible WPA Work

The issue of collecting facts is tied to the responsibility WPAs have in the ongoing lives of their writing programs. My notion of "responsibility" comes from Viktor Frankl's *Yes to Life: in Spite of Everything* (2020). In this text, recently translated into English, Frankl's particular framing of the choices we make—and have to make, really, on a daily basis resonates particularly strongly with the work WPAs find themselves doing.

Toward the end of *Yes to Life* (2020), Frankl highlights the untouchable nature of the past: we cannot un-ring the bell of history or make the past better than it was. Our accomplishments and our failures—both individually and as a society—are frozen in the past, untouchable. However, we live our lives on the ragged edge of that past. Each moment we live carries with it a responsibility: "precisely to bring what has not yet happened *into* the world" (105, original emphasis). This has to happen, according to Frankl, "as part of our daily work, as part of our everyday lives" (105). Each moment, for Frankl, is a chance to do something new, to put something into the world that ends, that moves away from past pain and suffering. Furthermore, we don't just have the *opportunity* to do so; it's a responsibility we have, a duty to do what we can to actualize the moments of our lives in ways that bring about lasting change.

This is a stunning responsibility, to be sure. And Frankl (2020, 106) is not unaware of the challenges:

> It is terrible to know that at every moment I bear responsibility for the next; that every decision, from the smallest to the largest, is a decision "for all eternity"; that in every moment I can actualize the possibility of a moment, of that particular moment, or forfeit it. Every single moment contains thousands of possibilities—and I can only choose one of them to actualize it. But in making the choice, I have condemned all the others and sentenced them to "never being," and even this is for all eternity! But it is wonderful to know that the future—my own future and with it the future of the things, the people around me—is somehow, albeit to a very small extent, dependent on my decisions in every moment. Everything I realize through them, or "bring into the world," as we have said, I save into reality and thus protect from transience.

We can see in this passage Frankl's recognition of the weight of the responsibility he claims we all have: the terrible duty to not only bring change into the world but, in doing so, to consign a range of other options, in each passing moment, to oblivion. This understanding of responsibility informs my use of "facts" in this text: we have a responsibility, as WPAs, to make sense of the facts that get constructed in and through our programs and to see how we can get new facts that will let us tell new stories, which in turn can help us make sure that what we bring into the world is something more just, more kind than what came before.

In understanding the responsibility of the present moment, though, Frankl argues that we have to be aware of the past—that there are persistent inequities we have to work to shed with each new moment. And our responsibilities to address these persistent inequities move far beyond our past, individual contributions to them. Frankl separates *guilt*, even collective guilt, from *liability*. An individual might not be *guilty* of a particular past act but still be *liable* to contribute to the effort to remove the negative effects of that act in the continuously unfolding present. They have the duty to make a decision in a moment—and, thus, for all eternity—to remove those negative effects, to whatever extent possible. This notion of responsibility can be particularly helpful to WPAs as they seek to understand and revise the functioning of their programs in light of (and as part of) the ongoing social injustices that permeate contemporary society. This chapter sets the stage for taking advantage of the potential for action that each new moment, day, week, semester, and academic year offers to meaningfully and sustainably improve writing programs in lasting ways.

The Responsibility for Framing and Telling Stories

An understanding of how we can responsibly take up WPA work—in Frankl's sense, that is—begins by articulating a sense of social structure in which the facts WPAs are searching for operate. My understanding of social structure in this text is, at heart, interactional: social structure is not something that exists *outside of* interaction but rather is something that *emerges from* interaction. This understanding, for me, comes from the study of ethnomethodology (Garfinkel 1967), which is the situated study of social order. Etymologically, "ethnomethodology" means "the study of members' methods." *Which* members? The members of the social action being performed: drivers and pedestrians navigating an intersection (Liberman 2013), contestants engaged in a game of tic-tac-toe (Garfinkel 1967), and students forming a line at a university bookstore (Livingston 1987). All of these situations involve people creating—through, for example, language, body movement, the position of objects—shared understandings we all work together to act on. These facts do not emerge from individual consciousness; rather, people work together to generate, operate on, and coordinate through these social facts.

For example, when I stand behind a person at a register, I am, in my action of waiting, creating a line. Should someone arrive after me to check out, they would co-construct anew the social fact of the line by standing behind me. We can call this a fact because it is *treated* as a fact; it is something that others who become members of the situation acknowledge in their words and actions. They act *as if* the line exists and should be used, and so it is. A newcomer to the situation can walk in, see the register, me, and the person behind me, and recognize our actions: we are waiting in line. He then acts off of that recognition by getting in line behind us—an act we recognize in turn. We have established the social order of the line, just here, just now, and in just this situation.

Ignoring facts like these—or, rather, attempting to—also has consequences. Say someone walks in and walks directly to the register. Social order does not unravel here. We can still ascribe an action to the newcomer: he's a line cutter. There are ways the line handles this too, from grumbling to outright heckling. The response would trigger another set of interactions that continue to create social facts (such as the line cutter versus the line dynamic) the members of the group (that is, the people in the coffee shop) would operate on.

As the reader can see in this example, for ethnomethodology, what counts as a fact is created in the ongoing interaction of people (people in line and line cutters), objects (the register), and talk (grumbling or heckling). What comes to count as a fact is contextual, situated. Facts emerge from and in interaction, and they are consequential for the members of those circumstances in which they arise. Through an ethnomethodological orientation to the production of social facts in our program, we can begin to get the information we need to responsibly tell stories about writers and writing in our program.

The Program's History as Interactionally Accomplished

The case for ethnomethodology that I make above is related to Linda Adler-Kassner's (2008) use of Erving Goffman's work on framing. Adler-Kassner draws on Goffman and his concept of framing to make sense of how we might counter problematic stories about writers and writing with new stories. She argues that frames—defined by Stephen D. Reese (2001, 11) as "organizing principles that are socially shared and persistent over time"—work their way from symbols to signifiers and are strengthened over time through repeated use. The ethnomethodological lens I articulate above helps us to see how, in the program, such frames might be accomplished, day in and day out, for another first time by particular actors, objects, and contexts. Such an interactional framing is not unheard of in our field (see Overstreet 2019), although I have a different starting point with ethnomethodology.

But ethnomethodology, though excellent at helping us understand the situated production of order, does not pay close attention to the history *behind* that production of order. I might be able to see the interactional work of pedestrians and drivers at a busy intersection, but tracing the history of that intersection—or, for that matter, the complex lives of particular people who go through that intersection—is less easily visible. As WPAs, we need to understand how our programs develop over time and how we might bring together the idiosyncrasies of the moment and the broader social and historical patterns that continue to shape the program. The concept of *social contracts*—and, as we'll see below, *racial contracts*—can help us bridge the historical and the interactional.

Talcott Parsons (1937) made what Harold Garfinkel (2019) saw as a monumental insight into sociology. Rather than seeing social contracts as something that emerged from the work of rational individuals, as Hobbes did, he viewed them as something that *led to* rational individuals interacting. That is, a social contract exists independent of any one individual or one set of individuals and is set into motion when individuals come together.

Parsons's idea of a social contract, when aligned with Garfinkel's (1967, 9) take-up of this notion in his study of the routine grounds of social order, can help us frame how background expectancies can be formed "for another first time" through interactional work. A social contract is not (or not *only*) in our heads, recipe-like knowledge ready to be enacted. We are always working through a contract, realizing it anew as we produce social order while making our way in the world, with our attention to enacting a contract operating at various levels of conscious awareness.

Building on the work of Garfinkel (2002), we can consider, as an example of this, the start of a class meeting in a typical first-year composition course. Let's say class starts at 9:00 a.m. and the previous class lets out at 8:50 a.m. So, between 8:50 a.m. and 9:00 a.m., the previous class will file out, and the new class will file in. The teacher would be part of this "filing in"—walking to the front of the room, maybe setting a laptop and a coat on a desk at the front, and starting to write the agenda for the meeting on the board. This work by the teacher is a set of recognizable practices—in doing such work, the teacher acts as the teacher in the classroom, preparing for the start of class. Students, meanwhile, are also engaged in recognizable actions—pulling out notebooks and books, sitting in chairs, engaging in quiet conversation while waiting for the clock to strike 9:00 a.m.

What we have here, then, is the co-construction of some social facts as we saw earlier in the chapter: who the students are and who the teacher is. But we also have a third: the fact that class has not yet begun. The students and the teacher are working together to *prepare* for a class, to *assemble for* a class, but also to *not yet begin* the class. And there are good reasons for that: some students might be coming from the other side of campus or still trying to find parking, and they have the expectation that class will begin at 9:00 a.m. and not at 8:55 a.m. At (or around) 9:00 a.m., the teachers and students will work together to begin class, to recognize it as having begun, and will use that fact to shape their interactions.

In this work of establishing some rather straightforward social facts, we see students and teachers working off of some shared sense of a contract: what the teacher can do and is expected to do (be at the front of the room, write on the board, start class on time) and what the students can do and are expected to do (be roughly on time, sit in a chair, wait for class to start). Again, these are not the result (entirely) of explicit prior knowledge by the students and teacher. The members of this class constitute themselves as a class through not only prior knowledge but also interactional work and engagement with surrounding materials (e.g., blackboard, desks, chairs). We can imagine the thinking-perceiving-saying-acting combinations at work here as the (re)construction and (re)enactment of a social contract—agreed-upon courses of action. The establishment of that contract is always a little bit new, a little bit different, a little bit improvised, but it is nevertheless a *contract*, an agreement (spoken or not) between social actors.

This notion of a social contract can help us understand how facts are instantiated from one moment to the next, one class meeting to the next, one semester to the next. It can help us frame the way we see writing programs operating. But we need to do one more thing before this frame is useful for us: we need to understand social contracts as always fundamentally *plural*. We are never working with and on one contract. Rather, the histories of our engagement with others travel with us to each new interaction, and those expectations shape the contracts acted upon in each next moment of interaction.

Understanding the plural nature of contracts will help us recognize and understand the disconnects across multiple moments of contracts-in-use that we will see when we study the writing program. In particular, they will help us understand the ways race, gender, class, and other aspects of othering emerge through interaction. We can look to two sources to guide us through this: Charles W. Mills's *The Racial Contract* and Anne Warfield Rawls and Waverly Duck's *Tacit Racism*. By bringing these two texts together, we can see how race, gender, and class may be enacted from one moment to the next.

Mills's (1997) work on social contract theory culminates in the Racial Contract, a political, moral, and epistemological exploitation contract that separates "white" from "non-white" and assigns different roles, privileges, and powers. Mills notes that "all whites are *beneficiaries* of the Contract, though some whites are not *signatories* to it" (11, original emphases). While Mills usefully historicizes the Racial Contract and provides a powerful explanatory framework through it, I have, in my own administrative work, struggled to use it as a lens to see the ways race operates in a program. To mobilize this within an ethnomethodological framework, I turn to Rawls and Duck (2020) and their notion of tacit racism.

Rawls and Duck (2020) draw on ethnomethodology and conversation analysis to show that two groups of participants in studies—one identifying as white (and from a largely white community) and one identifying as Black (and from a largely Black community)—have different patterns of turns at talk that they rely on. In other words, the social contracts that each community leans on are different, leading to circumstances that can enact, to greater or lesser effect, the Racial Contract. For instance, in chapter 1 of their book, Rawls and Duck note that different rules shape introductory sequences between the two groups. The disconnect in these expectations for sequences can lead to racialized conclusions that further reinvent and transform the Racial Contract and, by extension, other social contracts in action.

Attending to interaction calls attention to the production of multiple contracts in action, showing how social worlds are constructed just-here, just-now, in just-this-place, and at just-this-time-in-history. And we can think not only of race but of gender, socioeconomic status, and so on. It can be a starting point for the kinds of intersectional, interdependent frameworks that Laura Gonzales and Janine Butler (2020) call for. Understanding facts as emerging from interaction, and with a background of social contracts working with and against one another for another first time as new facts are produced, is our starting point for not only looking for the production of facts but for starting to explain how and why they may have come to be. Across the next three sections, we will put these ideas to work as we begin to collect artifacts that will help us, in chapter 2, build accounts of facts and fact production in this writing program.

How Does the Program Perpetuate Itself?

The previous sections provide a sense of how the reader might imagine facts as getting established and perpetuated: people, objects, and talk interact to produce aligned understandings that are treated like facts, much like the line at the register above. This interactional work enacts, for a next first time, a social contract for action. This social contract is actually plural (that is, multiple contracts are enacted at once) and is emerging from a history of past situations in which social contracts have been constructed for and by the people, objects, and talk in the current situation.

What I have just described probably seems like a bit of a mess. The agreement is ongoing, the contracts are multiple, and the histories that individual actors, objects, and snippets of talk are working from are plural and, at times, competing. Yet the formation of a line seems unproblematic. Turns at talk do not seem to be, for the most part, contentious (though they certainly *can* be, of course). This seems to be a very messy way of describing the ordinary.

In fact, that's exactly what it is. But it doesn't describe the ordinary as messy so much as it *uncovers* the messiness of the ordinary. What we perceive to be rather unproblematic talk is the result of a great deal of interactive work that is, by its very nature, effaced. It's not until a contract is breached that this work becomes visible, for the most part (thus the struggles Garfinkel [2002] and others had to find *perspicuous sites* of social order in action). Part of the accomplishment of ordinary action is that it *seems* unremarkable.

But if the production of facts is so messy, how do organizations survive? After all, the university seems to move through the semester, from one to the next, without much trouble, at least on the outside. Devastating though the pandemic has been for higher education, the fact is that most US institutes of higher education in 2020 and 2021 were able to open their doors, in person or online, for over a year and still move students into and out of classes. If there's an underlying cacophony of activity, where might we look for such stability? How might we be able to frame our writing programs as perpetuating themselves over time?

To think about the perpetuating of writing programs, we need to think about two ways in which programs are, in part, stabilized: with text and with buildings. Texts help stabilize social order. They become the things we turn back to, again and again, when producing social order. We look to stop signs, street signs, and maps while driving. We turn to syllabi, assignment prompts, and rubrics while teaching. And we look to semester schedules, teacher constraint forms, and classroom availability lists when building course offerings. Texts such as these bring people together with some sense of regularity, allowing particular facts—who the teacher and students are, what counts as which grade in a class, who gets assigned what section of which course—to be interactionally reproduced again and again.

Helping texts along are buildings (see LaFrance and Cox [2017] for a particularly compelling tracing of what buildings and space can do). The classrooms we meet in have some affordances and not others, invite certain kinds of activity and problematize others. We draw off of the buildings we are in just as we draw off of the position of the bodies of others to decide where we are and what we are doing—and, in the process, create facts that we and others operate off of. The combination of facts and buildings guides our use of talk and tools to co-construct facts again and again, week in and week out, semester in and semester out.

Even with the help of these artifacts, though, you are likely imagining that the facts produced are multiple, contradictory, and, in some ways, likely problematic. And that's the thing: they are. What we are looking for when we examine a program is not a grand, cohesive narrative anchored by complementary facts but a spotted, contradictory, somewhat confusing set of narratives driven by facts that complement and contradict one another in bewildering ways. It is important to see *both* the complementing and the contradicting, the smoothness as well as the messiness. It is only when seeing both that WPAs can understand the way a program creates and solves problems—and, in doing so, perpetuates itself. The concept of social contracts, as will be seen in chapters 2 and 3, will be a useful tool in not only tracing the complements and contradictions but in using them as a starting point to bring forward principled, meaningful change to a program.

The next section addresses what new WPAs need to know about a writing program. This will serve, in the section after that, as a starting point for artifact collection. In this work, readers will be looking for artifacts that help them understand how facts are interactionally created and operated on in this program and how these facts get stabilized over time through texts and organizational space. These facts will be both complementary and contradictory and may, at times, seem to have little relation to one another. But it's through this messiness that WPAs will be able to see (1) how problems get created and solved in their program and (2) what starting points they have for developing, in later chapters, meaningful and principled change.

What Do We Need to Know?

All writing programs are different. There are, after all, more than 4,000 institutions of higher learning classified by the Carnegie system, each of them serving different populations and with different missions in mind. That said, however, all writing programs have similar problems to solve: classes need to be staffed, writing needs to get assigned and assessed, and so on. These basic similarities create a broad set of categories of what WPAs need to learn across programs. Of course, the specifics of the program readers are working within will lead them to revise, add to, or delete from these categories, but the list below provides a useful starting point.

The first and most basic thing WPAs need to know is *what does your program do?* Is it a first-year writing program? A writing across the curriculum program? A writing center? Readers can think about this in two ways. First, they can see what the program calls itself—what it says on the website, how its members talk about it, and so on. Second, they can see what other programs on campus call it: deans and provosts, department chairs, different kinds of programs on campus. What do they imagine the program to be and to do? When do they turn to the program? For what purposes? These two approaches might give us wildly different answers. And that would be (in addition to very interesting) very good to know when starting to assemble facts and mobilize them into stories in chapters 2 and 3.

The next question to turn to is *where is your program?* I mean this in a physical and an organizational sense. Where, on campus, might we find your program? Where is space set aside for it? Where's the program office? Where does the program interact with students? Does it have its own classroom spaces, or are they shared with other programs? Where are offices of the faculty and staff who run the program? This is often something visible on a map, on a course website, or on a schedule of course offerings. A program might be far-flung, with classes operating throughout the day all over campus. Or perhaps the students come to the program in particular classrooms in a particular wing of a building (or in a particular writing center).

Knowing physically where the program is can be a starting point for understanding some of the ways facts get produced in the program. Does a teacher who has to move all the way across campus have time to talk with her office mates between classes? Probably not. So, what's the effect of this? How does this teacher contribute to the facts that are produced in and as part of this program? Obviously, this is just one example of how the physical work of the program comes to matter. But I hope it makes clear the ways it is possible to use the physical layout of the program to better understand, in addition to other questions that get answered, how the program perpetuates itself.

In addition to understanding the physical layout of the program, readers also need to know how the program operates organizationally. So, where is the program located in the larger structure of the institution it is part of? To whom does the program director answer? What other units on campus does it directly interact with? Toward what end(s)? How is funding of the program coordinated, and by whom? These questions provide an understanding of where the program fits in organizationally.

The first two questions I posed gave a sense of the work of the program and where it sits within the broader institution. Next up is knowing the ebb and flow of program life, not just in space but in time. So, the next question WPAs need to ask is *what is your program's calendar?* There is a lot to this question. Some aspects of answering it are rather straightforward—for instance, the academic calendar of the college or university is going to shape course offerings, grading deadlines, and so on. But there are more and more nuanced timing issues relating directly to the program: hiring new faculty, assigning course loads, organizing professional development, and so on. An additional consideration is the timing of particular days and weeks: when might most administrative help be available? What time does the program office open and close?

The final question WPAs need to ask is *who constitutes your program?* The program, after all, is run *by* and *for* people. It does particular things for them, allows them to act in particular ways. Who are these people? What students, teachers, and staff work together to make this program happen? What is their relationship to one another? When and how do they interact, and for what purposes? What expectations might they have about the program, and how do they see those expectations as being met? Answering these questions doesn't just tell WPAs who constitutes the program; it provides clearer motivations for the operations of the program, its place in the university, and the day-to-day, week-to-week, and semester-to-semester way it operates.

As readers can no doubt see, all of these questions, to one degree or another, overlap and interact. The timing of the program's operations is influenced, at least in part, by the folks who run it and the students it serves. Thinking about these questions individually, however, can be useful in making sure that nothing falls through the cracks. The next section explores possible artifacts that can generate answers to each question.

What Artifacts Can We Get?

As you were reading the previous section, you were likely thinking about the many ways we might go about answering these questions. If I want to know, for instance, what the ebb and flow of activity in a program office looks like, there's a great deal I can do. I can look up schedules and calendars on the program or university website. I can interview folks who work in the program. I can perform an ethnography that would trace the work of staffers in the office throughout a full calendar year. I can record, transcribe, and analyze turns at talk to understand the moment-to-moment production of facts in the office.

As all of these examples suggest, a range of commitment levels is available to get answers. A search of a program website might take a few minutes. A full, detailed ethnography of an office might take years to work up. Time, however, is rarely on a WPA's side. If you're a new WPA reading this, you might have a year or so, at best, to get up to speed. If you're a graduate student in a WPA course, you might be looking through a program you adopted from a distance and have only a few meetings, some emails, and perhaps some shared texts to use, in addition to the single term you'll be in the course. WPAs have to be strategic in their selection of materials and let our artifact selection be guided, in part, by the time and resources we have available to expend on the work. After all, we're burnin' daylight.

This sort of negotiation of resources is nothing new, and it is not necessarily a long-term problem. For instance, for a new WPA learning about a program, there are probably certain things they don't need to expend energy on right out the gate; there might be aspects of the program that run smoothly and that they can take a closer look at once they have a better sense of broader issues. Likewise, someone who adopted a program in a WPA course might have issues the WPA wants them to look into. In both cases, some things come to the fore more than others, and readers can use this to guide their artifact collection as it emerges. Programs and their larger institutions are always more complex than they let on (see, for instance, Scafe and Eodice 2021).

To get started, though, readers can think about what artifacts might usefully address the questions posed in the previous section. Once they have a sense of these artifacts, they can decide how much energy they need to spend generating answers to these questions and let that guide the collection of artifacts. Below, I identify some useful artifacts that might help readers address each of the questions.

WHAT DOES YOUR PROGRAM DO? What does it look like, on the ground, when your program is in action? What are the course offerings? What workshops, presentations, and other activities occur? You might look to department calendars, course descriptions and offerings, and any ongoing assessments that might be up and running. More informal aspects of the program, such as brown bag lunches or Slack channels, might turn up in discussions with colleagues in the program.

WHERE IS YOUR PROGRAM? Looking at a campus schedule and campus maps, where is your program in action? At what times of day? Where might you find program offices and the offices of faculty and staff? Are there spaces dedicated to meetings or activities for large groups? You should also find organizational charts to see where your program fits in the overall structure of the institution. Meetings with faculty, staff, and administrators in other programs can point to formal and informal collaborations, as well as the potential for further collaborations.

WHAT IS YOUR PROGRAM'S CALENDAR? Starting with the academic calendar, see what the flow of activity is like throughout the year. You can interview faculty and staff to see when and how annual reviews work, when schedules are assigned, when enrollments happened, and what celebrations/symposia are expected. You can meet with students, faculty, and staff to see what less formal events happen throughout the year as well and which people are involved in them.

WHO CONSTITUTES YOUR PROGRAM? The obvious answer to this question is "students, teachers, and staff," but you want to know more about those folks than just the labels. Where do students come from? What do they need? What training and expertise do faculty and staff have? You can get some of these answers from demographic data provided by your Office of Institutional Research (OIR) and your program's personnel records, but you'll also benefit from collecting new data in terms of surveys, interviews, and documents such as syllabi, meeting minutes, and so on.

These suggestions are not exhaustive, of course. You may also note that the suggestions offer a range of difficulties—anything from scouring a website to organizing interviews with upper-level administration. You want to be conscious of your time, your goals, and the resources you have available throughout the course of your study. In the next section, then, we take a close look at organizing your collection of artifacts.

Planning Artifact Collection

Artifact collection can be a time-consuming process—even more so if artifact collection and analysis are happening somewhat concurrently (which they will be—more on that in chapter 2). What readers have to think about next, then, is how they might organize this artifact collection to make the best use of their time and attention.

A good place to begin this thinking is with your own calendar. How long do you plan to collect and analyze data? What deadlines do you have? Do you have an end-of-year report to prepare? A term paper at the end of the course to write up? Whatever the deadline, you can work back from there to see what artifacts you can get of those you think you need. You will also need a sense of how many hours a week you can devote to this project, as well as any other competing projects and issues you'll need to navigate around.

In your reading of the section above, you have probably thought about what artifacts seem most important to you—and, in turn, what artifacts are low- or high-hanging fruit you can easily (or less easily) access. Using the questions and examples in the previous section, take some time to generate a list of artifacts you might like to collect. Once you have this list together, you can identify the artifacts that will take considerable time, effort, and planning to obtain. You might have to arrange a meeting with a provost, for instance, which is challenging even in slow times on campus. Or, you might be looking to meet with all of your faculty throughout the term. While making certain that you cover all your bases is difficult, the week-to-week scheduling of individual teachers is not, particularly early on.

Using (1) the artifacts you think you need, (2) the time line you have, and (3) the available hours you have per week during that time line, write a rough schedule for yourself of how you'll take on this work. My emphasis here is on the word *rough*; particularly if you are a new WPA, you'll likely have various events take you by surprise throughout the term. In my first year at UMaine, the moving company arrived in town with all my stuff on the second day of the semester. Needless to say, I struggled to get a lot of writing done that week. You also might run into information that leads you to the realization that you'll need new artifacts. You cannot plan for the unexpected, but you can be ready to adapt your plan as necessary. Beginning with the tough-to-schedule events (like meeting with a dean) and working backward to the little-scheduling-needed events (like looking through websites), you can have a general sense of what you need to do week to week to keep the project moving forward but still be ready to adapt those plans when the unexpected comes along.

In chapter 2, you will set this plan into motion and begin not only collecting but also studying artifacts to build facts and relate them to one another in ways that will let you generate detailed accounts of ongoing fact production in the writing program. The fact building and artifact collection will be going on simultaneously, similarly to a grounded theory approach (Glaser and Strauss 1967). This ongoing construction, revision, and development of facts will not just mobilize your facts but will lead to new artifacts you will want to look for, all of which will help you understand the rationality at work in and through the production of facts in your program. But the simultaneous path of artifact collecting, fact building, and account rendering will occur within the broad contours of the schedule you've just mapped out.

Resources

The resources below are a mix of current work in writing program administration to help you further develop your thinking on collecting artifacts and understanding society as interactionally accomplished.

Ansley, Jennifer. 2020. "Queering Ethos: Interrogating Archives in the First Year Writing Classroom." *Composition Studies* 48 (3): 16–34.

Conti, Maria, Rachel LaMance, and Susan Miller-Cochran. 2017. "Cultivating Change from the Ground Up: Developing a Grassroots Programmatic Assessment." *Composition Forum* 37. https://compositionforum.org/issue/37/arizona.php.

Gomes, Matthew, and Wenjuan Ma. 2019. "Student Expectation Auditing and Mapping: A Method for Eliciting Student Input in Writing Program Assessment." *Writing Program Administration* 43 (1): 111–139.

Oddo, John, and Jamie Parmelee. 2008. "Competing Interpretations of 'Textual Objects' in an Activity System: A Study of the Requirements Document in the _Writing Program." *WPA: Writing Program Administration* 31 (3): 63–88.

O'Meara, Katherine Daily. 2023. "Learning, Representing, and Endorsing the Landscape: WPA as Cartographer." In *Toward More Sustainable Metaphors of Writing Program Administration*, edited by Lydia Wilkes, Lilian Mina, and Patti Poblete, 97–122. Logan: Utah State University Press.

Pinkert, Laurie A., and Kristen R. Moore. 2021. "Programmatic Mapping as a Problem-Solving Tool for WPAs." *WPA: Writing Program Administration* 44 (2): 58–80.

Serfling, Nathan A. 2019. "Crafting a Pedagogical Identity: A Multiple-Method Examination of an English Department's Writing Pedagogy." PhD dissertation, Old Dominion University, Norfolk, VA.

2
Identifying Facts and Rendering Accounts

As chapter 1 progressed, readers may have noticed a change in emphasis between the first third of the chapter and the last two thirds. As the advice on artifact collection increased, the theoretical language of the first part of the chapter (as well as the introduction) tended to fall to the background. This is deliberate—I wanted to provide the reader with a chunk of text that would serve as an easy reference when digging into artifacts, planning meetings, scheduling visits to archives, and so on. But the theoretical framing never departed from the work of chapter 1—it was merely backgrounded, informing artifact collection and ready to be brought more explicitly forward in the identification of facts and rendering of accounts of fact production. In this chapter, I bring that theoretical language to the foreground to make sense of our analytical moves and the accounts we begin to render.

Chapter 2 is designed to guide readers through the identification of the facts on the ground in a writing program. These facts will be used to *render accounts* of what happens in the program. "Rendering accounts" is how I'll describe the mobilization of facts to understand how the program operates. At this stage, there is no identifying the underlying values of actions or any articulating what stories of writers and writing the program is telling (that happens in chapter 3). Right now, the goal is to see how different facts fit

https://doi.org/10.7330/9781646426416.c002

together and how they might be articulated in a way that matches the varieties of lived experiences that reproduce those facts.

A useful example of account rendering might be a problematic elevator in a building. Say there's a building that regularly houses writing courses. It's on the edge of campus, far from faculty offices. The elevator breaks down frequently throughout the term. When it *is* working, it doesn't hold many people and moves slowly. Furthermore, the path to the building itself is a busy one between classes; a significant chunk of the university population is active between the faculty offices and the building.

This establishes a few facts: (1) classes are frequently held in the upper floors of (2) a building far from faculty offices (3) that is hard to get to in a timely manner (4) and that has an unreliable elevator. These facts can be chained together into an account that highlights problems with holding classes in that particular building, especially during normal class times. Note that I have not highlighted any values or said anything about students and writing. I've simply brought facts together that render an account of how one aspect of the program operates.

Once multiple accounts are in place, it will be possible to start seeing consistent values at work, as well as the subtle ways stories about writers and writing are told and retold. The accounts rendered are important to seeing not just the production of facts but how those facts work together in particular ways and toward particular ends. The work of this chapter will be focused on moving from the artifacts to those accounts. Ideally, it will do so with the schedule set up in chapter 1.

Facts and Rationality: Articulating the Relationship

In the introduction and chapter 1, I traced a broad framework for fact production: facts are socially produced in interaction as people work with objects, talk, and one another to generate aligned understandings. These understandings are perpetuated in part through texts, objects, and buildings, which create a framework for the recurrence of similar patterns of social order. These productions of order bring forward, modify to greater or lesser extents, and reproduce multiple a priori social contracts that emerge from shared but individuated histories involving experiences with race, gender, and social class, among other items. The inherent and effaced messiness of social order, of the production of facts, is something writing program administrators (WPAs) will have to contend with in analyzing the artifacts identified in chapter 1. It will be helpful to rope rationality and reason into this framework a bit more tightly so there is no risk of operating on the problematic assumption that reason somehow stands apart from the ongoing production of social facts. There is no *outside* to the production of facts, and that includes our own work to understand the operations of the program.

In chapter 1, I argued that facts are something socially accomplished; they emerge in the flow of interaction among people, talk, and objects. But the production of facts, of things we take for granted in our work in the program, does something else: it perpetuates an aligned *rationality*, a sense of what counts as reasonable for people in a particular moment, for particular purposes, within the broader context of the program. When I trace the facts a program constructs, I am also getting a sense of the rationality the members of the program build together over time. As the chapter (and the rest of this book, really) progresses, it is important to keep this interactional aspect of rationality in mind. When we try to understand what makes people think they and others are being rational, we aren't turning to an external notion of rationality but rather looking closely at the work they do *to make themselves and others accountable in ways this program has considered rational*.

Pulverizing Artifacts

If facts are everywhere, if the production of facts is everything, if there is *no outside to fact production* and no place to stand to objectively see it in action, then the challenge of analyzing artifacts is to identify which facts are produced in which ways. What is needed are facts that connect to accounts, which in turn connect to principles and stories. These are the kinds of facts that can guide interventions in a program, that can help WPAs understand the directions in which a program needs to grow to serve its population of students, its constituents on campus, its local community, and the needs of the discipline of writing studies.

In chapter 1, you identified a wide range of artifacts: texts, objects, interviews, observations, and so on. This range of artifacts makes the process of analysis more difficult, but it also makes sure you can triangulate your findings to make certain that the contradictions found are not the result of a flaw in an analysis but of the ways the program operates on the ground. In this section, I outline a rough guide to analyzing artifacts, and I draw on some of the assumptions and language of grounded theory (Glaser and Strauss 1967) to do so.

Grounded theory (GT) has a complicated relationship with the ethnomethodological basis of facts, rationality, and reason I articulated at the start of this chapter. This process has more to do with the theoretical underpinnings of GT than the ways in which it may, at the early stages of the research process, be enacted. My mobilization of grounded theory's assumptions at the early stages of the research process is not, then, the kind of classic grounded theory (CGT) that Barney G. Glaser (1992) would argue for. It can best be thought of as repurposed constructivist grounded theory (Charmaz 2014). The theoretical framing throughout the text so far serves as a *sensitizing framework* (Nathaniel 2011) for using some grounded theory processes. Furthermore, I will not be using the GT processes to lead readers to articulate a middle-range theory. Instead, the chapter will remain tightly focused on artifacts to generate specific facts and narrow accounts.

Grounded theory can be thought of as *constant comparison*; that is, researchers are constantly collecting data and comparing them with other bits of data. This constant comparison is an act of violence at heart: grounded theory *pulverizes* (Brandt 2016) the data the researcher collects, allowing us to pull various facets of our records apart and put them back together to generate meaningful theories about what is happening. Throughout this section, I'll be keeping with this act of pulverizing, although the process will look a bit different than the coding that might normally be seen in a grounded theory study.

Where to begin such pulverizing? It can be identified by looking through the work of chapter 1—the prioritizing and scheduling of the collection of artifacts—to see what might come first. One of the most helpful features of GT is its flexibility: researchers move back and forth across the data collected in the ongoing acts of comparison, and future acts of analysis can lead the reader to reanalyze earlier data. So there's little risk of starting with the lowest-hanging fruit to begin pulverizing.

Let's say, for instance, that an early task in the list you developed is to collect records of past DFW rates (that is, the rates at which students earn a D or an F or withdraw from a course) in the program and also to conduct early interviews with some staff. You've got the time in your schedule to do this during the first week of the term, so you can schedule time to collect artifacts in the form of numbers (the DFW rates) and interview notes with your staff. These two seem disconnected (and, for all you know, they are), but that doesn't mean you can't start to pulverize both artifacts in meaningful ways, looking to see how (or if) they might be brought together. If you're taking notes in your interviews with staff, for instance, you might listen to them tell you how they do their jobs, toward what ends, and at what times of the day/week/year they do particular things. You'll walk away with a list of notes that you then have to make sense of. We can do this through the first act of pulverizing: open coding.

Open coding (Saldana 2009) is a process by which we apply descriptive labels to particular segments of artifacts to help us understand how they work in the writing program. A staffer might note that the biggest challenge to assigning instructors is in the weeks leading up to the start of fall semester, when student numbers change, other parts of the teaching schedule shift and pull teachers out of first-year composition sections, and so on. You might have jotted down "big challenge—weeks before fall semester—shifting numbers of Ss + Ts." You might describe that as something like "schedule shifting," which you can define as "movements within the teaching schedule before the semester begins."

As you may have noticed, these codes are going to need definitions that you can turn back to time and again. It's for this purpose that we are going to need a *code book*, a notebook or file that lets you pull together the definitions of different codes so you have them available to reference as you get more data (or to revise as needed based on those new data). Code books can be completed in Word documents, on spreadsheets, in notebooks, or in qualitative software. For the purposes of the examples that follow, I will treat them as notebook entries, which I have a preference for when coding for WPA purposes.

But code books, on their own, won't be enough for you to trace your thinking. You'll also need *memos* to trace your thinking throughout the process. Memos are a chance for you to step back from your codes, to start to pull pieces of different codes together, and to see a broader picture in action. Perhaps you note that "schedule shifting" comes up not only at the start of the term but in meetings with teachers throughout the term as they think about the demands of the coming semester. You could do some memo writing about this: why does it happen? For what purposes? With what consequences?

For the purposes of this work, the grounded theory approach I articulate above need not stand on its own. Data collection methods in writing programs are numerous (e.g., Grouling 2022; LaFrance 2019; Restaino 2012), and many different orientations can be brought to bear on the process of identifying facts and generating accounts.

Identifying Facts

In the previous section, I drew on open coding and memoing to identify broader patterns across artifacts. At this point, these codes and memos begin to cohere to reveal the kinds of facts that are produced and reproduced by the various artifacts from the writing program. Sometimes a fact (or more than one) will emerge from a single artifact, such as a file on DFW rates. Sometimes a fact will emerge across multiple artifacts. The task in this section is not to regulate facts and how they emerge but simply to follow the analysis performed earlier to see what facts can be found. Facts (as accounts do, below) have their genesis in a memo. As you are looking across artifacts and the coding and memoing you've done with and to them, you want to look for *recurrence* and *reflexivity*. These two concepts look different across different artifacts, but I can give rather capacious definitions of each to help get you started.

When we are looking for *recurrence*, we want to see where people talk, act, and move *as if* a similar thing is happening/created/in use again and again. This is recurrence as an intersubjective accomplishment, not as something that can be concretely pointed to absent social action. Say there's a particular time of the semester—for instance, around midterms—when teachers seem to grumble about work not being submitted on time. What we're looking at, when identifying facts, is not the broader story of "kids these days ignore deadlines" but rather how people come to construct *late work* at this point in the semester. What counts as *late work* at this time of the term? How does it come to be?

At first blush, this might seem rather straightforward—the students hand in work after a deadline, and the teacher marks it as late. But this seeming simplicity may actually gloss over some of the complex interactional work that makes late work happen to begin with. By looking across perspectives—at students and teachers as they navigate midterm deadlines—you can start to see a bit more of what's going on. This more developed perspective may help you generate more effective accounts that can lead to more useful interventions in the program in later chapters.

Take what you have here and see what makes *late work* recur at midterms. You can look across your notes from a great many artifacts to see how this fact emerges. Perhaps you see that the pattern of large assignments—say, four essays per term—means that the second essay tends to land just before midterm exams begin in large lecture courses (something that overlaps with first-year writing enrollment). You might also note that scaffolding into that second term paper is light: students draft rather little in the weeks leading up to it and thus end up doing the bulk of their composing as the deadline closes in. Furthermore, you might see from your meetings with students that the weight of the essay grade (say, 15% of a grade on average) is not as heavy as the midterms in, for instance, a biology class (say, 50% of a course grade).

When you put all of these artifacts together, you can see how the fact of *late work* gets constructed: students find themselves crunched for time, with a number of major assignments, and they prioritize their attention. Perhaps they even wager that losing a percentage of a grade on a late paper is worth it if they can add a few points to a more heavily weighted grade in a course in which they feel more uncertain about their grades. Now, this is only bringing a few perspectives to bear on the issue and doesn't give you *all* of the details we might find useful. But you can see how you've started to make sense of *late work* as a recurring fact around midterms that is mutually constructed by the teacher and the students. This is a good starting point, from which you might be able to add dimensions when we collect more artifacts. For instance, a number of students may simply be struggling with time management, and you have not heard from them yet because of said time management issues. But you can work that into our fact when further artifacts come in.

What you would have at the end of this, then, is a memo that describes in detail a fact you've pulled together from one or more artifacts. The second thing we need to attend to is *reflexivity*; that is, people who make up the program must act *as if* the fact exists—it must shape their social action going forward. Now, which "people" are affected will vary, of course; for instance, the data on student persistence rates might not be directly shared with teachers but will be treated as real by other administrators and various interested parties on campus. But some sort of engagement with a fact is important, as it's through this reflexivity that the facts become real (and thus consequential).

Characterizing facts with recurrence and reflexivity gives you a capacious sense of what a fact is. This capaciousness is important if you are to understand how you can go about seeing the full range of social action that makes up a writing program. Writing programs reach far beyond classrooms in a range of ways, and this definition of facts helps you trace this multidimensional activity.

In the work you'll do to identify facts, you'll find yourself with a great many memos of different lengths and levels of detail that uncover one fact or another. The varying degree of these memos is not of concern; I may need to say less about how the fact of DFW rates in a course is constructed than I do about the concept of late work because there's a more intuitive (to me) sense of how those rates came to exist. At no point in our articulation of facts will you gain an external, objective place from which to decide what is a fact and what is not. Tracing the construction of facts is a process of discovery, of seeing for the first time and from a new perspective how a writing program is made real.

Generating Accounts

Now that you have some facts to work with—and you will likely continue to work with facts as you cycle through the process of collecting and analyzing artifacts—it is time to consider how those facts might coalesce to *generate accounts* of how the writing program operates. Accounts are the stepping stones between facts and the principles and stories that emerge from them. The act of producing accounts gives a bit of breathing room: it enables the examination of how facts relate to one another in productive ways (for our purposes, that is) without worrying about the broader arc of a story or the details of a particular principle. It's a useful middle ground, a problem space of a sort, that can help WPAs step back and see (parts of) the bigger picture.

You've seen research that highlights accounts in other WPA studies, even if they don't use the word. Stacy Wittstock's (2022) careful examination of the "boss text" of the Analytical Writing Placement Exam (AWPE), for instance, emerges from the friction she detailed by generating accounts around the AWPE. Furthermore, you've probably begun to see some accounts emerge as you start to grasp various facts. As an example, you might have seen some changes in both grading policies and DFW rates over time. Is there a connection here? Perhaps; perhaps not. The goal when generating accounts is to start writing up these potential connections, to articulate how closely related facts work together. Eventually, we will need to ask things of these accounts: you will need to consolidate them, ask questions of them, and use them to craft principles and stories.

This process begins by turning our attention to the lists of facts that have been generated. Through working with codes, through the various memos that have been written, you now have a number of facts, as well as a trail of your thinking that led to the descriptions of those facts. As you're doing this work, you're likely to have a sense of how closely some facts relate to one another. For instance, you may notice that discussions of feedback and discussions of workload seem to coincide. You can use this as a starting point for generating accounts.

In a new memo, start to generate a list of facts that seem to bear relationships with one another. This does not have to be an exhaustive list—you will likely think of a number of straightforward connections rather easily, which is a fine place to start. In your memo, put those facts together in a list or a table of some kind. With this memo as a starting point, look through your artifacts, codes, and memos for the facts you've generated, and start to put in writing the connections you see across these facts.

Remember that the role of writing up accounts here is not to generate conclusions or actionable insights—this is something that will emerge in chapter 3. Instead, you're looking to put facts together in sense-making accounts. When you finish writing up an account, you should have a good idea of how a particular aspect of the program works. For example, you might note the relationships among several facts connected to the start of the semester in each first-year writing class. You've found that (1) almost all first-year writing courses have waitlists at the start of the semester; (2) a significant number of first-year writing teachers have shared that waitlisted students arrive in class on the first day; and (3) sorting out the needs of waitlisted students takes up a considerable amount of time on the first day of each class. These facts jump out at you as seeming to relate to one another.

So, how might you write up the account with those three facts in mind? How might you join them together so we can understand how these facts get produced? It would be helpful here to think back to the theoretical framing that has been emerging throughout this text: that reason, logic, and meaning are situated accomplishments, emerging *just-here, just-now, with-just-these-people-and-tools-and-talk*. What we need, then, is what Harold Garfinkel (2002, 2019) refers to as a *literal* description of what is happening.

Garfinkel uses the word *literal* in a different way than might be expected. He realizes that the act of turning an event into writing is a violence to that event, something that by its nature transforms the event. But he worked, throughout his career, to understand how writing might be used to *render* accounts of events, to write about them from the inside, from the perspective of the members engaged in the event. Your accounts need to do the same thing: they need to show how people engaged in the event you are attending to are making sense of the social facts they are constructing and reflexively engaging with.

You need to keep in mind, while doing this, that we can never *fully* render a literal image of a situation. The totality of a situation always escapes us, leaving our descriptions partial, even at their best. But there's a space between the impossibility of a fully rendered situation and an account that, in Garfinkel's language, "turns into words" (quoted in Liberman 2013, 3)—failing to capture anything about the lived experience of facts getting produced. It's in this space that your accounts need to fall.

Letting Garfinkel's description of *literal* guide you, turn your attention to the facts that have been uncovered so far. How might a member of the program, a person who participates in the ongoing production of facts that constitute it, engage with certain facts? How might you see them moving through space, interacting with others, and constructing a chain of facts that contributes to the overall production of the program?

Consider the three facts used as an example earlier in this section about the start of the term:

1. All first-year writing courses have waitlists.
2. A significant number of these waitlisted students show up on the first day of class.
3. Sorting out the waitlist situation consumes a considerable portion of the first class meeting.

You can stitch these facts together as an account by taking the point of view of someone involved in the situation. In a separate memo, you might articulate the experience as reported by teachers. You can start with the email requests to over-enroll; then move to the hectic frenzy of the start of class, with students coming to the front of the room to announce they are on the waitlist; then discuss the shortage of desks in the classroom; then outline the process of considering over-enrollment; then email students about decisions, newly opened slots in the class, and options for enrolling in other sections. Writing out this process can give you a sense of what it is like to experience (and, in that experience, produce again) these facts from the teacher's point of view.

But the teacher is not the only one working to construct these facts. There are also students, which you can break into two groups: those who are enrolled in the class, and those who are waitlisted. Each of these groups can have a separate memo; you can articulate what their situations were prior to enrolling, what their course loads are, what requirements they have for graduation, and so on. You can start to figure out what it's like to be in the precarious situation of being waitlisted, as well as what it's like to watch this unfold while waiting for class to start on the first day.

Finally, you might also step away from the classroom and rope in facts about how the writing program staff deals with late enrollments and what the rules are for enrollment in the institution at large. Once you have these memos written (about the teacher, the students, and related institutional items outside of the classroom), you can bring them together to make a multi-perspective account of fact production. This account, as you can no doubt see from the explanation above, can be dense. It need not be, of course, and perhaps it's not necessary that it is; maybe after a brief sketch of how facts fit together, you feel you have enough detail to understand how the facts work together and can move on. As you are engaged in the cyclical process of working with artifacts, facts, and accounts, you will have to make judgments about what you need to prioritize and what not to prioritize in terms of detail and attention. As you end up crafting principles and stories, you might find that you need to articulate some accounts further, which you'll be able to do thanks to your record of artifacts, codes, and memos.

Consolidating Accounts and Finding Gaps: Preparing for Principles and Stories

Following the process throughout this chapter, you've developed a number of *facts*—anything from the results of recurrent kinds of student-teacher interactions to the records we have on DFW rates in individual courses. You've also drawn on these facts to generate some *accounts*—a tied-together set of facts that tell us something about how facts relate to one another. For instance, you might have found facts about student perceptions of engagement with online learning and other facts about student persistence in online offerings in your program. The accounts you render about how these facts relate to one another can help you say a little bit more than each fact might by itself.

That said, however, you will also have a number of facts just sort of hanging out—facts that don't seem to get pulled into the accounts you've gone about rendering. These facts are not (or, at least, not necessarily) unimportant; you might just need more facts to build accounts, or you might need to see connections across accounts (the stories we'll talk about in chapter 3) to see where the facts you've found fit in. In this section, we'll work through the accounts and stray facts you've worked up to prepare for the work to come—of tracing principles and telling stories.

The work of this section can begin by thinking about how the accounts might be *consolidated*, or put into some sort of relationship with one another. You might not be able to see, yet, how *all* of these accounts relate to one another. What you are looking for at the moment are the accounts that bear some sort of relationship you can see with the data at hand. It is from these relationships that you will start to pull together stories about writers and writing.

An example here might be helpful. Say that you've developed an account about persistence rates for students who have accommodations. Students who receive accommodations from the accessibility office on campus are slightly more likely to struggle throughout the course, as evidenced by final grades and completion rates. This account pulls together facts from final grade reports, concerns raised by the accessibility office, and broader data about student accessibility at your institution. So, we've pulled together some facts from different places that tell us something useful: the program struggles to adequately support students who need accommodations.

Let's say also that there are some facts about *receiving* accommodations from the accessibility office, including reports of being swamped and in need of additional help (in particular, more hands to make the work lighter). Students, as a result, are not able to receive their accommodation letters until well into the term, which means they are already in a hole they might have to dig themselves out of when they get the paperwork sorted. So we now have an account about student persistence with accommodations and an account of students struggling to receive timely accommodation support from the institution.

These accounts bear some kind of relation to one another, and, if I designed my example correctly, the relationship is rather obvious. But you don't need to develop these accounts into a story just yet, and you don't need to say anything about the values underpinning how this situation came to be. Instead, you just have to note that the two accounts are related in some way. It's easy, particularly in such a seemingly straightforward situation as the one I just gave, to start to attribute causation or identify solutions from a couple of accounts jammed together. You might think that the struggles of students with accommodations are the result of paperwork delays, for instance, and turn your attention in that direction.

But this could be problematic on a number of fronts. First, unless your writing program is designed *much* differently from every one I've ever heard of, the WPA will not be able to say or do anything to influence the accessibility office. So, there's no way to act on a story as told by putting the problem in the accommodation office. Second, you don't know that the delay in notice of an accommodation is the problem—many teachers I know are happy to honor a needed accommodation without waiting on official notice. If enough teachers in a program honor an accommodation while waiting on notice, the delay will have little sway on overall DFW rates.

What you need, it seems, are more facts and more accounts. But you cannot let this particular case (that is, accommodation issues) be what shapes your prioritizing of your resources and attention. Rather, you need to see what other accounts there are and how they all seem to relate (or not) to one another and from there identify how you might best prioritize issues and manage the limited time you have to engage such problems. Consolidating accounts, seeing the links across accounts without jumping ahead to telling stories and proposing solutions, gives you the bird's-eye view needed to do just that.

You can develop this bird's-eye view by looking through the accounts we've generated and grouping them together (a concept map is often useful for this exercise, though it is not the only way to do it). This will help you see some straightforward relationships that can become the starting point of our later creating of stories. The accounts related to one another should cover a good portion of the facts you've uncovered. But there will be both facts and accounts that are isolated, disconnected from everything else, it seems. This is a strong signal that you need to know more about those facts and accounts and that there might be information that is as yet invisible to you.

Once you've identified connections across accounts and highlighted the facts and accounts that seem disconnected, you're ready to start working to uncover principles and articulate some of the stories about writers and writing being told through this program. In chapter 3, we begin to articulate some principles, principled practices, and stories those principled practices tell in this program. These broader visions of the program operation will be the jumping-off point for the interventions you craft in parts II and III.

Resources

The resources below are a mix of current work in writing program administration to help you develop your thinking about the many ways you can generate accounts. As you can see from the discussion above regarding "rationality," there are a great many ways for people to efface the work they do to (re)produce social order time and again. These resources provide different methods and mechanisms for making the effaced work of producing rationality visible for the purposes of generating accounts. The "Exploring Writing Programs" section can give WPAs ideas for investigating the production of accounts in their own programs. "Exploring Writing Program Connections" provides resources for thinking beyond the boundaries of a program.

EXPLORING WRITING PROGRAMS

Graziano, Leigh, Kay Halasek, Susan Miller-Cochran, Frank Napolitano, and Natalie Szymanski. 2020. "A Return to Portland: Making Work Visible through the Ecologies of Writing Program Administration." *WPA: Writing Program Administration* 43 (2): 131–151.

Inoue, Asao B. 2016. "Friday Plenary Address: Racism in Writing Programs and the CWPA." *WPA: Writing Program Administration* 40 (1): 134–155.

LaFrance, Michelle. 2023. "Practice, Work, and Further Possibilities for IE." In *Institutional Ethnography as Writing Studies Practice*, edited by Michelle LaFrance and Melissa Nicolas, 17–31. Fort Collins and Boulder: WAC Clearinghouse and University Press of Colorado.

Wood, Shane Alden. 2018. "Intersections of Genre and Assessment: Systems, Uptakes, and Ideologies." PhD dissertation, University of Kansas, Lawrence.

Wood, Tara. 2021. "Writing Program Administration and the Title IX Controversy: Disability Theory, Agency, and Mandatory Reporting." *WPA: Writing Program Administration* 44 (2): 40–57.

Young, Vershawn Ashanti. 2023. "Foreword: A Forenote from an Angry Black Man—Blackness Should Always Be Center." In *Black Perspectives in Writing Program Administration*, edited by Staci Perryman-Clark and Collin Lamont Craig, vii–xiv. Urbana, IL: National Council of Teachers of English Books.

EXPLORING WRITING PROGRAM CONNECTIONS

Champoux-Crowley, Alexander J. 2022. "Negotiation and Translation in First Year Composition WPA Work: Transformative Professional Knowledge to Composition Practice." PhD dissertation, University of Minnesota, Minneapolis.

Fodrey, Crystal N., Meg Mikovits, Chris Hassay, and Erica Yozell. 2019. "Activity Theory as Tool for WAC Program Development: Organizing First-Year Writing and Writing-Enriched Curriculum Systems." *Composition Forum* 42. https://compositionforum.org/issue/42/moravian.php.

Friedman, Sandie, and Robert Miller. 2018. "'Give All Thoughts a Chance': Writing about Writing and the ACRL Framework for Information Literacy." *WPA: Writing Program Administration* 42 (1): 72–88.

Garrett, Nathan, Matthew Bridgewater, and Bruce Feinstein. 2017. "How Student Performance in First-Year Composition Predicts Retention and Overall Student Success." In *Retention, Persistence, and Writing Programs*, edited by Todd Ruecker, Dawn Shepherd, Heidi Estrem, and Beth Brunk-Chavez, 93–113. Logan: Utah State University Press.

Grayson, Mara Lee. 2023. "Working within the Rhetorical Constraints: Renovation and Resistance in a First-Year Writing Program." In *Systems Shift: Creating and Navigating Change in Rhetoric and Composition Administration*, edited by Genesea M. Carter and Aurora Matzke, 165–187. Fort Collins and Boulder: WAC Clearinghouse and University Press of Colorado.

Johnston, Emily R. 2023. "Negotiating Dominance in Writing Program Administration: A Case Study." In *Systems Shift: Creating and Navigating Change in Rhetoric and Composition Administration*, edited by Genesea M. Carter and Aurora Matzke, 189–202. Fort Collins and Boulder: WAC Clearinghouse and University Press of Colorado.

Morton-Aiken, Jenna. 2023. "Flexible Framing, Open Spaces, and Adaptive Resources: A Networked Approach to Writing Program Administration." In *Systems Shift: Creating and Navigating Change in Rhetoric and Composition Administration*, edited by Genesea M. Carter and Aurora Matzke, 321–344. Fort Collins and Boulder: WAC Clearinghouse and University Press of Colorado.

Voss, Julia, and Kathryn Bruchmann. 2023. "'It's Complicated': Scheduling as an Intellectual, Networked Social Justice Issue for WPAs." In *Systems Shift: Creating and Navigating Change in Rhetoric and Composition Administration*, edited by Genesea M. Carter and Aurora Matzke, 293–320. Fort Collins and Boulder: WAC Clearinghouse and University Press of Colorado.

3
Articulating Principles, Principled Practices, and Stories of Writers and Writing

Chapter 2 ended with a number of facts, many of which have been worked up into accounts that relate them to one another in various ways. With these accounts, you can start to trace the workaday world of the writing program and its operations. As will be seen in this chapter, these accounts can help us keep facts tied to the ground, to the working world of the program, so that what becomes visible is not just what a program and its people *profess* to value but what values they actually live out. It is in the ongoing production of these facts that you can start to identify the potential for action your future work with the program has, as well as the ways you might responsibly make use of that potential.

Relating Principles and Facts

Throughout this text so far, I have been talking about facts as drawn from recurring patterns of interaction well beyond the program, socially produced and treated as real. Now, thanks to the accounts we've generated, you don't need to move straight from facts to principles. The middle ground offered by accounts allows you to see a bit more of the bigger picture your facts are connected to. But if facts as I've defined them are at the root of how we are going

https://doi.org/10.7330/9781646426416.c003

to identify principles, then we need to make sure we understand the relationship between fact and principle before we move on.

How, then, might we go about defining principle? At the start of this text, I drew on Linda Adler-Kassner's (2008, 2016) work to get a sense of where we were headed. Adler-Kassner (2016, 461) defines principle as "those beliefs and values that lie at the core of what we do." She specifies them as "those 'die on your sword' elements, the lines you absolutely won't cross in making the decisions, choices, and sometimes compromises that comprise the everyday life of the WPA" (461). Later work that resonates with Adler-Kassner's notion of principle also highlights less violent imagery, such as culture building (Baez and Carlo 2021), sustainability (Cox et al. 2018), and unrecognized strengths (Ghimire and Wright 2021). Adler-Kassner's notion of principle helps writing program administrators (WPAs) decide not only what to do but also what to value in terms of their time and attention, in terms of the fights they are willing to have with other interested parties about the direction of their program.

My use of facts in relation to principle complicates Adler-Kassner's position slightly. If reason is emergent from interaction, from context, and from the multiple, laminated social contracts as I describe them in chapters 1 and 2, then surely our values, the beliefs we have, also emerge from interaction—furthermore, they interact with the facts as we see them. So what we value is influenced by the facts we see produced, both on a moment-to-moment basis and over time. But, conversely, the social facts we produce are influenced by that which we value.

This influence of facts on values and vice versa doesn't undercut principles in a serious way: because of the recurrence of the kinds of interaction we tend to have (and that, by extension, make up what we see as "broader" social structures such as a writing program), we can articulate the ways we tend to prefer to act in certain recurrences, and we can talk about more portable values within those moments that carry across to other, seemingly related circumstances. So far, so good.

But if what we value is shaped at least in part by the production of social facts, then there will always be aspects of our values that are unknown to us, because we haven't had cause to engage with them yet. The full span of our values always runs beyond our horizons, and we can always have the capacity to be surprised by new challenges to what we value. Furthermore, there may be circumstances we find ourselves in in which we end up *contradicting* that which we profess, in other circumstances, to value.

Such contradictions do not make us hypocrites—or, at least, not any *more* hypocritical than the average person. Values are difficult to articulate, challenging to live out, and always a little in flux in all their detail. As long as we lack omniscience, we'll lack the ability to live a fully principled, uncontradicted life. And omniscience might only make us aware of the problem without offering a solution, so even that one is a "maybe."

The alignment of a fact and a principle is a principle lived out. The clash of fact and principle is a principle that is not brought to bear, that does not (in the lived experience of the principled actor) apply, or that has not, for whatever reason, been investigated. In the next section, you'll turn to the accounts that seem to suggest some sort of underpinning set of values, that offer clues suggesting that this account matters in some significant way to the people constituting the program. That will help you later to identify contradictions, recruit more viewpoints, and set the stage for enacting meaningful, lasting, and sustainable change in the program.

Generating Principles from Accounts

Principle as I am working with the term in this book is at least partly aspirational in nature: it's a value that is worth fighting for in the bureaucracy of higher education. Your task, in this section, is to look through the accounts you've drafted to see what sorts of values seem to be underpinning them. When program staff worry about failure rates in the program, when teachers complain about particular issues of student writing, and when students respond positively to particular course offerings in evaluations and exit interviews, you get the sense that there's something going on behind the scenes. People worry about failure rates in the program because they sense it means something is amiss—that something they value isn't being met or addressed in some way. When teachers complain about a particular issue in student writing, it means they are not getting what they want out of the classroom. Likewise, when students respond positively to a course offering, it means they *are* getting what they want (or perhaps more than they realized they wanted) out of the classroom.

In all of these instances, values are at work. The values shape, at least in part, the ways these people make sense of the situation. Your task is to comb through these accounts to see the constants in those values. What *consistently* matters to teachers, to students, to staff? What *recurring* things come to light across these accounts? You might start by looking for a particular word or phrase; from there, you can draw on other accounts to articulate it into a more detailed principle. Let's look across three hypothetical accounts as an example of how you might go about this work.

The first account features responding to student writing: the students and teachers discuss the need for frequent, timely feedback on student writing. The second has to do with assignments themselves: an overwhelming opinion is leaning in favor of what scholarship in teaching and learning refers to as *spaced practice* (students receive multiple, low-stakes assignments rather than fewer high-stakes assignments). The third is about grades: teachers in the program favor mostly (although not exclusively) labor-based grading contracts, and student reporting of their experiences with these contracts has been positive.

So, there are three accounts that discuss

1. Feedback on student writing
2. Spaced practice
3. Labor-based grading contracts.

These three accounts overlap in several ways. First, they deal with the intersections of student writing and teacher assessment. Second, they reflect classroom practice—and, more specifically, key mechanisms through which curricula are delivered. Third, they inform how teachers make sense of course outcomes. So, how might you put these accounts together in a way that helps you see a principle at work? You can begin doing this by turning your attention to what underpins these accounts. What is it that the teachers in this program and their students seem to privilege when discussing each of these topics?

One item that jumps out is *lowering anxiety*. Teacher feedback that is turned around quickly often helps students locate themselves in relation to course outcomes: they don't have to guess at how they're progressing, because the recent feedback they received *told* them that. Similarly, spaced practice provides more formative feedback opportunities, so students don't have a huge percentage of their grade tied to any one event. Finally, with labor-based grading contracts, students don't have to worry about identifying a particular level of quality in their writing and meeting it; instead, the work of the course can be a place to explore ideas and try out new things while knowing concretely what to expect in terms of grades.

Lowering anxiety as an underpinning concept seems to work for teachers as well; frequent feedback opportunities (and more formative moments) allow teachers to see a great deal of student writing and may lower their concerns that perhaps students are not "getting" a concept, idea, or approach. Labor-based grading, likewise, takes judgments of qualities off of their plates and lets teachers engage with student writing meaningfully instead of as a means of assessing course progress.

We can identify one more underlying value of these accounts at work for teachers: they seem to value engaging with students and student writing on the students' terms. Without having to judge writing, without ramping up to high-stakes assignments, and with more opportunities to engage with student writing, these teachers can keep the ball in the students' court, so to speak.

So, you now have two different values at work that you can find (we can probably find more, but two is enough for this example). First, there is *lowering anxiety*. Second, you have *respecting student motives and goals*. It remains to be seen whether these are two different values or two different facets of a more abstract value; as you begin working up more and more principles, you will start to see how abstract you can make the principles you detail while also keeping them useful.

One potential way you can bring these values together is by seeing one of these values as an outcome of the other. So, perhaps *respecting student motives and goals* is best performed by *lowering anxiety* in any given class, on any given assignment. That would mean you could write out a principle like this:

> This writing program respects student motives and goals by creating multiple, low-stakes opportunities to write, discuss writing, and move toward course outcomes.

Does this work as a principle? Perhaps. This is where you would turn back to the accounts. Does this principle provide a broad, underlying explanation for much of what is seen in these accounts? Can you see this value at work across the accounts you have derived it from?

If the answer to these questions is *yes*, then you have a potential principle to work with. Of course, there will be contradictory aspects of the program—moments in which this value isn't enacted or perhaps is contradicted. For now, though, what you need to do is identify the principles you can find across accounts, articulate them as best you can, and make sure that what you articulate has an honest connection to the accounts you've drafted and the facts that underpin them.

Drawing on the example above as a guide, take time to articulate some of the principles you see emerging across the various accounts you've drafted so far. What values seem to underpin these accounts? What do the people in your program believe in, try to enact, and insist on working toward? Furthermore, what values might they be enacting that they may not be aware of working toward? What lurks in the corners that everyday program operations tend not to look at? Once you have a few values worked up, you can start to think about how you might define, from these principles, the *principled practices* at work in the program.

Articulating Principled Practices

As I mentioned earlier, *principled practice*, for a WPA, is decision making that is informed by values, by expertise in the field, and by the particular needs of the contexts in which the WPA is working. Now that you have some principles to work with, you can identify those that are enacted in ways that (1) are informed by expertise in the field and (2) address the particular needs within the contexts of the program. These principled practices will be the grounds on which you build the stories about writers and writing that the program is telling and the starting point from which you begin to make principled, productive, and meaningful programmatic change in the short and long term.

It's important to remember the direction in which these principled practices will be taking you, because you have no doubt discovered some practices that clash with your values, what you know about writing as a discipline, and what the students and teachers in the program need. It is important that you know about these factors, but they cannot be the building blocks for a program you want to run. They contain within them inherent issues that will lead to a program that, in various ways both great and small, fails its constituents. Principled practices build on the bedrock of values while looking ahead to the future with a wider landscape of knowledge than local traditions or individual preference would permit.

The articulation of principled practice, of course, begins with principle. You've already tightly linked the principles you've found to particular accounts. The connection between accounts and principles can give you a start on this: obviously, the accounts you've drafted are enactments of the principles you've found. Starting from these connections, look for enactments of principles that relate to what we know about writers and writing. By way of example, you can turn back to the hypothetical principle I worked up earlier in this chapter. Your value of *respecting motives and values through low-stakes opportunities to write* is connected to three aspects of the program: feedback, spaced practice, and labor-based grading contracts. What in these accounts can be linked to what the field knows about writers and writing?

Quite a bit, of course. Spaced practice has been demonstrated to be superior to massed practice, and we can tie several strains of research to that. Likewise, writing studies has been looking into grading contracts for some time (e.g., Danielewicz and Elbow 2009), although recent work by Asao B. Inoue (2015, 2019) has raised further awareness and anchored grading contracts exclusively to labor. And feedback has long been discussed in the field as well, burgeoning with the work of Nancy Sommers (1982) in the 1980s and continuing along several different research lines ever since, up to and including books (e.g., Ferris and Hedgcock 2013) and feedback-dedicated journals, such as the *Journal of Response to Writing*. You could go even further beyond the specifics of the classroom to theoretical perspectives that would shape assessment, such as Ruth Osorio's (2021) disability-as-insight approach or Lisa Blankenship's (2019) theory of rhetorical empathy. Clearly, there is quite a bit to work with.

But it's important to remember that not all links that you'll find between research and a particular principle are going to be worth transforming into a principled practice. A *principled* practice has a particular value for the people in your program: it's a signature practice, one that demonstrates who they are and what they do at their best. When your teachers think of themselves *as* teachers, it's the principled practices (and both aspects—the principle and the practice) that come to mind. And it's that act of valuing that you'll have to focus on as you identify tentative principled practices.

Consider, for instance, this notion of spaced practice. My use of it in the example above is just part of a hypothetical example. But if I were articulating my *own* principled practices, I wouldn't mention spaced practice. I use that approach because it's been proven to be useful, not because of its direct connection to my own values. If more research demonstrated that massed practice worked better, I would do that instead. The research you focus on, much like the practices themselves, have to be things you can see are demonstrated as valuable in the accounts.

We can demonstrate that a practice (and its connection to research) is valuable by examining the second component of describing a principled practice: it addresses particular needs in the contexts of the program. So, if you look at the three accounts from which the principle of respecting student motives and values arises, what particular needs do you see in those accounts that the practices address?

Perhaps, when you look into it, you see that teachers began using labor-based grading contracts as a response to reports that first-generation students in the program were receiving lower grades in the course than their peers. Labor-based grading contracts were enacted to combat this issue. They helped create a context for students to find and pursue their own goals in a class, through the values they held, without causing those goals and values to hamper their reported accomplishment of course outcomes. What you would have here, then, is a practice (labor-based grading contracts) in line with a principle (respecting motives and values of students), connected to research (Danielewicz and Elbow 2009; Inoue 2019) and responding to particular needs of the program (addressing the needs of first-generation students). In other words, you have a potential principled practice.

This is, to be sure, a rather specific principled practice. Perhaps looking across spaced practice and feedback, you might be able to make this principled practice a bit more abstract: maybe you could talk about *respecting student labor* through an umbrella of options involving curricular strategies, feedback, and grading policies. But that might not be possible or even useful to the needs of you and your program. It will be up to you and the members of your program to define the limits of principled practices.

Your task at this point is to look across the principles you articulated and triangulate across the principles, the accounts, the research in the field, and the context of your program a handful of principled practices: things that drive your program, that show your program at its best. Once you have done that, you can start to explore the kinds of stories that are getting told by the program.

Telling Stories with Principled Practices

You have done a great deal so far in this book: you've identified facts, which you've worked up into accounts, which you've looked across to uncover principles, which you've highlighted and specified further through principled practices. These principled practices are indeed useful on their own: you can use them to talk with new students at orientation, with interested folks in other departments, and with accreditation committees about what your program looks like, in action, at its best. You can help students understand what the program is asking of them, what the rationale is behind those asks, and so on.

But your program's principled practices also need to work together to promote a positive understanding of student writing and writers in the program.

You need to know not just what you do but what the things your program does convey to outsiders about student writers and writing. Toward that end, then, you can start to think about how you can tell coherent, principled, and integrated stories through the everyday operations of your program.

Stories pervade both our lives and our work as not only WPAs but also teachers of writing (see, for instance, Haswell and Lu 2000). Adler-Kassner (2008) provides a great roadmap for thinking about how you can tell stories to interested parties about student writers and writing. In this section, I walk you through how you might use the principled practices you just articulated to think not about how to create a story but rather about how your program is *already* telling stories about writers and writing through the enactment of those principled practices. By doing this, you will be able to get a sense of how the program interacts with other interested parties when talking about student writers and writing, where you want to revise those interactions, and what kinds of new stories you might want to tell.

You can start to see these stories by looking across the principles and principled practices you just identified. This can help you see both the abstract stories you and your program tend to tell (or try to tell) and what these stories look like "on the ground" of the workaday world of your writing program. I'll walk you through this with an example. Let's consider, for instance, the values of the College Composition program at UMaine. Our program has identified five principles that shape our work. When we design classroom activities, respond to student writing, draft assignments, and so on, we should do so in ways that

> Respect the importance and complexity of writing as a social practice
> Support students as they repurpose past writing practices for academic purposes
> Respect student labor
> Introduce students to the social purposes of academic writing through a meaningful, legitimate, and collaborative semester-long project
> Reflect ethical, responsible assessment practices.

Now, what might these principles look like in action? If you were to step into an English 101 classroom at UMaine, what might you see that would call your attention to these values?

If I were to think about the ways we practice these principles in the classroom, I could point to a number of practices in three broad categories: feedback, assignment design, and peer interaction. It's within these three categories that you can most easily see how these principles come to life in our classrooms in English 101. You'll see assignment prompts that don't try to "flatten" writing by demanding a particular paragraph structure, a particular number of words or pages, or a particular formatting. You'll see feedback that calls back to previous assignments while priming students for the next one, that values the work students have done by looking at what *is* in the text rather than what's missing. And you'll see class discussions that emerge from and contribute to student work while constantly bringing to the surface for investigation the language of our *Portfolio Assessment Rubric*, which is what students' final portfolios will be scored according to.

As you look across the principles and their classroom instantiations, then, what might be some stories that can be told about student writers and writing? What do people in the program keep saying about students and what they're able to do when they engage in the act of writing—and, by extension, what that writing itself can later accomplish? The stories that are developed here need to be, as Adler-Kassner (2008) points out, *new* stories of student writers and writing. The stories need to help us counter pernicious myths about what students can and cannot do, what they do and do not accomplish in the classroom, through writing. They can also help us tell new stories about writing and the teaching of writing more broadly, since, as Lori Salem and Peter Jones (2010) note, orientations toward (and thus stories about) these topics can vary widely across a program.

If I'm looking across the principled practices of the UMaine composition program, then, I would be able to see stories that, rather than identify students' struggles, celebrate student accomplishment. Our students regularly work successfully with difficult texts. They learn to articulate challenging ideas that are at the very edge of what their current rhetorical powers allow them to do. And they pass our portfolio review in massive numbers.

I'm not trying to tout how wonderful students at UMaine are. I mean, I *am*, but what I am also trying to do is demonstrate that if we can point out our values and how those values are lived—and if those values that we articulate resonate across the program—then we can say something meaningful about student writers and student writing that can help us challenge common (and damaging) stories about them. Our values don't just shape our actions—they also *tell us something* about what's going on in the program; we can use that to change narratives of student writing and writers on our campuses.

We can begin this work by turning to the principles and principled practices we've developed and thinking about how we might challenge some commonly held understandings about student writing and writers. As part of helping our students respect the complexity of writing as a social practice, for instance, we regularly ask them to read difficult texts. They struggle with these texts, of course—they're difficult. And they've rarely encountered anything like them before. But through the course of the semester, they come to not only understand the texts but to learn to develop new lines of inquiry with and through them. This is something we can draw on to say "wow, look what our students are capable of."

What I've done here is identify a principle (respecting the complexity of writing as a social practice), connect it to a practice (reading difficult texts), and draw from those two practices something (1) our students are capable of and that (2) counters a common and problematic story (for instance, that students are struggling readers). Because it's coming from our principled practices, I know it's tied to research (giving students appropriately scaffolded and challenging tasks is tied to higher student achievement). Because it's tied to our principles, I know it's tied to recurring facts and accounts throughout our program. And if I wanted to, I could do more than just tell this story in meetings or in hallway conversations: I could start to generate data that can be shared in reports, publications, and presentations both on and off my campus.

Recruiting Viewpoints and Acknowledging Contradiction

As this chapter moves toward its close, you now have a number of facts, accounts, principles, principled practices, and stories about writers and writing. The last three items in that list—principles, principled practices, and stories—have an important outward-facing function: they tell interested parties outside the program what our program is about. But, like all stories, many items are left out. There are contradictions, competing viewpoints, and uncertainty in the program. It's important to acknowledge these internally, even if it would contradict external messaging to roll this into a statement of principles and the telling of stories.

The first thing to do, then, is to roll out these principles, principled practices, and stories for review by your program. You'll have to create a window for feedback, then orchestrate some kind of revision, as necessary, to make sure concerns brought up during feedback are addressed. A good example of this is the establishment of what we call the UMS-OS, or the University of Maine System Outcomes Statement.

Years ago, the University of Maine System (UMS) created transfer agreements among the schools in the system and the community college system for a range of courses, with English 101 chief among them, if only because everyone has some version of English 101. But there was little beyond that agreement besides bureaucracy: English 101 might look quite different across the various campuses the transfer agreement brought together.

Thanks to a grant from the vice chancellor for academic affairs, WPAs at all UMS campuses came together and wrote the UMS-OS, which provided common language and shared goals for English 101 courses throughout the system. The work of these outcomes would not be as dynamic as, for instance, the multi-institutional approach Steven Accardi, Nicholas Behm, and Peter Vandenberg (2022) trace, but it would be an important step in greater multi-institutional writing support across the state.

The process of drafting the outcomes went smoothly, and a first pass at a finished document came together in about a year. At the end of our first semester of work, we established a draft document that was circulated among teachers of English 101 at various campuses. This period of feedback led us to crucial revisions that, later, teachers in various programs felt they were more able to work with.

As you go about developing your principles, principled practices, and stories of writers and writing, it will be important that you try to make sense of the divergences in those stories. There are always contradictions, paradoxes, and uncertainties in a program, and to ignore them is to ignore the important voices of some members of the program—and thus to shortchange its potential for development (see Belanger and Gruber 2005 for a practicum-focused example). We will discuss how to work through problems and clashes of principle that arise in part II, but the principles and principled practices in this chapter need to be shared and mutually understood, and they must emphasize the overlaps while leaving room to work through the divergences in the future.

So, how do we do this? And, more important, how do we do this in a way that is even somewhat timely? If we need to wordsmith every word (and, if you're in an English department, you're going to do need to do that), how can we keep things moving in a timely manner?

To begin with, you will want to organize groups of interested parties that can look at and offer feedback on your principles and principled practices. You'll want all interested parties to have a say in what you develop, but you also don't want to try to work through the feedback of forty people or so at once.

You might want to start with a small committee of program members who can represent different constituencies. For instance, when our program revises our *Portfolio Assessment Rubric*, we're sure to have a mix of teaching assistants, adjunct instructors, and full-time folks involved. You might do something similar for a first pass at writing and reading principles, principled practices, and stories.

This small committee would not be the end of the feedback, but it might be able to anticipate objections and concerns by people in the program that you—as a new WPA—might not know as well. This can lead to a revised set of principles, principled practices, and stories that can make for a more productive discussion with larger groups of interested parties.

These larger groups can be addressed in a range of ways, depending on the needs of your program. If your program is heavily involved in service learning, you might want to have meetings with community members so you can be certain that the principles and principled practices you develop resonate with their needs and are sensible to them. You might want that meeting to be separate from, say, faculty members, at least at first.

Since you're using the principles and the principled practices as a launching point to tell new stories of writers and writing, you'll want to make sure those in the program (or, in the example above, those working directly with it) have first say in what counts as a principle and a principled practice—and if there's a contradiction, how a principle or principled practice might be able to work around that contradiction. Once the people in your program know how to make sense of and interpret these principles, you can move on to other, more adjacent interested parties. For instance, if you're in an English department like I am, you may have colleagues in your department who have no engagement with your program. It may be helpful in terms of departmental support to get their insights into your principles and principled practices, but you wouldn't want their voices to wash out those of your faculty (this can particularly problematic if you have a large adjunct corps). You might, if you are in a position to do so, also use the principles to shape the direction of the larger department you're in, as Christine Farris (2021) demonstrates.

Once you've obtained the necessary nods for your principles and principled practices, you'll be ready to tell new stories of writers and writing—and, more important, you'll be in a position to begin developing ambassadors for your program, people who can tell the stories for you. At this point, you've developed a good sense of how your program operates—what it does best, how it does it, and where it's capable of improvement. Here, at the end of part I, you have a sense of how your program can operate successfully now and how you might make it work better in the future.

The Challenge of Change

As you pull these principles, practices, and stories together, you're probably starting to realize that in articulating what was previously not articulated, you are, indeed, changing things: you're making concrete what was previously unspoken or abstract, and you're shaping (if only subtly) the ways the program operates. This change isn't just necessary; it's unavoidable. By engaging with this program, by participating in its operations in some way, you are bringing change to the program. This isn't a bad thing, by the way; it would be strange indeed if you moved into a position of power in a program and nothing really changed.

I bring this up because some tension might emerge from this change. As Laura J. Davies (2017) notes about grief and a new WPA, this tension might be something that, at least temporarily, cannot be helped. Understandings of writing and teaching writing change over time (Olejnik 2019), and *you* will change through your experiences with the program (Rose 2005), so you might have understandings about how a program should run that go against what some others think. Furthermore, if you are stepping into a program that has a high number of people in liminal positions (adjunct instructors, teaching assistants), there may be real concern about security of employment, of working conditions, and other issues. Often, these teachers have little control over what their supervisor is able to do; they have to trust that the person they are working for will treat them well and will give them the circumstances they need to thrive. Building that trust takes time. This can be true in more friendly employment environments as well (i.e., Norgaard 2017), depending on the larger structural tensions at work.

So the tensions that might, from your perspective, seem as if they are created by you are, in at least some way, a necessary part of the transformation of the program that happens merely because a new person has stepped into the WPA position. It is my hope (and my experience, if only in part) that the work you do to listen, to build from the ground up in the ways part I has guided you, will allow this trust to be built, will help people see that you value them, their work, and their contributions to the program.

This trust is going to be important for the work coming up in part II and is absolutely crucial to the long-range planning you'll be doing in part III. Part

II is, in large part, responding to the circumstances you can now see in the program thanks to the work you've done in part I: in many instances, you'll be providing much-needed results that respond to problems perceived by people in the program. By demonstrating through the work of part II that you are listening to the concerns of the program, you'll be better able to build a long-lasting ethos that can serve as a bedrock for you as you build your program.

Resources

The resources below can help you think through the details of developing principles, principled practices, and stories. The resources under "Principles" directly attend to values and how you might explore them. "Principled Practices" resources highlight ways principles might be enacted through practice. "Stories" resources provide WPAs with methodologies, metaphors, approaches, and ideas for generating stories about writers and writing.

PRINCIPLES

Broad, Bob. 2003. *What We Really Value: Beyond Rubrics in Teaching and Assessing Writing*. Logan: Utah State University Press.

Dibrell, Denae, Andrew Hollinger, and Maggie Shelledy. 2023. "Fugitive Administrative Rhetorics." *WPA: Writing Program Administration* 47 (1): 148–162.

Rylander, Jonathan J., and Travis Webster. 2020. "Embracing the 'Always-Already': Toward Queer Assemblages for Writing across the Curriculum Administration." *College Composition and Communication* 72 (2): 198–223.

PRINCIPLED PRACTICES

Buyserie, Beth, Anna Plemons, and Patricia Freitag Ericsson. 2017. "Retention, Critical Pedagogy, and Students as Agents: Eschewing the Deficit Model." In *Retention, Persistence, and Writing Programs*, edited by Todd Ruecker, Dawn Shepherd, Heidi Estrem, and Beth Brunk-Chavez, 151–166. Logan: Utah State University Press.

Powell, Pegeen Reichert. 2017. "Absolute Hospitality in the Writing Program." In *Retention, Persistence, and Writing Programs*, edited by Todd Ruecker, Dawn Shepherd, Heidi Estrem, and Beth Brunk-Chavez, 135–150. Logan: Utah State University Press.

Reid, E. Shelley. 2018. "Beyond Satisfaction: Assessing the Goals and Impacts of Faculty Development." *WPA: Writing Program Administration* 41 (2): 122–135.

Shea, Kelly A. 2017. "Kindness in the Writing Classroom: Accommodations for All Students." *WPA: Writing Program Administration* 40 (3): 78–93.

STORIES

Babb, Jacob. 2023. "Seeing the Forest and the Trees: A Rhizomatic Metaphor for Writing Program Administration." In *Toward More Sustainable Metaphors of Writing Program Administration*, edited by Lydia Wilkes, Lilian Mina, and Patti Poblete, 35–48. Logan: Utah State University Press.

Carter-Tod, Sheila. 2020. "The Importance of Documenting Oft-Unspoken Narratives." *WPA: Writing Program Administration* 44 (1): 148–156.

Craig, Sherri. 2016. "A Story-less Generation: Emergent WPAs of Color and the Loss of Identity through Absent Narratives." *WPA: Writing Program Administration* 39 (2): 16–20.

Sanchez, James Chase, and Tyler S. Branson. 2016. "The Role of Composition Programs in De-normalizing Whiteness in the University: Programmatic Approaches to Anti-Racist Pedagogies." *WPA: Writing Program Administration* 39 (2): 47–53.

Sanchez, Raul. 2015. "Theory Building for Writing Studies." *WPA: Writing Program Administration* 39 (1): 141–157.

Zenger, Amy A. 2016. "Notes on Race in Transnational Writing Program Administration." *WPA: Writing Program Administration* 39 (2): 26–32.

PART II

The Little Picture

As I mentioned at the start of part I, Coach B. paid relentless attention to detail. Pad level, foot placement, hand placement, communication before the snap—nothing was too small to pay attention to. "For want of a nail" was a recurring phrase in his daily work with the offensive line. But Coach B. also put those details into a greater context for us. We didn't learn only how to, say, cut block a linebacker but how to cut block a linebacker as part of a series of choices throughout a game, one that ended with our team having more points on the board than the opponent. We had to know what we were doing, but we also had to know *when* to do it so our choices could have the most powerful effect on the outcome of the game. In part II, you'll mobilize what you've learned about your program to develop a set of priorities for growing and changing it in the "short" term (figure 4.0).

You completed part I of this text with a number of resources at your disposal. You have some facts, accounts, principles, principled practices, and stories about writers and writing that you can draw from as you manage, develop, and transform your program. These are all designed to help you with everything from planning change to communicating about the good your program does. In part II of this text, we turn our attention to what I refer to as "the little picture," or the near-term plans for you and your program. This

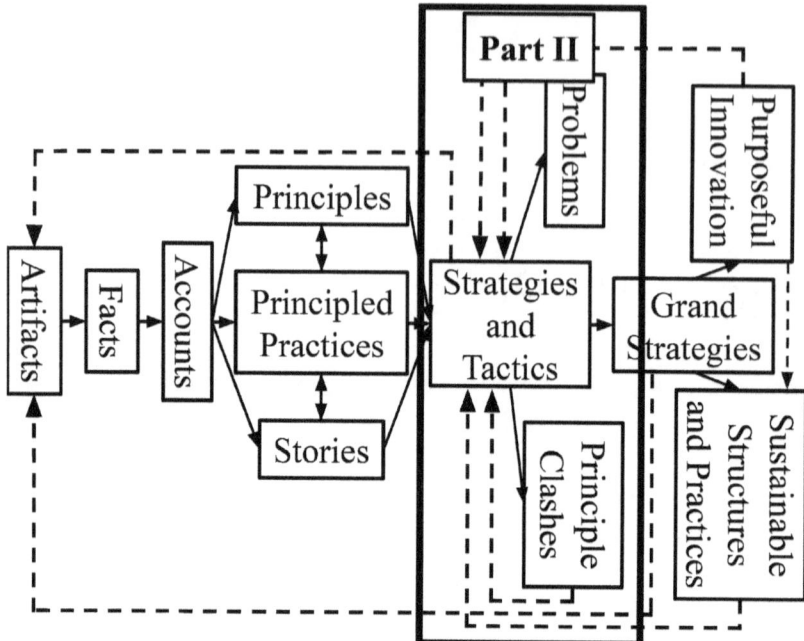

FIGURE 4.0. Part II's role in the work of this text

"little picture" is designed to help you make short-term plans for up to the next one to three years. With the work of chapters 4, 5, and 6, you'll be able to articulate a vision of the near future of your program, identify the resources that will help you get there, and adjust to changing circumstances, as needed.

Part II, then, helps you mobilize the empirically grounded claims you established in part I to make changes to your program. Many of the changes you make will be informed by the planning you do in chapter 4. There, you'll identify some strategies (that is, long-range plans running up to three years into the future) and tactics (day-to-day plans to bring those strategies to life) that will position you and your program to address immediate and pressing concerns and to position the program to address emerging midterm concerns. In chapter 4, you'll identify the ways your program needs to change and articulate, in a broad sense, a vision of how it will take on those changes throughout the course of one–three years.

With that plan in place, chapters 5 and 6 then walk you through issues that arise as you enact those changes. Chapter 5 addresses the easier (but still difficult) kind of changes you need to make: those that address long-standing issues in the program. I refer to these issues as "easier" to address because you have the wind at your back, so to speak: the people making up your program have likely long recognized these issues but did not have the resources (time, money, people) to deal with them. The fact that you're addressing these issues will be perceived positively, even if navigating the changes can be challenging.

Chapter 6 turns our attention to a tougher aspect of enacting programmatic change: resolving clashes of value between you and your program. What do you do when teachers in your program enact a value that conflicts with your own—or, sometimes more confusingly, try to enact the same value in ways you see as problematic? How do you sort through the complex web of experience, values, institutional memory, and long-term consequences for students and teachers to chart a path forward for yourself and your program?

You should wrap up part II with a clear, detailed plan for the future that has the capacity for adjustments to address the unexpected. If you're a pre-tenure WPA, this would be the kind of plan that leads into a third- or fourth-year review; it will tell your review committee what you had planned to do and how that work was carried out. If you're in a rotating WPA position, this might be a list of the goals for your term as WPA before you step down. If you're a graduate student who has adopted a writing program, this might be the sketch of program development you would offer your adopted WPA.

Having the details for this short-term plan will set us up to think about the long view of the program—that is, how you might imagine your program developing across decades. This is the work of part III, and it emerges from the short-term issues you're addressing and the new information you gather from that experience. This long-term vision, when ironed out, gives the people in your program (and you) a sense of direction, a way in which the program can be seen to be moving and that individual actions in research, teaching, and service are moving the program toward.

4
Developing Strategies and Tactics

In this chapter, we'll look through what you've found out about your program, the ways you would like to change it, and the mechanisms of change that are available to you to craft a short-term plan for programmatic change. For most readers, this planning will be for about one to three years. If you think about the work of part I stretching out over an academic year, then the work of part II would involve planning from the end of that first year up through a major annual review (usually in the third or fourth year, if on the tenure track). If you are a rotating writing program administrator (WPA)—that is, someone who rotates in and out of the WPA position with several other colleagues—then this might comprise your term of service. If you're a graduate student planning a fictional future for an adopted writing program, this chapter is an opportunity to think through what it means to run a writing program on a day-to-day basis while also planning for the future.

Thinking in the Short Term: One to Three Years

It probably sounds strange to many readers to think about the "short term" as consisting of three years. After all, that is most of a doctorate for many people. But when you are thinking about implementing stable and lasting change in an institution as complex as a writing program (or, for that matter, in higher education, broadly speaking), change often takes time. It takes time to plan, to implement, to expand. As Laura J. Davies (2013) demonstrates, change is always slower than WPAs want it to be (paradoxically, the changes people *don't* want always seem to happen far too quickly).

An initial plan stretching from one through three years is a fine starting point for enacting some change based on what you found in part I. It's a short enough time frame to be responsive, and it's a long enough time frame to see real results emerge. In this chapter, you will think about targeted transformations of the program: how you can go about making real change happen and seeing the impact of that change on the program.

Depending on the structure of your institution, a "short-term" view of one to three years can mean two–six semesters or three–nine quarters/trimesters. It's within this time frame that you are going to target, organize, and enact change in your program. To do this, you will be drawing on Linda Adler-Kassner's (2008, 2016) notions of *strategies* and *tactics*. You will also do concept mapping to help you envision the things you need to prioritize and organize. But first, you are just going to map out a couple of years and identify what you can anticipate.

Using a calendar or a spreadsheet (I prefer to work on Microsoft Excel, but that's a personal preference—this can work just as well on most programs, as well as on a sheet of paper), create a schedule for the next one to three years. I recommend trying to map out a full three years for the moment—a map doesn't commit you to much and helps you think about a slightly wider time frame. If you end up deciding just to focus on a single year, you won't be any worse off for having tried to look a bit further into the future.

You can organize this calendar however you'd like—for example, month by month or week by week. When working across three years, a month-by-month calendar usually works for me. With this calendar in place, then, mark off the following events:

1. SCHEDULED DEPARTMENT OR COLLEGE SELF-STUDY EVENTS. These happen on a somewhat regular schedule. There are events (like the pandemic) that can knock those numbers around, but within a one- to three-year span, you can probably identify any that have been slotted.
2. SCHEDULED ACCREDITATION REVIEWS. These are usually tied to the self-study work. You might not know all the details of the review, but you will be able to find out when your institution is due and at least mark off the year.

3. PLANNED INITIATIVES AT THE COLLEGE/UNIVERSITY LEVEL. Initiatives are not hard to find in academia. You can probably identify a few that are kicking off in the near future on the university website, or you may have heard about them in department/college faculty meetings. Not all of these initiatives will impact your program, but if there are events or launches around initiatives that may affect your program, you should note them.
4. PROFESSIONAL EVENTS. The Conference on College Composition and Communication's (CCCC) and Council of Writing Program Administrator's (CWPA) annual meetings are worth putting down on paper. You might not know the exact date of these meetings several years ahead, but you want to make sure you are aware of them, as they are potential venues for promoting your program within the discipline.
5. CAREER MILESTONES. You should be able to access the requirements of your annual reviews, the time line for reaching out to external reviewers, and so on. Be sure that you're aware of these moments, and have them accounted for on your schedule.
6. PERSONAL MILESTONES. You don't put your life on hold while you're building a program. You might get married, have children, buy a house, and so on. Friends and family will live their lives, and you'll want to be there for that as well. Obviously, you can't plan out all of your personal life three years in advance. But you might know about some things that are on the horizon, and you should mark those events down so you can protect your personal time.
7. PROGRAMMATIC REVIEWS YOU WANT TO HAVE. Erika Lindenmann (1979) points out the value of external reviews, and the Consultant-Evaluator Service can effectively help your program through this. You might want to schedule one of these reviews in the next few years, in which case you might want to slot it into the time line.

Once you've worked through this list, you'll have a sense of some of the big events in your life over the next few years. You can use this to help you get a sense of your program's wider ecology (Ryan 2012) and to articulate how you are going to go about pursuing strategies and tactics for your program in the coming years.

Strategies and Tactics: Adler-Kassner's Approach

Now that you have a sense of what's on the calendar, you can turn your attention back to Adler-Kassner's (2008, 2016) notion of *strategies* and *tactics*. By "strategies," Adler-Kassner (2016, 466) is referring to "those long-term visions that we have that are closely linked to principles and values." You've already spent some time, in part I, articulating what you see as not only the principles but also the principled practices that make your program run. In various places and for various reasons, when people see your program in action, they see particular principles enacted in particular ways. Your task is to generate a vision of one to three years of work to identify how you might best put forward, build on, and (when necessary) revise your principled practices in targeted and effective ways.

Consider, for instance, a hypothetical principled practice of frequent, formative one-on-one conferences in first-year writing classes. This might enact, say, a principle that values student-teacher interactions. By having frequent one-on-one conferences and having them focus on developing students' thoughts rather than on an evaluation of student progress, teachers in the program can be certain that these conferences create the conditions for rich and productive student-teacher engagement.

Now, in other parts of the program, this value (student-teacher interactions) might not be as visible as it could be. Obviously, there are aspects of running the program (such as managing course enrollment) to which this principle doesn't apply. But there are other aspects that it could easily apply to and is not. Let's say, for instance, that the end of the term in an upper-division writing course tends to focus on independent work and peer review, with the teacher in the background as students move toward course outcomes. That's not necessarily a bad thing, but perhaps it is difficult to see a valuing of student-teacher interactions here.

This would be a great place to enact a strategy. Perhaps the particulars of this course can be taken into consideration, and the teachers in the program can get together to develop a list of texts to read, guest speakers to bring in, and conferences to attend that can help them identify, explore, and evaluate alternatives to the end of this course. Over the course of two years, these teachers might have some reading groups, try new approaches, and generate a list of recommendations that move forward the value of student-teacher interaction at the end of this particular course offering. The end result would be more than just a principle applied in a new way; it would also give you the chance to more deeply interrogate what the program means when it says it values student-teacher interactions.

Notice that when I was discussing the enactment of a strategy, I talked about more targeted activities: reading lists, conferences, and so on. These particular activities can be thought of, in Adler-Kassner's (2008) language, as a *tactic*. Tactics are "the tools/actions taken as part of a strategy" (94). WPAs enact tactics to support and forward their strategies as part of the day-to-day work of being members of the program.

Your task in this chapter is to identify the short-term visions you have and the ways some of your other goals, ideas, and thoughts can be treated as tactics that can move the program toward the visions you have developed. But before you start shuffling, sorting, and prioritizing your visions of the future, you need to take a step back and start thinking big: you need to get a sense of *all* the things that matter to you based on what you discovered in part I, and you need to do so without too much judgment out the gate. In the next section, then, you dream big. After that, you'll settle into some targeted plans, particular strategies, and specific tactics.

Dreaming Big: Mapping Potential Change

I title this section "Dreaming Big" because it's here that you can imagine the many possibilities of the program you are now a part of. What, in your wildest dreams, might the possibilities of this program be? How might you build, with those in your program, a robust, coherent writing program that lives through its principles and is receptive to the many and changing needs of its constituents?

To figure out the answers to these questions, you can turn to concept mapping: creating a space where the many ideas we came up with in part I can turn into a heap of potential for action, connected (and disconnected) in various (and fascinating) ways. Thanks to the work you've done in part I, you now have a wide range of material at your disposal: you've identified facts, linked some of those facts into comprehensive accounts, and tied some of those accounts into wider stories of writers and writing. You've also developed some principles and principled practices to work with. So you have, at varying levels of scale, a good sense of what the program is doing and how you might develop it further.

Using a concept map, then, start to work out a sense of what you might be able to do. Don't worry, for the moment, about what is more or less possible—try to treat all of your ideas equally, at least for now. You can go about turning this big dream into an actionable plan in a bit. For now, you just want to see what the options are. The steps below can help you trace out a concept map.

1. Looking through the facts, accounts, principles, and stories you've developed, identify in a few words potential transformations to the program that you might make. These should be rather straightforward, such as "Revise Assessment through Anti-Racist FYC Goals Statement" (Beavers et al. 2021), with "re-localizing" (Asmuth 2022) in mind. Enacting these transformations isn't the issue; right now, you just need the potentials for action all in one place.

2. As the transformations accumulate, try to see how they might relate to one another, using connecting lines with descriptive language to help you make sense of those connections. So, for instance, you might see a "revise assessment through new goals statement" and "conduct disparate impact analysis of program" (Poe and Cogan 2016) as having a straightforward connection; the disparate impact analysis can help you make local sense of the need to make use of the new goals statement.

3. Once you've finished getting all (or most) of your goals in one place and have connected them in all the ways you can see, take time to write about what you feel is missing, undeveloped, or otherwise unfinished. You can come back to this writing as you organize your strategies and tactics below—having a parking lot for the hunches you have will help you make sure you're not losing sight of anything important.

Planning Change: Strategies and Tactics

You now have, in one place, all of the ideas you can think of about how to introduce change to this program that are connected, in some way, to the principled practices of the program, to your own principled practices, or both. But the work of the previous section deliberately avoided too much actual planning; you just took some time to dream, big and small, about the ways you can move this program forward. Now that the dream is down on paper (or some kind of document), you can start to see the ways you might bring some of these dreams to life over the course of the next one to three years.

To do this, I'll turn back to the concepts of *strategy* and *tactics*. Remember that a *strategy* is a broad vision (in our case, one to three years' worth of broad vision) that is enacted in the shorter-term work of *tactics*. For instance, I might use what I've learned about the circumstances of adjunct teaching in my program in my work from part I and, combined with what I know of the struggles adjunct teachers face both historically (Blank and Greenberg 1981) and today (Dorfeld 2022), want to do something about them. I might want to draw on Seth Kahn's (2017) guidance for helping adjunct teachers develop in order to enact a three-year strategy of co-developing career paths with adjunct teachers in my program. I want to plan trainings and workshops that scaffold these teachers into full-time positions at my institution or nearby institutions and help them move into the industry—whatever they want that my program can help them with. The *strategy*, then, is to set up and enact these plans for all adjunct instructors.

But this strategy is enacted slowly, on a daily basis, over time. From day to day, from week to week, I might be taking up particular activities—particular *tactics*—that move this plan forward. For instance, I might need to corral resources for these professional learning opportunities. Perhaps I need a grant or some kind of fundraising effort to get this plan off the ground. It's likely that I need more than one source of revenue. I will also need the support of other administrators: my department chair, for instance, might not take it well if the answer to "why do our experienced adjuncts keep leaving for better-paying jobs" is "because our strategy is working."

As these examples suggest, I have quite a bit to do if I want this strategy in motion in the next three years. Toward that end, then, I can think about how I can characterize this work in meaningful ways that are easily graspable, both to myself and to others. I need a list of tactics to attend to that avoid the pitfalls of providing no detail, on the one hand, and too much detail, on the other. If I boil down my work into two tactics—communicate with administrators and get funding, for instance—there won't be enough detail for me to work with on a daily basis, and things will fall through the cracks. But if I articulate several hundred tactics, I lose the forest for the trees.

What I need, then, is a set number of tactics that give me some detail and that I can incorporate more specific tactics into—like a dropdown menu of more specific actions I can articulate in the context of a particular tactic (which is, in turn, in the context of a particular strategy). So, let's say I have "co-create career pathways with adjunct faculty" as my strategy, with "coordinating with adjunct faculty," "finding funding," and "recruiting administrator support" as some of my tactics. I might have this organized in a bulleted list, as follows:

> *Strategy: Co-create career pathways with adjunct faculty*
> - TACTIC 1: Coordinate with adjunct faculty about concerns and needs
> - TACTIC 2: Find funding to support professional learning
> - TACTIC 3: Recruit administrator support.

Using these three tactics as a starting point (as I suggest above, others would be needed), I can start to identify particular actions I can take to enact these tactics in, say, a single semester. So, I might draw on the work of Robert Samuels to consider how I might get a sense of adjunct faculty needs and concerns. A working group that emerges from that tactic would help you develop a sense of what I might ask for.

Now, as for Tactic 2, let's say I spend your first semester establishing a working relationship with someone in the fundraising arm of the university. I might also comb the archives of my department and program: what major anniversaries are coming up? Are there particular individuals who need recognition, which can double as a fundraising event? We can think of each of these as more specific tactics.

For Tactic 3, "recruit administrator support," I might want to spend a semester putting together a moral and material case for taking on this challenge, which I can present to my department chair, dean, and perhaps provost to ensure their goodwill in the effort. And I might also imagine, in detail, a future with a revolving door of adjunct instructors who work for the program briefly and move on to other, full-time positions. Perhaps that can be an end-of-term report to follow the presentation. So, my bulleted list might be expanded as follows:

Strategy 1: Co-create career pathways with adjunct faculty

- TACTIC 1: Coordinate with adjunct faculty about concerns and needs
  - Surveys to identify general trends
  - Establish a working group
  - Write series of recommendations to inform Tactics 2 and 3
- TACTIC 2: Find funding to support professional learning
  - Have regular meetings with someone in fundraising
  - Review program/department archives
- TACTIC 3: Recruit administrator support
  - Plan presentation for chair, dean, provost
  - Present to chair, dean, provost
  - Write report of possible futures involving career pathways for adjunct faculty.

So, I have a strategy that has a finish line three years in the future. I have two tactics that run into the much nearer future (for instance, once I have administrator support, the recruiting can end). And I have more specific instantiations of those tactics that I can point to as goals for a much shorter period of time (and, likewise, with much easier targets to hit).

With this example to work from, your task now is to look through the mapping you did earlier to articulate a set of strategies, specific tactics, and short-term instantiations of those tactics. You should consider this set of strategies and tactics to be a good start, and that's about it; you'll be revising your tactics and your strategies as you go along, and you'll be doing so in response to learning more about the conditions of your program and the needs of the people in it. Making adjustments to your plans so they better assist your people and your program is, obviously, a good thing—although it doesn't always feel great to scratch out a strategy and revise it.

This work of corralling what you have into strategies and tactics, of planning for the near term, is the first of several steps toward enacting programmatic change. You are doing *some* assessment of your dream changes in this step; you're putting them into some sort of relationship to one another, making some changes as you do so, and you're identifying the ways these various plans of yours can work together.

One thing you're not doing much of at this point is thinking through the relative weight of each strategy—that is, its cost for you, for the program, for those in it. You've no doubt noted some ideas you have that will take you far longer than three years to put into effect or those that might easily crowd out others, but you aren't yet far down the "what is the cost of this" road. And that's fine—it's actually what we cover in the next section. For now, you just want a sense of how the dreams you established earlier can be made into a reality through the lenses of *strategies* and *tactics*.

It's helpful to think of the tactics as dropdown windows underneath each strategy. So your strategy and tactic breakdown might look like table 4.1. This kind of setup can help you articulate particular tactics and what a single semester (or single year) of implementing those tactics looks like. Taking Tactic 2 as an example, once you've planned and presented to your administrators, you can slot in the next steps of your plan.

A Sense of Cost

Now that you have organized your dream changes to the program into a series of interrelated strategies and tactics, we can start to make sense of the cost—to your institution, to your own schedule, and to the program itself. Some of the changes you're suggesting here will be easy to work with and implement. Others will be costly. Most will be somewhere in between. The reality that

TABLE 4.1. Enacting a strategy

Strategy 1: Co-create Career Pathways with Adjunct Faculty
TACTIC 1: Coordinate with adjunct faculty about concerns and needs
Surveys to identify general trends
Establish a working group
Write series of recommendations to inform Tactics 2 and 3
TACTIC 2: Find funding to support professional learning
Have regular meetings with someone in fundraising
Review program/department archives
TACTIC 3: Recruit administrator support
Plan presentation for chair, dean, provost
Present to chair, dean, provost
Write report of possible futures involving "off-ramps" for adjunct faculty

something is expensive in terms of time, effort, or resources does not make it a bad idea, just as something that is low cost is not necessarily a good idea. What you want to be sure of is that the expense of rolling out a strategy/tactic is commensurate with the gain. Toward that end, then, you can start to imagine what it might look like to operationalize these strategies and tactics.

First, take time to bring your list of strategies/tactics and your three-year calendar together. Try to plot the particular strategies and tactics you're thinking of enacting in the calendar. You should get a sense of what this is going to cost you in terms of time and energy across the three-year span. Some of the strategies and tactics will require daily attention, while others will need attention on and off.

Once you have a sense of how your strategies and tactics will fit into a calendar, think about not just the big events you have coming up—personal and professional—but about how this work will fit into your release time for WPA work. Most WPAs I know and talk with don't have a course reassignment that is on par with the time being a WPA takes. For instance, my own reassigned time works fairly well *during* the semester but does not account for the incidental work I need to do between semesters, either over winter break or over the summer.

That said, though, even if my release time isn't exactly what I'd like it to be, I can at least use it as a rough gauge of whether I am putting in an appropriate amount of time. So, if I have one course release per semester for WPA work, will I be able to enact the eight strategies and forty tactics I have mapped onto my calendar? Not likely. So I'll have to focus in on the strategies and tactics that (1) I want to prioritize and (2) I have time to prioritize.

These are not always the same thing. I might really want to pursue an overhaul of my assessment process *and* write an in-house textbook, but these two things are deeply time-consuming. So I have time for one or the other but not both at once. However, I might also want to start raising the visibility of my program throughout the university and the region. This is time-consuming, but it's a bit more flexible. I might choose to present (or encourage colleagues to present) at local conferences, find my way onto certain university committees, and so on. These are demands on my time and attention that can pair nicely with either the revised assessment process *or* the in-house textbook (though, again, not both).

Using your calendar as well as your sense of what you have the capacity for within your reassigned time, you can revise your strategies and tactics to a manageable number. You may want a separate spreadsheet (or document or sheet of paper) for this, one with your prioritized and organized strategies and tactics in place. You can make these strategies and tactics even more manageable by turning to other interested people in the program, the university, and the surrounding community.

Recruiting Support: Finding Interested People

Because your time, energy, and resources are limited, it's ideal, when you get the chance, to draw on someone else. It's at this point that you can think about people who might be helpful as you are advancing a particular strategy (or even, at times, a particular tactic). Lining up support for a change to the program ahead of time is a way to not only spread the workload but to spread the political cost of making such a change. WPAs have potential allies and potential sway in places they might not expect (see, for instance, Miles 2000), and unexpected limits and possibilities crop up when working collaboratively (e.g., Schell 1998). So, it's important to take the time to think as widely as possible about who might help you do the work you want to do and how you might want to work with them.

Interested parties in your program exist in a wide variety of places: there are upper administrators committed to the success of your course, department chairs and support services that would be interested in working with you, community members who might like to collaborate with your program or build off of its accomplishments, and—of course—the students, staff, and teachers who make up your program. All of these interested parties are folks you can turn to in an effort to recruit support for the strategies and tactics you would like to take up.

In this section, you won't be doing actual recruiting—that is going to be part of the work you take up in chapters 5 and 6. Rather, you'll be starting to generate lists of interested parties who might be willing to work with you on particular strategies and tactics. Now that you have a sense of the cost of some of the changes you'd like to implement, you can investigate the interested parties who might help you spread out the cost of these changes, so you might be able to use *their* political capital to enact one strategy while using your own on another.

For this, turn your attention to the right-hand column next to your strategies and tactics. In that column, write down the names of people, programs, and initiatives (on campus, in a university system if you have one, in the local community, or in the discipline) that might help you bring these strategies and tactics to life. Once you have their names, you can do additional writing to articulate how they can help you defray the political cost of your changes.

Much as when you articulated the cost of change in the previous section, you will be trying to assess these interested parties—for the moment—with somewhat limited information. You might be wrong about a few (or more than a few) of these folks, but that's alright—you can adjust your plans later to account for that once you know more. Right now, you are trying to draw on what you know to make sensible, straightforward plans that can be presented persuasively to people to recruit support. As you'll see when you try to articulate interested parties and costs, this in and of itself is enough work on its own.

Once you have a sense of who might be able to help you enact the strategies and tactics, you can revise your estimates of your time and effort. You might realize that if you are able to recruit departmental support for a professional learning series, you will have the time to take up a smaller strategy you otherwise might not have time for. Or you might have recognized someone (or some program) capable of taking up a strategy or tactic you don't have time for yourself. Obviously, at this stage, such potential alliances are theoretical—you won't get into building them out until chapters 5 and 6—but having the sense of the possibilities in front of you is helpful and can give you a notion of how you might be able to reallocate your time and effort.

Making Room for the Unexpected

Throughout this chapter, we've discussed what it means to plan, in a short span of years, for change and innovation in your program. What we have not yet discussed is how we might make room for the unexpected. As someone who found himself (like so many others) leading a program through a global pandemic unprecedented in living memory, it seems wise to at least mention that the best-laid plans may also go awry, that there will always be unexpected shifts in the terrain that we are not ready for, and that we, as WPAs, need to remain flexible to adapt to those changes if our program is to remain relevant and meaningful. And, as Justin H. Cook and Jackie Hoermann-Elliot (2022) note, we might need to reexamine our notions of failure and success in accomplishing various goals as we do so.

Yet as wise as the idea seemed, I had trouble thinking about what I might say in this section. How can we make room for the unexpected? How can that which we do not know and, by definition, cannot anticipate be accounted for in the work we do?

To start to think about answers to these questions, I looked back over my writing during the early months of the pandemic—how I tried to conceptualize the problem in writing to myself, how that conceptualizing shaped my solutions to the recurring questions of "what fresh hell is this" and "what the hell am I going to do now," and how the results of my actions fed back into my further conceptualizing of the problem in the future. What follows is hardly scientific, although it got the job done during a pandemic, so maybe it's not that bad.

One of the first things to do to make room for the unexpected is to be ready to **go back to your principles** to make sense of that unexpectedness. It's through those principles that we can start to see coherent courses of action that make sense to both ourselves and others. For instance, UMaine made the decision to go all remote in spring 2020, just before spring break. So, we had about two days of classes left, then a week off (which was later extended to a week and a half), and then we were all remote going forward.

There were a lot of ways to respond to this, of course. I could have made any number of decisions, and any of them would have had limits and possibilities. But the language that kept popping into my head when I was thinking about what to do was "dead ends." I didn't want to send our program down a dead-end road, to ask teachers and students to do things in these circumstances that (1) were not workable and (2) there was no clear way out of. Thinking through my principles helped me find a way forward that, even if imperfect, at least gave us something to build on.

I thought a great deal about my principles when I was drawing up plans. To begin with, I thought about *labor*: the labor of students, of teachers, and of the members of my administrative team. How might I create the circumstances for them to do sustainable, useful labor? I also thought about *accessibility*: how can I create an online version of English 101 that is accessible for all students, regardless of circumstance, in less than two weeks?

Through the twin lenses of *respecting labor* and *creating an accessible program*, I started to find answers to "what the hell am I going to do now." ("What fresh hell is this" remained an open question until the writing of this book, at the very least.) If I wanted to respect the labor of students and teachers, I had to begin to imagine an online course that could operate successfully with the technology the teachers and students had and with the pedagogy they were already familiar with (and had established during the first half of the semester). If I wanted a program that was *accessible*, then what I created had to work with students facing the starkest of limitations: those in low-income and rural households, with slow or no internet access and perhaps added financial pressures due to lost wages.

The solution I came up with was this, in a nutshell: classes would meet via Zoom, with discussions happening both in real time and in Google Docs. Assignments were to be submitted through the learning management system (LMS) options the teachers were using before the pandemic. Attendance would be encouraged but not required; students who could not attend in person could check and add to the Google Doc asynchronously, if needed. Teachers who were comfortable with various technologies could use them, provided that students still had asynchronous options for the work.

This solution was far from perfect, to put it mildly. But it gave teachers focused tech options that allowed them to translate some aspects of their pedagogy online, and it gave flexibility to students with slow or no internet access. And it gave us a base to work from: as we learned new things as the rest of the semester unfolded, we had an approach that was consistent and reliable (as long as Zoom didn't crash). It also gave us important data about how students were handling work in remote environments, what challenges they were facing, and so on. This would prove useful to us a few months later, as we began envisioning and planning for a remote fall semester.

Was the solution successful? I would say it got the job done, based on the end-of-term student success rates. That success confirmed for us that we were on the right track. With more information about remote teaching, with new knowledge about the nature of the pandemic and what students and teachers alike needed, I was hopeful that we could build a more effective set of strategies in future semesters.

This gets us to the second step of dealing with the unexpected: **building on the small wins**. Working from principles got us to an approach that, while imperfect, did what it needed to do. From there, the program had the wind at its back, so to speak, so it could take on the challenging work of building out a remotely offered fall semester. The success helped direct our attention through research about online literacy instruction and the torrent of unfolding information about how spring 2020 had impacted the lives of students and teachers. The small wins of spring 2020 for us were a starting point to get more small wins, to move more confidently in a direction that was in line with our principles and, by extension, helpful for students and teachers when things became (unbelievably) even more chaotic in fall 2020.

After working from points of principle to build on small wins, we need to **integrate the unexpected into the program**. The unexpected isn't just a hurdle to overcome; it's a chance to learn more about what you value, what your students and teachers need, and what you can do to make your program better. We've learned a great deal about how students learn, what supports students need to be successful in English 101, and what obstacles we have been unintentionally putting in their way under the mistaken impression that we were helping them. This information will result in a program that looks fundamentally different, in both large and small ways, once we move into a post-pandemic world.

Obviously, you could break down the three steps I outlined above into more fine-grained processes. I think that keeping these three steps as open as I have, though, will make them more adaptable to a wide range of circumstances—in other words, they can help us be more prepared for that which we do not expect. These steps do overlook the fraught and sometimes contentious work of responding to the unexpected. Things like recruiting constituent support, building (or mending) alliances, and plotting short- and long-term strategies still have to happen; doing them requires a great deal of interpersonal effort. But these three steps, I hope, offer at least a rough guide to getting through it.

At this point, you've got a good sense of the strategies and tactics you'd like to focus on to bring about change in your program. You have a conceptual lens for thinking about the cost of these changes, as well as a general approach to making room for the unexpected. You've even had the chance to get feedback from various interested parties in and outside of your program, so you can spread the cost of these changes around.

In chapters 5 and 6, we deal with the next step of the process: dealing with issues that arise while bringing about change with these strategies and tactics.

In chapter 5, we turn our attention to commonly understood problems—the issues that many in the program see and would like to have addressed. In chapter 6, we turn to clashes between your values and those in the program you've stepped into.

Resources

The resources below can be helpful as you develop various strategies and tactics. "Exploring Strategy-Tactic Combinations" provides a bit of an overview of how strategies and tactics might be explored together, with an eye on the bigger picture of how each informs the other. "Thinking through Strategy" calls attention to the types of long-term plans Adler-Kassner means when she talks about strategy. "Thinking through Tactics" calls similar attention to tactics.

EXPLORING STRATEGY-TACTIC COMBINATIONS

Adler-Kassner, Linda. 2012. "The Companies We Keep, or the Companies We Would Like to Try to Keep: Strategies and Tactics in Challenging Times." *WPA: Writing Program Administration* 36 (1): 119–140.

Adler-Kassner, Linda. 2018. "Taking Action in the Age of Reaction: Constructing Architectures of Participation." In *Writing for Engagement: Responsive Practice for Social Action*, edited by Mary P. Sheridan, Megan J. Bardolph, Megan Faver Hartline, and Drew Holladay, 3–13. New York: Lexington Books.

Cheramie, Deany M. 2004. "Sifting through Fifty Years of Change: Writing Program Administration at an Historically Black University." In *Historical Studies of Writing Program Administration: Individuals, Communities, and the Formation of a Discipline*, edited by Barbara L'Eplattenier and Lisa Mastrangelo, 145–165. West Lafayette, IN: Parlor Press.

Fedukovich, Casey, and Sue Doe. 2018. "Beyond Management: The Potential for Writing Program Leadership during Turbulent Times." *Reflections* 18 (2): 87–115.

Gunter, Kim. 2023. "I'm Just Playin': Directing Writing Programs as Improv." In *Toward More Sustainable Metaphors of Writing Program Administration*, edited by Lydia Wilkes, Lilian Mina, and Patti Poblete, 215–234. Logan: Utah State University Press.

Lehn, Jeanette. 2019. "A Renewed Critical Pedagogy: Rethinking Activism within Writing Program Administration." PhD dissertation, Florida State University, Tallahassee.

Maraj, Louis. 2022. "Unlike Conventional Form(s) Of: Beyond Reparative Antiracism." *Composition Studies* 50 (3): 40–58.

Spiegel, Cheri Lemieux, Darin Jensen, and Sara Z. Johnson. 2020. "Don't Call It a Comeback: Two-Year College WPA, Tactics, Collaboration, Flexibility, Sustainability." *WPA: Writing Program Administration* 43 (3): 7–19.

Teagarden, Alexis. 2023. "Representing the Basement." In *Toward More Sustainable Metaphors of Writing Program Administration*, edited by Lydia Wilkes, Lilian Mina, and Patti Poblete, 145–156. Logan: Utah State University Press.

THINKING THROUGH STRATEGY

Adler-Kassner, Linda, and Susanmarie Harrington. 2010. "Responsibility and Composition's Future in the Twenty-First Century: Reframing Accountability." *College Composition and Communication* 62 (1): 73–99.

Beckett, Jessica Marie. 2017. "Negotiating Expertise: The Strategies Writing Program Administrators Use to Mediate Disciplinary and Institutional Values." PhD dissertation, Virginia Tech University, Blacksburg.

de Mueller, Genevieve Garcia, and Ana Cortes Lagos. 2023. "Building an Antiracist WAC Program." In *Making Administrative Work Visible: Data-Driven Advocacy for Understanding the Labor of Writing Program Administration*, edited by Leigh Graziano, Kay Halasek, Remi Hudgins, Susan Miller-Cochran, Frank Napolitano, and Natalie Szymanski, 253–263. Logan: Utah State University Press.

Ding, Huiling. 2019. "Development of Technical Communication in China: Program Building and Field Convergence." *Technical Communication Quarterly* 28 (3): 223–237.

Elder, Cristyn L. 2023. "From a Faculty Standpoint: Assessing with IE a Sustainable Commitment to WAC at a Minority-Serving Institution." In *Institutional Ethnography as Writing Studies Practice*, edited by Michelle LaFrance and Melissa Nicolas, 113–128. Fort Collins and Boulder: WAC Clearinghouse and University Press of Colorado.

Gindlesparger, Kathryn Johnson. 2020. "Trust on Display: The Epideictic Potential of Institutional Governance." *College English* 83 (2): 127–146.

Huot, Brian. 2003. *Rearticulating Writing Assessment for Teaching and Learning*. Logan: Utah State University Press.

Townsend, Martha A. 2007. "Negotiating the Risks and Reaping the Rewards: Reflections and Advice from a Former jWPA." In *Untenured Faculty as Writing Program Administrators: Institutional Practices and Politics*, edited by Debra Frank Dew and Alice Horning, 72–96. West Lafayette, IN: Parlor Press.

Wible, Scott. 2023. "Forfeiting Privilege for the Cause of Social Justice: Listening to Black WPAs and WPAs of Color Define the Work of White Allyship." In *Black Perspectives in Writing Program Administration*, edited by Staci Perryman-Clark and Collin Lamont Craig, 74–100. Urbana, IL: National Council of Teachers of English.

Workman, Erin, Madeline Crozier, and Peter Vandenberg. "Writing Standpoint(s): Institution, Discourse, and Method." In *Institutional Ethnography as Writing Studies Practice*, edited by Michelle LaFrance and Melissa Nicolas, 81–96. Fort Collins and Boulder: WAC Clearinghouse and University Press of Colorado.

THINKING THROUGH TACTICS

Cavazos, Alyssa. 2019. "Encouraging Languages Other than English in First-Year Writing Courses: Experiences from Linguistically Diverse Writers." *Composition Studies* 47 (1): 38–56.

Clinnin, Kaitlin. 2021. "In the Event of an Emergency: Crisis Management for WPAs." *Writing Program Administration* 45 (1): 9–31.

Condon, Frankie, and Vershawn Ashanti Young, eds. 2016. *Performing Antiracist Pedagogy in Rhetoric, Writing, and Communication*. Fort Collins and Boulder: WAC Clearinghouse and University Press of Colorado.

Giordano, Joanne, Holly Hassel, Jennifer Heinert, and Cassandra Phillips. 2017. "The Imperative of Pedagogical and Professional Development to Support the Retention of Underprepared Students at Open-Access Institutions." In *Retention, Persistence, and Writing Programs*, edited by Todd Ruecker, Dawn Shepherd, Heidi Estrem, and Beth Brunk-Chavez, 74–92. Logan: Utah State University Press.

Graziano, Leigh, Kay Halasek, Susan Miller-Cochran, Frank Napolitano, and Natalie Szymanski. 2023a. "Introduction: Making Work Visible Work through Data-Informed Advocacy." In *Making Administrative Work Visible: Data-Driven Advocacy for Understanding the Labor of Writing Program Administration*, edited by Leigh Graziano, Kay Halasek, Remi Hudgins, Susan Miller-Cochran, Frank Napolitano, and Natalie Szymanski, 3–23. Logan: Utah State University Press.

5
Identifying and Working through Problems

Now that you have a set of strategies and tactics you would like to work on, it's time to turn to the grittier bits of putting a plan into practice. In this chapter, you will address shared problems that arise (and that you anticipate arising) as you put your strategies and tactics into motion. Some of the problems you identify and work through in this chapter will be at the center of a particular strategy or tactic. For instance, if there are concerns about coherence across a particular multi-section course, you might have developed a strategy to enact a multi-year set of professional learning experiences aimed at increasing coherence. Or, there might be problems that get in the way of enacting a strategy or tactic. Let's say you want to increase multimodal writing assignments in your program as a strategy, but many classrooms lack the needed technology. You've got to solve one to do the other, but it wasn't a focus for you until you realized it had to be. In this chapter, we'll work on both of these kinds of problems.

This chapter focuses in particular on addressing shared problems: items, issues, and recurring situations that you and many members of the program you are part of agree need fixing. This is not to say that the agreement is unanimous or that agreement that there *is* a problem also means there is agreement on *how* the problem should be fixed but rather that there isn't anyone asking "why is this new WPA (writing program administrator) so focused on *that*." The motivations of your desire for change on the issues we're focusing on this chapter are rather obvious to all involved: there's a problem, it's persistent, and it needs fixing.

What Is a Problem?

Let's begin by identifying what a problem is. How might you define a "problem," for the purposes of this chapter? In looking over the research you did in part I and the strategies and tactics you developed in chapter 4, what characteristics might you look for to see a "problem" that can be addressed through the work of this chapter? Furthermore, what might be some counterindicators of problems? What might signal, in other words, that a particular issue is *not* something you'd want to cover with the work of this chapter?

As you were writing up your accounts, stories, and principles, you probably heard multiple references to particular issues: perhaps courses were not assigned until right before the start of the term, or maybe there was always a shortage of paper in the office at exactly the wrong moment of the semester. Some of these problems (as you might be able to see from my examples above) are not *really* things you need to address with a great deal of time or energy; perhaps a note to your administrative staff to order more paper in October would solve the problem, for instance. And sometimes problems arise simply because there aren't enough people to get certain things done. If you're stepping into a role previously filled by (1) an interim director or (2) no one, your presence—the presence of just one more person to shoulder some of the responsibility—can make some problems go away.

What you want to focus on now, though, are problems that endure. Some of these problems might be tied to broader social trends (e.g., de Mueller and Ruiz 2017) and so are tricky to trace out. Others might address particular student populations (Grijalva 2016) or perhaps your own emerging sense of self as a WPA (Fedukovich 2013). Maybe the annual assessment process is an ongoing problem: not enough people, or resources, or time, or attention is being paid to it for it to be successful. Or perhaps teachers in the program keep discussing the supports that are needed for particular groups of students in the program (see, for instance, George and Wetzl 2020). These problems have a few particular characteristics. First, the problems are **recurrent** across multiple people. This problem isn't arising because someone is grumpy but because persistent, recurring issues crop up as a result of it.

Second, these recurrent issues have a **cost** to them. Perhaps these problems are minimal and are minimized further with particular kinds of workarounds. But even if the cost is *small*, it's still there, still persistent; and this cost makes the problem worth addressing. The degree to which we want to spend time and energy to solve any one particular problem is something we can decide later. Right now, your task is simply to find the recurrent issues in the program that have a cost to them.

The third characteristic of problems is that they **endure** over time. These problems—that is, the ones on which you are going to bring your strategies and tactics to bear—are not passing issues; you can't wait for them to disappear on their own. And, to be sure, sometimes you have temporary issues like this crop up and that you have to attend to. Teaching circumstances early in the Covid pandemic are a good example of this; we might have been struggling at the moment to work through emergency remote teaching, but once the vaccines were distributed and the case counts dropped, we found ourselves in a much different situation. To be sure, that situation *also* has problems, but they're different kinds of problems.

There are, then, three characteristics that suggest a problem has emerged. When you see a problem that can be addressed through strategies and tactics, it has:

a. Recurrence
b. Cost
c. Endurance.

You can use these characteristics to start to identify which strategies and tactics seem to be addressing problems worth investigating for the purposes of this chapter. But you also need to think about another characteristic, one that needs a separate section for us to get at: the problems need to directly interact with the principles shared among you, the new WPA, and the program.

You've no doubt come across issues that speak to the characteristics above but that also highlight a rift between what you believe and what the constituents of your program believe. These issues *are* problematic, and they *do* need to be addressed. However, you will take them up in chapter 6. Dealing with underlying conflicting values is a tricky business, and it takes a different kind of focus than you will be working on in this chapter. What you want to address now are problems that have some popular support. That's what you're looking for.

What Problems Have You Found?

Now that you have a sense of how you might define a problem, you can turn your attention to what you see in your part I (and chapter 4) work that might fall under this category. Where do problems seem to exist in this program? In the next section, you'll be exploring what it might mean to articulate these problems, and in the section after that you'll be sharing these articulations with others. But for this section, you are going to see what *you* find to be problematic and how you might characterize those problems for yourself.

As you look through the facts, principles, and stories you articulated in part I, what stands out to you as a problem? How might you articulate that through the lens of the principles and principled practices you established in order to make sense of why this might be problematic? Remember that the problems you are working on at the moment are, in fact, tied to the principles the program constituents operate from, so however you articulate it, you are starting to uncover problems that are, to a greater or lesser extent, recognized by those in your program (or *will* be recognized, once you make it obvious to them). Maybe you are having struggles with your placement approach (e.g., Nicolay 2002). Perhaps you need to address a broader tension the program has with a larger unit (e.g., Graham et al. 1997). Or maybe you have issues with talking about writing to faculty in different disciplines (e.g., Adler-Kassner and Wardle 2022; Glotfelter et al. 2020).

A useful way to take on this work is to begin by articulating broadly what you see as a problem. Let's say there's something in the end-of-term assessment rubric that sets off my alarm bells: as I was watching the end-of-term assessment, the ways teachers were talking about student writers and writing seemed to go against the grain of the values established in other parts of the program. In particular, I'm concerned that the respect for student labor might not be centrally addressed through this rubric. So, I've got an area of the program that stands out to me as potentially problematic, a particular principle it (might) clash with, and a particular time and place where that clash might be evident. This is a useful starting point for finding problems we can work on.

Now that I have a sense of the problem, I can recruit facts I've already established, accounts I've already worked up, and artifacts related to those facts and accounts I might be able to glean some insight from. In this example, what directed my attention was the rubric, which can be a great focusing object: I can look at the history of the document, the ways people in the program have come to understand it, and how students develop a sense of it throughout a term.

Perhaps the structure of the rubric has issues that work against the program's valuing of student labor. If I trace its history, I might find that its structure is rooted in past attempts to atomize student writing: to identify particular characteristics in ways that value the reliability of scoring over its validity. For instance, the rubric might demand something like "two citations per paragraph" for students to receive a full score in the "citations" category. This certainly can make for reliable scoring by readers, but there's no connection to authentic writing beyond the course. After all, writers do not add a set number of citations per paragraph because they are told to; rather, they cite when needed to shape their text to their own ends. Can we really respect students' labor if we are making them labor over arbitrary aspects of a text in ways that don't connect to their future writing demands? Perhaps this is what is driving my concern with the rubric—not the citations in particular but the broader pattern of atomizing student writing.

So, I can start to draw a line from the origins of the rubric to its current iteration and, from there, to the clash with program principles that has emerged as a result of it. This is a good start, and no doubt the history of this document can help me see much of the reason it's become a problem. But it's important to remember that even with history informing our perspective, I can't see *everything* that is going on here. Histories are always complex, always partly (and sometimes mostly) occluded; and the ways such an atomized approach to evaluating student writing shapes assessment goes far beyond this particular end-of-term assessment. Assessment, as we all know, drives instruction, so whatever is going on in the assessment is *also* permeating what's going on in the classroom.

Now, to be sure, teachers might take issue with how *this* assessment shapes the classroom, but the assessment shapes it all the same. If I am teaching a first-year writing course and I know that students will need two citations per paragraph to pass the final assessment, that knowledge will be driving my teaching choices. In fact, if I've been teaching for a while, it might be baked into the way I approach teaching first-year writing. So, I've designed at least part of my course with that in mind. If a WPA is going to erase that aspect of our assessment, then I am suddenly going to have a gap between what I do and why I do it in my classroom.

What I'm getting at here is that solving one problem often creates others, and you have to be attuned to how far a particular problem might reach.

Knowing the reach of a problem can help you avoid a backlash when you go about solving it. Let's say I decide to get rid of the current rubric entirely and build a holistic assessment instead. While this is good for assessing writing—it increases validity—the program suddenly has a fair amount of work to do: we need to work harder on reliability, we need to reimagine how we might go about teaching such a course with this rubric in mind, and so on.

But actually *solving* the problem comes later. Right now, your task is just identifying problems and tracing out their impact. So, I know that the rubric is causing a clash, I can trace that back to the history of its development and use, and I can start to identify the reach of the problem (into classrooms, program reports, teacher trainings, and accreditation processes, for instance). As I articulate the problems and their reach, I might find that some problems intersect: perhaps the struggles of some classroom teachers in providing feedback are tied to the atomistic nature of the end-of-term assessment.

You can see in the example above the usefulness of such a tracing of problems and their impact. WPAs can see what other issues they have to address in resolving a problem, and they also see where they might usefully turn their attention. If adjusting the rubric, for instance, can also help a WPA address concerns about feedback (or some other problems), then they can imagine a more robust transformation of the program that is both in line with the values of that program and supported by the people who believe in those values.

There are many ways to look for problems, and you've likely already noted a few from your work in part I that you can start articulating (we do this in the next section). To help you, I offer a few questions to guide your work through your facts, accounts, stories, and principles:

1. What strategies and tactics did you develop in chapter 4 that address "problems," as defined above?
2. As you were composing principles, where did you note clashes between the principles being developed and the facts and accounts you had articulated?
3. Likewise, what clashes emerged as you generated your stories about writers and writing? Where did the stories seem to be at odds with principles, with particular facts on the ground, with the accounts you drew up?
4. What facts seem to stand on their own, now that you've generated your principles, principled practices, and stories? Where does there seem to be fact production that does not feed back into those three?

Answering these questions can get you to some functions of the program that you may want to pay closer attention to. In the next section, we work through how to help you articulate what problems there are and how they are perceived.

Articulating Perceptions of Problems

In the previous section, you identified some problems: recurring issues that have a cost to the program and endure over time and that conflict with the stories of writers and writing we tell, as well as the principles that underpin those stories. In the next few sections, we'll be recruiting constituent support—as well as disciplinary knowledge—to tackle these problems, prioritize them, and set our plans into motion. Before you do that, though, you need to make sure others agree that your characterization of a problem is, indeed, a problem.

You have a great sense of the program at this point, after all the work you've done. But you're still trying to get a sense of the lived experience of the program, what it means to work with others to keep this program running, day in and day out, year in and year out. So long as this gap exists (and it will be around for a while), you run the risk of a kind of ethnocentrism: you risk identifying problems from *your* perspective, not the perspective of your members.

For this reason, it's helpful to ask others in the program to characterize the problems you're seeing. They might be seeing something different but agree that a problem does exist. This isn't, in and of itself, a bad thing, as long as you are aware of it. In fact, such a multifaceted view of a problem can help with recruiting constituents, planning solutions, and implementing changes. Constituents who agree on a problem *also* need to see your solution as addressing their concerns about it; otherwise, you risk losing the support you might get from those people.

You can take up this work by turning to the potential problems you generated in the previous section. To begin with, you can make sure you frame the potential problems as "potential issues" rather than "problems." This gives your program members the chance to note that, in fact, something might not be a problem (or might not seem like one to them). Using the facts, accounts, stories, and principles, you can generate a description of the potential issues you've spotted that spring from the language they have already shared with you.

Second, make sure the potential issues you identify are brought up with those affected by them. If your program keeps being assigned a classroom that is, in fact, a glorified cupboard, you should be asking the teachers who tend to teach in that room (and the students who are taught in that room) about the issues. There may be problems that affect the entire program, of course, but there also might be issues that only affect particular members in particular ways—and you want to make sure those voices are heard.

Third, give program members a chance to say what they want to have done about the potential issues they identify as problems. To go back to the example in the previous paragraph, perhaps the students and teachers would like the small classroom if some technology was involved or if all the lights worked. Again, background your own judgment to get a sense of the problems they see themselves as having.

Fourth, get a sense of people's priorities. Which potential problems need the most time and attention? Have the most urgency? Need substantial resources? After all, you only have so much time in the day to get things done, and you only have so many resources. So, you'll need to make choices about what to prioritize and what not to prioritize. You may not agree with what you hear about these priorities, but at least if you know what they are and you make a different decision, you know that you need to make the case for that choice so your program members feel as if they are heard.

I've steadfastly avoided addressing *how* this information might be collected, largely because I don't know the size of your program, what your resources are, and what potential issues you've identified. You might have a handful of teachers you can meet with one on one. You might have fifty adjuncts working in your program and several other programs. Depending on the size, resources, and issues at hand, you might be able to use interviews, focus groups, a series of surveys, or perhaps some combination of the three. How you do that is up to you, and the resources at the end of the chapter can help you make those choices.

Recruiting Interested Parties

Now that you have some problems you can work through, you need to identify the interested parties who can help you solve them. Toward this end, you can turn to the list of interested parties you worked up at the end of chapter 4. This gives you an idea of people involved in the particular strategies and tactics you are planning to work up, as well as a sense of how much they can allay the cost of the particular problem solving you're about to engage in.

But simply putting names next to a program does not provide a particular way to bring those people into the problem-solving process. A constituent who might be helpful with recruiting financial support might not be a very helpful voice in, say, discussions of assessment. Recruiting interested parties is about more than just getting support for your ideas; it's also about putting interested people in positions to do the most good.

Let's think about what you might be able to do to recruit interested parties to mobilize solutions to a problem. There are a few things you'll have to line up first. You've noted that there's an issue, one that conflicts with existing program principles and one people in the program want to see addressed. Then you started to see how those folks identified the problem, what they thought about it, and what they thought might be needed to solve it. Now, you need to recruit these people—some of whom you've talked to, and some of whom you may not have spoken with yet about this particular problem—to bring about change. So, what might the first step be?

A good place to begin is to frame the problem. How might you synthesize those differing viewpoints to recruit folks to address the problem in a particular way? Drawing on what others have said about the problem, you can identify common ground, something everyone agrees can be said about the issue at hand. This common ground can feature prominently in how you go about solving the problem.

Once you've framed the problem, you can identify how the problem is of importance to particular interested parties and use that importance to underscore the value of their support. For instance, let's say the issue in your first-year writing program is that the program needs sustained funds for ongoing assessment. The problem—agreed upon by all of the program constituents—is that there is no money. You cannot run an assessment on no money, at least not ethically. But the lack of assessment goes beyond teaching concerns: accrediting bodies are deeply interested in assessment. So it might be valuable to your chair and your dean, and you can use that connection to make the argument for resources.

Finally, you can help constituents think about a payoff. What do they *get* from this support? In the example above, the payoff is rather straightforward: there will be assessment data from a large program on campus. That can be valuable in accreditation, but it also might generate data the Office for Institutional Research can build on in tracking retention of first-year students. How might you be able to frame constituents' involvement in solving this problem as something that has a payoff for them?

Recruiting Disciplinary Knowledge

So, now that you have a number of interested parties and ways they can be recruited to help you carry out the solutions to problems you've identified, we can think about how you might also recruit from your field. We can look in two places: position statements and resolutions from the major organizations in your field and from recent and germinal research.

POSITION STATEMENTS AND RESOLUTIONS. Statements from professional organizations such as the Conference on College Composition and Communication (CCCC), the Council of Writing Program Administrators (CWPA), the National Council of Teachers of English (NCTE), and the Modern Language Association (MLA) can provide useful starting points for conceptualizing problems and suggesting remedies. For instance, a recurring problem might be the size of classes: perhaps you have thirty students in each section of first-year writing, and your teachers are certain that this is too many, that they can't dedicate enough time to each student. This, they argue, exacerbates problems first-year students (who are often at higher risk of dropping out) already have.

Thankfully, our professional organizations have done some thinking about class size and made recommendations. These recommendations might not be followed by your upper-level administrators, but they can help underscore the concerns your teachers have raised and show the administration that they are not simply griping about their work and that there is an actual problem, according to what the experts in the field have told us.

Position statements, resolutions, and suggestions for best practice alone are rarely enough to figure out solutions to problems. Or, at least, that hasn't been my experience. But the fact that these documents cannot solve problems on their own does not mean they are not helpful. In fact, position statements and resolutions can guide our attention to particular texts, authors, and other organizations to help us put the problems we have in particular boxes, which can lead us to the literature we need to start envisioning solutions.

Let's take an example from student persistence rates. Imagine that you're concerned about the persistence rates of minoritized students in both your program and your university. You'd like to do something to address them. But what? And where do the position statements and resolutions fit in?

You can begin with the 2020 CCCC publication from the Special Committee on Composing a CCCC Statement on Anti-Black Racism and Black Linguistic Justice, or, Why We Cain't Breathe. The publication, *This Ain't Another Statement!*

This Is a Demand for Black Linguistic Justice (Baker-Bell et al. 2020), argues that "we cannot say that Black Lives Matter if Black Language is not at the forefront of our work as language educators and researchers!" The committee makes five demands, each articulated in some detail and with references to guide interested readers to the literature.

The publication has some language that may be of help to you in addressing your concerns. Demand #1 in particular stands out: "We demand that teachers stop using academic language and standard English as the accepted communicative norm, which reflects White Mainstream English!" You note that you use the phrase *standard English* in some of your program outcomes, so this demand has clear connections to the way your program operates. Demand #1 goes on to demand that "teachers STOP telling Black students that they have to 'learn standard English to be successful because that's just the way it is in the real world.' No, that's not just the way it is; that's anti-Black linguistic racism. Do we use this same fallacious, racist rhetoric with white students? Will using White Mainstream English prevent Black students from being judged and treated unfairly based solely on the color of their skin? Make it make sense" (Baker-Bell et al. 2020). This language—that is, the "you need this to be successful"—is something you may have heard in the hallways, at meetings, and so on. This only underscores that you might have useful language here for thinking through changes to your first-year program, particularly the language teachers in the program use to talk about language.

Obviously, you're just at the tip of the iceberg here. The CCCC Statement is a helpful document, to be sure, although other useful documents are available through CCCC and other organizations, and it would likely be useful to look at a number of them to put together a good framework for thinking through the problem you have. To keep this example simple, however, I am going to move forward with Demand #1 at the forefront of your attention. Through this language, you can start to walk through examples of how you might recruit recent and germinal research to your side.

Below, I use the terms *recent* and *germinal* deliberately: recent research helps you stay at the cutting edge of what our field is discovering about teaching, learning, writing, and so on. You don't want to be operating through assumptions from twenty years ago that have been disproven in the last five years. That said, though, older research isn't unhelpful just because it's old. Toward that end, I use the word *germinal*: you want to turn your attention to those publications that have had a lasting and positive impact on how we understand writing, writers, teaching, and learning. These germinal texts might have central claims that have been modified by later research, but the framing they provide still shapes the field today. It's useful to have these texts in mind both for understanding the research that came later and for making a compelling case to others in our field about the choices we are making.

RECENT AND GERMINAL RESEARCH. Now that you've been able to locate some position statements that address your problems, you can use those statements to guide your look into the available research on those problems. Thankfully, many of the issues WPAs face are not new; different people at different institutions have been wrestling with them—for better or worse—for some time. So, whenever you have a problem, there is generally not a lack of research to turn to. The problem is more often sorting that research, making it meaningful, and turning it into a compelling case that moves the program forward.

This involves more work than you might believe if you are to imagine using research. We tend to imagine (or at least *I* tend to imagine) fielding a question through email or at a meeting, typing that question into Google Scholar, and finding an article that gives us the answer. And sometimes that happens—if you've got issues about class size for writing classes, for example, Alice Horning's (2007) "Definitive Article on Class Size" will pop up in almost any search and do a lot of heavy lifting to help you solve your problem. But that's not usually how it works. Fields of study are contentious by their nature, so working through studies usually requires asking hard (and sometimes contentious) questions about the field itself (e.g., Kopelson 2013). The findings in our field are useful, of course, but you, the WPA, need to do the work of translating those findings into your setting, of understanding how what these folks found applies to your own circumstances, so that you can solve the problems you need to solve—and, most important, not create bigger problems along the way.

What does this mean, then, for you, the WPA, as you turn to recent and germinal research in the field? It means that the use of this research is more than just drag and drop: you will have to translate this research to your site, make it meaningful to your colleagues, and craft a compelling case for using it to transform your program. If you continue our example about issues of persistence rates through the lens of the CCCC Statement (2020), you can turn your attention to research on language instruction in postsecondary environments. These data can give you starting points for framing what is happening in program classrooms that might be negatively affecting student success. This idea of standard English as "what you need to succeed in the real world" seems to be an instance of a code-switching argument bubbling up. So, you can go to Comp-Pile and type in "code-switching" as a keyword, sorting by newest date first.

You get about 150 hits on this keyword (as of this writing, anyway), which is a good start. And if you look at the list of options, you might notice a blend of different kinds of publications: book reviews, qualitative studies, traditional scholarly arguments, and quantitative assessments. So, you've got a fair amount of work to do to integrate these different pieces into something usable by you and your colleagues. It might be tempting to look for a killer article—one that addresses something rather close to your concerns, that makes a compelling case on its own, and that can help you anticipate some of the counter-arguments that might come up along the way. And that's far from a bad thing to look for—I've never been lucky enough to find one, but surely one day someone will. However, it's also useful to get a wider sense of what the discussion of the field is like, particularly if issues of code meshing, code switching, and translingualism are not central to your own research agenda. Even seemingly disconnected research (such as the framing of assessment raters [Dryer and Peckham 2014]) might usefully inform what you do and how you do it. If you're breaking new ground for yourself, in other words, it doesn't hurt to look around.

Once you have statements, resolutions, recent research, and germinal research pulled together, you can integrate everything into the way you frame both the problem and the payoff to concerned program constituents. How you do this is up to you and will depend on the nature of the problems you are addressing. The resources at the end of this chapter offer some useful ways to begin mobilizing what we know in our field to address particular problems in particular programs.

Making and Enacting a Plan

Throughout this chapter, you've done a great deal: you've identified problems and perceptions of problems, you've identified interested parties in and around your program, and you've recruited disciplinary knowledge from a range of sources. You've stitched together an alliance of supporters—from those on your campus and in your communities to those in your discipline—so you can go about addressing some problems. At this point, you can start to put together a plan for resolving these problems through principled responses and with the larger context of the near-future plans we developed in chapter 4.

To begin with, look through your strategies and tactics to see how the resolution of particular problems fits in. Now that you have a better sense of how to work through some of these problems, how do they work with or against the other strategies and tactics you develop? How do they help some strategies and negatively impact others? Let's say, for instance, that a problem you've identified is a lack of easy-access resources for students. This problem resonates with two tactics you developed in chapter 4: (1) developing additional funds to support programmatic work, and (2) lowering the cost of the course for students. You might develop some open educational resource (OER) materials, which would help with (2). But those same resources also rule out a program-specific textbook, which would give you additional money in support of (1). So, you would have to think about how solving the problem you've identified fits into the larger framework of what you're trying to do. Could you make *some* additional resources OER but still have a course textbook? Or perhaps you could find other ways to raise funds while shifting to an entirely OER footing? How you answer the question is up to you and your program, but you want to make sure you solve problems in the context of your larger strategies and tactics.

Once you have a sense of what these problems will do to move your program forward in line with your emerging mission, you can start to think about a time line for implementing change. When, in the next one to three years, would it make sense for this plan to run its course? How might you go about enacting it given your other goals, particularly with regard to the resources you have at your disposal (e.g., financial, personnel)? Plot the resolution of each problem out on a calendar, trying to identify a reasonable and timely process for working through the plan you've developed.

Finally, once you've plotted out how to resolve these issues in concert with your overall tactics and strategies and your one–three-year time line, you need to consider how you might present the problem as solved. To whom will you communicate the success of this work? When? How? Do you need to just mention it in a few sentences to your chair or dean in an end-of-year report? Should you celebrate at the annual celebration of student writing? Does it need to be communicated at a staff meeting? Resolving long-standing problems in the program is indeed a cause for celebration, and it can give you and your team a sense that the program is making progress in some way, shape, or form.

TABLE 5.1. A process of resolving problems

Goal	Criteria	Notes
Defining Problems	Recurrence	
	Cost	
	Endurance	
Finding Problems	What strategies/tactics directly address problems?	
	What principle clashes do you see?	
	What clashes with stories do you see?	
	What facts seem disconnected from principles?	
Articulating Problems	Frame as "potential issues"	
	Ask those impacted about issues	
	Ask those impacted how they'd like the problem to be solved	
	Prioritize problem solving	
Recruiting Interested Parties	Frame the problem for interested parties	
	Show how the problem impacts interested parties	
	Identify a payoff for interested parties	
Recruiting Disciplinary Knowledge	Review related position statements and resolutions	
	Identify germinal and recent research	
	Integrate into definition of problem	
Making and Enacting a Plan	Fit problem solving into strategies/tactics in chapter 4	
	Put problems on a time line	
	Figure out how to communicate the problem as solved	

Conclusion

At this point, you have identified some problems, recruited interested parties, recruited disciplinary knowledge, and set in motion a plan to resolve the problems (table 5.1 can help you track this work). You're now able to engage, in a productive way, with the problems you identified in your earlier work. This puts you in a position to make headway in building your program in a way that has popular support: you're listening to your colleagues, identifying their concerns, and finding ways to address those concerns. This is not to say that you definitely *will* address those concerns, of course; you might not end up solving a problem, or you might create an entirely new problem. Such is the thrill of WPA work. But the point is that you're taking disciplined, principle-informed steps toward addressing issues.

What I have not addressed—in fact, what I have studiously avoided addressing throughout this chapter—is what happens when principles clash. That is, what happens when the principles *you* have clash with the principles that are already at work in the program you've begun to direct? What do you do then?

That's such a tricky issue that I've decided to devote an entire chapter to it, which is coming up next. But I put this chapter ahead of the next to encourage you to move in this order: to build trust and agreement with your program first before you have to address underlying disconnects. This is an important first step, because you do not want the people you're working with to feel that you're dismissing what they value (you also do not want to experience that feeling yourself). I recognize that it isn't always possible to go in this order—you might have to say "what you're doing is harming students and it needs to stop"—but I would hope that is the exception rather than the rule and that you can begin your work of building the program by making sure the program members are heard and that their thoughts and concerns are valued.

Resources

Below are resources to guide you as you develop responses to the problems you and others see in your programs. The "Framing WPA Problems" sources provide readers with a range of ways to make sense of the obstacles WPAs encounter. "Resources for Particular Problems in WPA Work" drills down into specific problems (e.g., professionalizing graduate students) and in particular contexts (e.g., small liberal arts colleges).

FRAMING WPA PROBLEMS

Burns, Michael Sterling, Randall Cream, and Timothy R. Dougherty. 2018. "Fired Up: Institutional Critique, Lesson Study, and the Future of Antiracist Writing Assessment." In *Writing Assessment, Social Justice, and the Advancement of Opportunity*, edited by Mya Poe, Asao B. Inoue, and Norbert Elliot, 257–292. Fort Collins and Boulder: WAC Clearinghouse and University Press of Colorado.

Craig, Collin Lamont, and Staci M. Perryman-Clark. 2016. "Troubling the Boundaries Revisited: Moving towards Change as Things Stay the Same." *WPA: Writing Program Administration* 39 (2): 20–27.

Jones, Natasha, Gerald Savage, and Han Yu. 2014. "Tracking Our Progress." *Programmatic Perspectives* 6 (1): 132–152.

Konrad, Annika M. 2021. "Access Fatigue: The Rhetorical Work of Disability in Everyday Life." *College English* 83 (3): 179–199.

Leverenz, Carrie S. 2016. "Redesigning Writing Outcomes." *WPA: Writing Program Administration* 40 (1): 33–49.

Malenczyk, Rita. 2017. "Retention≠PanoPticon: What WPAs Should Bring to the Table in Discussions of Student Success." In *Retention, Persistence, and Writing Programs*, edited by Todd Ruecker, Dawn Shepherd, Heidi Estrem, and Beth Brunk-Chavez, 21–37. Logan: Utah State University Press.

McNabb, Richard. 2008. "Rocking the Boat: Asserting Authority and Change in a Writing Program." In *The Promise and Perils of Writing Program Administration*, edited by Theresa Enos and Shane Borrowman, 64–71. West Lafayette, IN: Parlor Press.

Norris, Christine. 2008. "Exploitation, Opportunity, and Writing Program Administration." In *The Promise and Perils of Writing Program Administration*, edited by Theresa Enos and Shane Borrowman, 250–255. West Lafayette, IN: Parlor Press.

Ranieri, Paul, and Jackie Grutsch McKinney. 2004. "Fitness for the Occasion: How Context Matters for jWPAs." In *Untenured Faculty as Writing Program Administrators: Institutional Practices and Politics*, edited by Debra Frank Dew and Alice Horning, 249–278. West Lafayette, IN: Parlor Press.

Sanchez, Fernando. 2013. "Creating Accessible Spaces for ESL Students Online." *WPA: Writing Program Administration* 37 (1): 161–185.

Wilkes, Lydia. 2023. "From Putting Out Fires to Managing Fires: Lessons for WPAs from Indigenous Fire Managers." In *Toward More Sustainable Metaphors of Writing Program Administration*, edited by Lydia Wilkes, Lilian Mina, and Patti Poblete, 19–34. Logan: Utah State University Press.

RESOURCES FOR PARTICULAR PROBLEMS IN WPA WORK

Broad, Bob, Linda Adler-Kassner, Barry Alford, Jane Detweiler, Heidi Estrem, Susanmarie Harrington, Maureen McBride, Eric Stalions, and Scott Weeden. 2009. *Organic Writing Assessment: Dynamic Criteria Mapping in Action*. Logan: Utah State University Press.

currie, sarah madoka, and Ada Hubrig. 2022. "Care Work through Course Design: Shifting the Labor of Resilience." *Composition Studies* 50 (2): 132–153.

Faye, Sarah, Erika I-Tremblay, Dan Melzer, D. J. Quinn, and Lisa Sperber. "The Adoption of Contract Grading in a University Writing Program: Navigating Disruptions to Assessment Ecologies." *WPA: Writing Program Administration* 46 (2): 62–84.

Foley-Schramm, Ashton, Bridget Fullerton, Eileen M. James, and Jenna Morton-Aiken. 2018. "Preparing Graduate Students for the Field: A Graduate Student Praxis Heuristic for WPA Professionalization and Institutional Politics." *WPA: Writing Program Administration* 41 (2): 89–103.

Gladstein, Jill M., and Dara Rossman Regaignon. 2012. *Writing Program Administration at Small Liberal Arts Colleges*. West Lafayette, IN: Parlor Press.

Jackson, N. Claire. 2021. "Writing Program Administration at Public Liberal Arts Colleges." PhD dissertation, University of Louisville, Louisville, KY.

Jaxon, Kim, Laura Sparks, and Chris Fosen. 2020. "Epic Learning in a 'Jumbo' Writing Course." *Composition Studies* 48 (2): 116–127.

Lang, Susan M. 2016. "Taming Big Data through Agile Approaches to Instructor Training and Assessment: Managing Ongoing Professional Development in Large First-Year Writing Programs." *WPA: Writing Program Administration* 39 (2): 81–104.

Leon, Kendall, and Tom Sura. 2013. "'We Don't Need Any More Brochures': Rethinking Deliverables in Service-Learning Curricula." *WPA: Writing Program Administration* 36 (2): 59–74.

Osorio, Ruth, Allison Hutchison, Sarah Primeau, Molly E. Ubbesen, and Alexander Champoux-Crowley. 2021. "The Laborious Reality vs. the Imagined Ideal of Graduate Student Instructors of Writing." *WPA: Writing Program Administration* 45 (1): 131–152.

Oswal, Sushil K., and Lisa Meloncon. 2017. "Saying No to the Checklist: Shifting from an Ideology of Normalcy to an Ideology of Inclusion in Online Writing Instruction." *WPA: Writing Program Administration* 40 (3): 61–77.

6
Overcoming Clashes of Principle

In chapter 5, you explored how you might go about resolving problems you identified in the work of part I. But these problems were, at some level, consensus-driven: your new colleagues in your program have some agreement that these problems are *actually* problems, that they exist and need to be addressed. Throughout chapter 5, you worked your way to solutions to those problems, identified the cost, and explored how you might go about paying that cost. Though not easy work, these kinds of issues were at least not particularly contentious; they worked off of the beliefs people hold and let you make adjustments to the program through the problems they perceive the program as having.

This chapter explores a very different kind of problem: clashes of principle. The clashes of principle you will be centrally addressing are clashes between *your* principles and the principles of those in your new program. No doubt some of your values—perhaps many of them—overlap in productive ways. This isn't that surprising; after all, if you've been able to work your way through submitting an application for this job through a campus visit and contract negotiations, there must be some alignment between you and your program that you can work from. But the hiring process is not foolproof on that front (along with many other fronts), and even if you align on some issues, there might be considerable distance between the values the program lives and those you want to live as a writing program administrator (WPA) (see Bishop and Crossley 1996; Charlton et al. 2011; Gunner 1999; Kinney 2009; Stolley 2015 for further discussion of the complexities of WPA identity).

In this chapter, you'll tackle how to work through these sorts of problems. How might you work to resolve principled clashes, to work through them to new insights, or even just to exist peacefully with those whose values your principles clash with? You will look at how you might be able to leverage clashes of principle to grow everyone's understanding of both the problems at hand and your own values. As you'll see, the principles you've articulated are not set in stone; they are amenable to your changing understandings of the world. Therefore, examining clashes of principle can help you see more than you otherwise might about what it is you value and why.

Defining Clashes of Principle

If you think back to the discussion of principle in the book's introduction, you can imagine how difficult it is to define a clash of principle. Our principles—that is, the articulated version of them—are often the tip of the iceberg of what we value. When I say it's important for me to respect student labor, there's a *lot* going unsaid. I'm aware of *some* of this unsaid business—after all, I'm the one who wrote the principle, so I can get a good sense of what I've left out. But there's even more that I am not conscious of with this principle. This is true for a great many reasons, but I can quickly think of a relatively easy one: I haven't been in all possible circumstances where the act of respecting student labor is challenging, so I have not had to articulate every facet of this value.

You need to keep this iceberg metaphor in mind when thinking about clashes of principle, because you can very well find yourself running into what *feels* like a clash but, once you look across the principles you've articulated, the situation doesn't clearly run up against any of them. This is a useful learning opportunity; it's in these moments of perceptible but un-nameable discomfort that we can learn the most about our values, that we can come to new understandings of what we really value and why we value it. For the purposes of this chapter, though, we need to set these particular instances aside, at least for the moment. What you want to look for are direct, obvious clashes of principle. Let's say, for instance, that you have a principle that respects the complexity of the lives students live during (and outside of) school. Members of your program, in contrast, have clear-cut expectations for how their students should approach their classes: school is a job—one students need to show up on time for, do the work for, and keep at the center of their attention.

What we have here are two principles that, as currently articulated, are diametrically opposed to one another. Now, this is just an example—you might have principles that are not *diametrically* opposed to one another but that run up against one another nonetheless. But the point here is that the principles, as articulated, run into one another. What you're looking at are principles that, in some fundamental way, clash. You might think of principle clashes as *values working at cross-purposes*.

Noting Clashes of Principle

Noting clashes of principle isn't that difficult; you likely felt it in your gut when you saw the program operating in a way that didn't mesh with what you value. But, at least in the work of part I, we weren't thinking about implementing changes or transforming the program. Instead, we were working through what the program is, what it values, and why it has those values. The work you were doing submerged those clashes, pushed them aside so you could get on with fact production.

Now that you've produced those facts, though, and now that you've explored the challenges to the program (in chapter 5) that many constituents see as problems, you can turn your attention to these clashes. First, look through your notes from fact building, and look for facts and accounts that seem to run against the grain of what you value. It's important that you stick to this level of specificity to note the clashes of principle: since the facts are what hold up the stories of writers and writing in your program, it's only by looking at those facts that you can see where the clashes emerge.

Accounts are also important to look at, because sometimes the production of a fact in one moment can be negated or complicated by another moment. So, seeing the *sequence* of fact production can help you understand what is going on in the program. But getting to accounts is step two. In step one, you identify, in the facts you produced earlier, the moments at which particular recurring actions conflict with the values you hold for the program and its administration.

Once you have the clashes noted, you can start to do something with them. This gets us to the second step: looking for similarities across clashes. Do you see points at which clashes with your own principles intersect? Are there, for instance, moments in which your value of respecting student labor *and* your value of respecting the working loads of teachers are disrupted in the program? These converging moments of clashing with your principles can be a useful way to see how the constituents in the program package their understandings of the program together, how the knife cuts for them while they organize the world that is teaching in the writing program.

Let's sum this up in a few steps before you frame clashes of principle in the context of a "big-tent" writing program. First, identify, within the facts produced earlier, potential clashes of principle between your values and the values of those in the program. Then, once you have potential clashes identified, look within those clashes (that is, across multiple facts and accounts) to identify patterns of clashing. You might find a range of one-off clashes of principle, but you are looking for *patterns* of clashing so you can identify those you might most productively engage with.

Respectful Program Transformation

You will need to make sure that the ways you work through clashes of principle remain respectful, particularly of those who were part of the program before your arrival. Although they might have values that differ from yours, the long-standing members of a program have been, at least in part, responsible for the program's long-term success. In the work you do to transform the values of the program, then, you need to make sure you keep that in mind, that you are willing to be certain that voices are heard, that people don't feel they've been left out in the cold.

Now, that's a much easier thing to *say* you're going to do than it is to actually *do* it, but it's not impossible. And, to be sure, there may be folks who are part of your program who don't want to change at all and don't care to see themselves as part of the program transformation you're leading. You can't help that. But what you *can* do is make the program and its ongoing transformation a place where people who are interested can see themselves. That is, in the end, what a community is: a place where you feel you belong. You want to give teachers in the program a chance to feel like they belong, even if it's through rapid change.

So, how do you go about doing this work? How do you engage in respectful program change? In the next two sections, you'll take up the work of recruiting interested parties and disciplinary knowledge to build compelling cases and bring around those who might lean against programmatic change or, perhaps, the particular changes you're interested in making. But for right now, you can start to put in the hard work of making these changes respectfully.

I can draw an example from a recurring issue: respecting student ideas. Oftentimes, as Nancy Sommers (1982) points out, teachers can appropriate the text of students, pushing them not into further exploring their own ideas but into exploring the particular areas that seem of value and interest to the teacher. This can also happen at the level of syntax and diction, by the way: teachers can push particular edits not because the original writing was incorrect but because it didn't have the sound they wanted it to have.

I frequently run up against this issue. It's easy to see this as a clash of principles, but it really isn't, in a lot of ways. These teachers see themselves as helping their students' ideas "be clear" or "connect to the needs of the audience" or something. The teachers are, in your eyes, working against students' ideas and not giving those ideas the respect they deserve, but in the eyes of the *teachers*, what they're doing is just fine. They are preparing students for the writing future courses will demand of them.

Such a situation is often a great way to start to bring about a transformation of the program and its values. The teachers you're talking to will say they value what their students have to say and that their feedback is intended to make what they say more effective to the audience they are trying to reach. So, what you have to do here is come to a shared understanding of what's happening and why it is at odds with something you value.

One thing to keep in mind in situations like this is that you are focusing on one aspect of teaching (feedback) and on a particular issue in that aspect of teaching (when appropriation happens). Feedback is not *all* teaching is, and appropriation is not the only thing the teacher does with the text. This is probably intuitively obvious, but a fixation on troublesome connections can easily obscure that very real fact. If I am making suggestions that another teacher in the program should change the way they give feedback, then they might not hear "changing this can make your feedback better" but rather "what you are doing is hurting students." And that last one is much tougher to take than the former. Furthermore, the teacher might have convincing evidence to the contrary: students who speak highly of working with them, who go on to do great things with writing in their careers. In short, the teacher might be (1) hurt and (2) convinced I'm wrong; after all, they've got the goods (anecdotes of successful student outcomes) and I don't.

What I can do, then, is begin to build a framework for how to talk about feedback so that our value clashes can clash a bit less. For instance, when we talk about feedback, we might discuss the many ways our feedback impacts students, as well as the context in which it happens. As Carol Rutz (2006) demonstrates, no feedback happens in a vacuum: there are class meetings, discussion posts, prior assignments, and on and on—in other words, there is a great deal of relationship building (for good or for ill) that we can draw from to shape our feedback. So, by expanding the range of what we're discussing when we talk about feedback, we can end up building our collective relationship while nudging our values (slowly) into some kind of (tentative) alignment.

If we were to break down this process into a series of steps, it might look like this:

- STEP 1: Break down the patterns of clashes you've identified into a series of targets for professional learning and discussion.
- STEP 2: Frame each of those targets in a wide context, allowing many principles to be brought to bear (and respected) so subsequent changes to the program might be tied to values that do align.
- STEP 3: Create pathways to feed the results of the discussion into future work so the clash between values can continue to be resolved over time, through the daily work of those in your writing program, through the strategies and tactics you set into motion.

Recruiting Interested Parties

Now that you have worked out some ways to engage in respectful program transformation, you can consider how you might recruit interested parties to this work. As an example, let's turn our attention back to strategy 1 in chapter 4: co-creating career paths for adjunct faculty. This particular strategy hits on a value that means a great deal to you—creating opportunities for people in your program. The end result might cause some problems on your end, in that you might find yourself with sections that need to be filled in short order. If you're not in a large metropolitan area, replacing some of those teachers might be challenging. But, if you really do value making certain that people are given a decent wage, are given the benefits and financial support they need to live their lives, and you can't just snap your fingers and make them all full-time employees, this may be the best way to go about living your values.

But this strategy might also lead to conflict with those who disagree with your value—or, at the very least, disagree with carrying it out. Perhaps there are program constituents who believe that contingent faculty, for one reason or another, *belong* in the adjunct ranks and that it's not the job of the program or the university to help them do something they should be able to do on their own. If they don't like being adjuncts, they might argue, they can go somewhere else. We don't need to help them do that.

This is an expression of values that operates in diametric opposition to *your* values and, more urgently, to the strategy you've created to solve a problem you and others would like to take a shot at solving. What you need to do here is more than just identify people who can help solve the problem: you need to promote what you are doing, let it gain momentum, *show* that it's gaining momentum, and allow the success of what you are doing to change the minds of those who might disagree with you.

If you were to think about career paths for adjunct faculty, who might you turn to in order to support this effort? What parties might be interested? Adjunct instructors may find this of interest—although you shouldn't assume that, as some people may be teaching classes as part of a range of other activities in their lives and may not wish to change their current circumstances. If so, that's fine. But no doubt, many adjunct faculty may want more stability in their careers, more income, health insurance, and other benefits. So, while you cannot assume that *all* adjunct faculty would be interested in your effort, you can rest assured that at least some will.

But these adjunct faculty don't have much power institutionally. You can't ask them for money, for instance, to fund professional learning events. You can't arrange for meetings with them to recruit a broader base of support. What you need to do is think about the people with more authority than you (or adjunct faculty) have: chairs, deans, and so on. Who in those ranks might be willing to help you enact this strategy, and to what extent?

At this point, there are plenty of options. The easiest (and least costly) approach is something akin to career counseling: asking adjunct instructors what their goals are and how professional learning support can be geared toward making those goals come true. This can lead adjuncts to other institutions or different fields, with onetime (or recurring) financial support. Let's say you have an adjunct instructor interested in moving on to secondary teaching in the area but who isn't sure about how to go about getting credentialed, finding a job, and so on. You can help them with most of this work: for example, understanding the (often labyrinthine) website of the state's Department of Education website, finding the sites that cover the local secondary teaching job market. In Maine, as in most states, we have a National Council of Teachers of English (NCTE) affiliate (the Maine Council for English Language Arts) that hosts a yearly conference and other activities, which acts as a great, low-cost networking and professional learning event. Bringing these sorts of resources together for an interested adjunct is not always easy work (even with the relatively straightforward example I picked), but it's relatively straightforward, has low overhead, and may rather easily garner the support of upper-level administrators.

But there are other approaches to doing this kind of work: you could *create* full-time teaching positions for adjunct faculty at your institution, in your program. This is a far more difficult sell, although there are administrators who are not content with the plight of contingent instruction in higher education and want to help whenever possible. But even with such support, it might be too heavy a lift for those on your side; you might just need to spend time recruiting more support and finding more interested parties until you can get some (even a little) movement on that front.

As you can imagine, those working *against* your principle of creating career paths for adjunct faculty would find it far easier to fight back against more expensive options. In the former, university resources that might be spent elsewhere are diverted to this goal, whereas in the latter, most of the "cost" might be resources already set aside for professional learning and your own professional time. This isn't to say that someone might not have something to say about the latter—higher education does seem to be, in my experience, the place where unsolicited opinions are loudly shared—but you might have more room to move, more opportunities to build momentum, by starting with the smaller tasks.

Even as you're supporting these faculty and letting some clashes stand where appropriate, you can still leave the door open for those opposed to join in, to be swayed by the successes of your work, and thus to contribute to more aspects of the program. Let's consider a tenured faculty member at your institution who, for some reason, doesn't like to see funding going to adjunct teachers. It might be wise to find out *why* this pushback is happening. Some of the reasons might be ridiculous—there are people, after all, who can only pick themselves up by pushing others down—but there also might be legitimate concerns from that teacher's history in the program. Perhaps a loss of well-trained adjunct instructors in the past devastated the program, and the faculty member is concerned that this would happen again.

Whatever the reason, it would be good to know it. Understanding the rationale can be an important step toward leaving the door open. If the teacher is concerned about, say, limited resources, you can demonstrate how the professional learning you support for adjunct teachers comes back to the entire program and perhaps actually creates *more* opportunities for professional learning across the board. If the teacher is concerned about losing well-trained teachers too quickly, perhaps you can detail broader plans for bringing in and training new teachers, for establishing more tenure-line or non-tenure-track ranks that would give way to a stable teaching corps, and show how the work you're doing now is a step in that direction. If you can demonstrate that you're addressing needs even if you're moving in a direction a program constituent might not like, there's a better chance of bringing that person over to your side in the future or perhaps on a different issue.

So, what steps can we abstract from this example when it comes to recruiting interested parties? First, create a context for your ask. What bigger picture does what you're asking for fall into? How might this help with a broader strategic vision for the university? Second, generate a series of small steps for pursuing your goal so you can let momentum build. Third, glean as much information as you can about your opposition as you progress through these steps so you can work around them and, when appropriate, gain their support.

Recruiting Disciplinary Knowledge

Much as you did with problems in chapter 5, you can use disciplinary knowledge to build a foundation for working through clashes of principle. And, much as in chapter 5, you have two different starting points: you can start with the field's position statements, or you can start with recent and germinal research on the issue at hand. Throughout this section, I am going to work through how you might mobilize these resources, using an example: the teaching of 'grammar' in first-year writing courses. Note that I have 'grammar' in scare quotes. I am working from the point of view of how people *talk* about 'grammar,' which often includes stylistic decisions, punctuation, and so on. Grammar, in the vented frustrations of teachers and other interested parties, often becomes what the speaker needs it to become.

Here's the scenario: some people in other departments are complaining—loudly, frequently, and without regard to whether anyone actually *asked* them—that students are coming into their program and "can't write a sentence" and that this is primarily because they "don't know grammar." They would like your program to address this issue. Never mind that the examples of grammar they provide have nothing to do with *actual* grammar: this is a story about student writers and writing, and it has sway not only with people in other departments but also with a significant portion of your own teaching faculty, many of whom think they need to devote more time to "the basics." Writing programs can be useful in helping faculty in a college or university develop new insights about students and their writing (Olds 1990), so this is an issue worth addressing. Your task is to make a case for your own position by drawing on what we know in the field of writing studies, connecting it to the particularities of your context in this program, and building alternative pathways to talking about (and working through) this particular issue.

This issue of 'grammar' as it's discussed here clashes with several of your own principles: that we need to respect students' language use; that writing is a complex act, and trying to isolate particular aspects of it does not help people grow as writers; that error in student writing, however conceived, tends to grow and change along complex trajectories, not simply by slowly disappearing. So, what do you do? You have interested parties who don't believe what you do. You have teachers in your own program who don't believe what you do and would like to enact teaching strategies that would run counter to some of the program's other values. How can you work through this issue? How might you bring position statements, resolutions, best practices, recent and germinal research to bear on these matters so you can create ways of engaging with these folks without also contradicting what it is that you value?

POSITION STATEMENTS AND RESOLUTIONS. Much as in chapter 5, position statements and resolutions can provide useful starting points for understanding the broad lay of the land in the field. Position statements, resolutions, and best practices can usefully act as intersections of a number of research publications, opinions of scholars, and so on. These statements might be in need of an update—obviously, these organizations do their best to keep them up to date, but sometimes they take time to cycle through. And sometimes the available statements don't *quite* hit the nail on the head, but they still provide a decent starting point. Let's turn back to our scenario to see what this might look like.

If we turn to the Conference on College Composition and Communication (CCCC), we have a few statements like the CCCC Statement (2020) that address issues of "standard English" and other language. If you look at the 1974 statement "Students' Right to Their Own Language" (SRTOL), you can find useful phrases to help you discuss language varieties. Likewise, you can turn to the Statement on Second Language Writing and Multilingual Writers (2020) to find helpful language about how the kinds of explicit 'grammar' instruction advocated by the parties you are working with create additional and unnecessary burdens on multilingual students.

But these arguments, though useful, do not really address the demands made by interested parties. They are not arguing that *particular* students can't write—they are arguing that *all* students (or at least most) can't write. As a result, they might see the turn to multilingual writers as addressing the needs not of a particular few but rather of the student body as a whole. It's this wide-ranging nature of the problem that seems to be the inciting thought for a holistic reform of first-year writing to focus on "the basics." So, while useful, these statements on their own won't be enough.

If you turn to the Council for Writing Program Administrators (CWPA), the *Framework for Success in Postsecondary Writing* (Council of Writing Program Administrators et al., 2011) offers some useful language. One of the aims of the *Framework* is to help students develop "knowledge of conventions" (9). The language in this section usefully locates issues of "correctness" in the particular demands of genre and context (9). Here we have a useful point that speaks directly to the stated complaints: correctness is inescapably *situated* in particular writing demands. First-year writing cannot make students great writers in biology—that's the job of the biologists. But first-year writing *can* provide a springboard for that kind of work, can help students make sense of the demands that are made of them at the sentence level.

Now, the *Framework* does not mean we should ignore the CCCC Statement, SRTOL, or the statement on multilingual writers. Rather, we should think about the *Framework* as being able to set the stage in this discussion, since it speaks directly to the problems presented by the interested parties. We can use this particular document as a foundation from which we can bring in other statements.

Another document, "Some Questions and Answers about Grammar," offered by the Assembly for the Teaching of English Grammar (ATEG 2002), provides useful language about what we mean by "grammar" and what one might expect from its instruction. This document has some useful language—phrasing such as "teaching grammar will not make writing errors go away." Here, even an assembly advocating *for* grammar instruction is pointing out that this kind of instruction won't solve the problems these people see their students as having.

With language from the ATEG Q&A and the *Framework*, you can start to directly address some of the concerns of program constituents. Using language from the CCCC Statement, SRTOL, and the statement on multilingual writers, you can be certain that what you pull together is addressing a range of student needs and that the initial framing of the problem is not driving the discussion. You might think of the ATEG Q&A and the *Framework* as the basis from which you can direct attention to the ideas about writing, language, and power put forth by the CCCC Statement, SRTOL, and the multilingual statement. This can set a broad frame that you can fill in with recent and germinal research.

RECENT AND GERMINAL RESEARCH. Recent and germinal research, as in chapter 5, provides you with useful texts to make a more compelling case to interested parties—particularly to interested parties who disagree with you. You can turn to scholarly argument, qualitative research, and quantitative research to make your case. To continue the example from above, there is a great deal of research on the teaching of grammar in K–16 classrooms.

Since you're looking to argue that grammar instruction (variously defined) is not going to be a helpful approach for students in first-year writing courses, you are in luck that considerable evidence supports that claim. You can look to George Hillocks's (1986) meta-analysis and pair it with Steve Graham and Dolores Perin's (2007) meta-analysis to show that there is, in fact, a *negative* effect size associated with the teaching of grammar. In other words, grammar instruction can do far worse than nothing: it can actually *decrease writing proficiency*. So, you have quantitative measures that can support your position. You can also turn to qualitative approaches to exploring issues of grammar and standard English ideologies, such as those of Bethany Davila (2016, 2017), which can be put into useful conversation with the meta-analyses already mentioned. Resources like these can help you point out that teaching writing is complicated, and people don't even agree on what counts as error, grammar, and other factors in the many ways they talk about writing and student writing.

Now that you have a set of overarching documents (the position statements) and some key findings (recent and germinal research) recruited to your position, you can set yourself up to work through the clash of principles. You can begin this work by highlighting the evidence on your side: that grammar instruction can have a negative impact on student writing. You can contextualize this a bit further if you put the findings in conversation with what you know about your particular context: the backgrounds of your students, the expectations of their degree path, and the like. Finally, you might use both the findings and the context to think about alternative pathways to discuss and enact in your teaching, which can inform programmatic strategy and tactic development. If you know that the kinds of grammar instruction being asked for can negatively impact student learning, what are you doing that you

TABLE 6.1. Addressing clashes of principle

Goal	Criteria	Notes
Note Clashes of Principle	Identify clashes	
	Look for patterns	
Create Respectful Program Transformation	Break patterns into targets for professional learning and discussion	
	Frame targets in a wide context	
	Create pathways to feed into future work	
Recruiting Interested Parties	Create a context for an ask	
	Generate a series of steps for your goal	
	Gather information on opposing viewpoints	
Recruiting Disciplinary Knowledge	Highlight supporting evidence	
	Connect evidence to context	
	Use findings and context to develop alternative approaches	

know *can* support student learning, and how can you build on that? Recruiting support in recent and germinal research, connecting to context, and finding alternative pathways for you to work together with colleagues can set the stage for eventual development of more aligned (or, at least, less diametrically opposed) values in the program.

Conclusion

You've spent this chapter figuring out how to go about addressing clashes of principle in your writing program: points at which your values and the values of your program are at odds. This is a challenging (and often uncomfortable) place to be. However, as I've tried to point out throughout the text, this is not a matter of imposing your values; it's a place to learn more about your values, to encourage others to learn more about theirs, and to work together toward a new sense of what all of you value and, by extension, what you want your program to do. Table 6.1 provides a general overview of your work throughout this chapter so you can keep yourself organized (either by writing on it or creating your own spreadsheet with a similar layout). As you take up the work of this chapter, you'll find yourself returning to the strategies and tactics you developed in chapter 4, revising and refitting them as necessary while you try to resolve these clashes or at least get to a state of détente between you and those members of your program with whom you have principled disagreements.

You are now at the close of not only chapter 6 but of part II. The work of this chapter guided you through (and around) clashes of principle so you might be certain that you're working with and for a program that aligns—as well as possible—with what you value. Making plans that stretch for several years, figuring out how to solve seemingly intractable problems, and working through clashes of value in respectful ways are incredibly difficult tasks, and—at least for me—it seems that each semester and year, that work tends to begin anew. But, for the purposes of your early work with the program you are now directing, you have gained a sense of what the program is like (part I), and now (in part II) you have developed a plan to bring this program into the future. In part III, you'll turn your eyes toward a longer time frame and identify a broader trajectory of your program through grand strategies, piloted innovations, and the creation of sustainable structures and practices.

Resources

Below are resources that may inform or guide your work as you address clashes of principle in your program. Each text offers a different way of seeing what's happening in your program, from thinking differently about development (Eubanks and Vanovac 2020) to a close look at how textbooks operate (Taylor 2019).

Alexander, Jonathan. 2017. "Queer Ways of Knowing." *WPA: Writing Program Administration* 41 (1): 137–149.

Baca, Isabela. 2021. "Hispanic-Serving or Not: La Lucha Sigue in Academia; the Struggle Continues in Academia." *Composition Studies* 49 (2): 70–78.

Banks, William P., Michael J. Faris, Collie Fulford, Timothy Oleksiak, G Pat Patterson, and Trixie G. Smith. 2020. "Writing Program Administration: A Queer Symposium." *WPA: Writing Program Administration* 43 (2): 11–44.

Bastian, Heather. 2019. "The F-Word: Failure in WPA Work." *WPA: Writing Program Administration* 43 (1): 94–110.

Carter-Tod, Sheila. 2023. "Nothing New: Systemic Invisibility, Epistemological Exclusion, and Faculty and Administrators of Color." In *Making Administrative Work Visible: Data-Driven Advocacy for Understanding the Labor of Writing Program Administration*, edited by Leigh Graziano, Kay Halasek, Remi Hudgins, Susan Miller-Cochran,

Frank Napolitano, and Natalie Szymanski, 27–38. Logan: Utah State University Press.
de Mueller, Genevieve Garcia. 2016. "WPA and the New Civil Rights Movement." *WPA: Writing Program Administration* 39 (2): 36–41.
Del Principe, Annie, and Jacqueline Brady. 2018. "Academic Freedom and the Idea of a Writing Program." *Teaching English in the Two-Year College* 45 (4): 351–360.
Elder, Chris L., and Bethany Davila. 2019. "Responding to Bullying in the WPA Workplace." *Writing Program Administration* 43 (1): 73–94.
Eubanks, David, and Sarah Vanovac. 2020. "Divergent Writer Development in College." *Journal of Writing Analytics* 4 (1): 15–54.
Heckathorn, Amy. 2019. "The Professional Is Personal: Institutional Bullying and the WPA." In *Defining, Locating, and Addressing Bullying in the WPA Workplace*, edited by Chris L. Elder and Bethany Davila, 151–171. Logan: Utah State University Press.
Hillin, Sara. 2017. "We Are All Needed: Feminist Rhetorical Strategies for Building Trust among Colleagues." In *Surviving Sexism in Academia*, edited by Kirsti Cole and Holly Hassel, 287–295. New York: Routledge.
Jack, Jordynn. 2022. "The Cognitive Vernacular as Normative Mandate in Habits of Mind." *College English* 84 (4): 335–355.
Kynard, Carmen. 2022. "Fakers and Takers: Disrespect, Crisis, and Inherited Whiteness in Rhetoric-Composition Studies." *Composition Studies* 50 (3): 131–136.
Nicolas, Melissa. 2017. "Ma(r)king a Difference: Challenging Ableist Assumptions in Writing Program Policies." *WPA: Writing Program Administration* 40 (3): 10–22.
O'Neill, Erin. 2008. "Irreconcilable Differences: One Former WPD's Cautionary Tale." In *The Promise and Perils of Writing Program Administration*, edited by Theresa Enos and Shane Borrowman, 72–78. West Lafayette, IN: Parlor Press.
Sicari, Anne. 2020. "Complaint as 'Sticky Data' for the Woman WPA: The Intellectual Work of a WPA's Emotional and Embodied Labor." *Journal of the Assembly for Expanded Perspectives on Learning* 25 (1): 99–117.
Tang, Jasmine Kar, and Noro Andriamanalina. 2016. "'Rhonda Left Early to Go to Black Lives Matter': Programmatic Support for Graduate Writers of Color." *WPA: Writing Program Administration* 39 (2): 10–15.
Tarr, Kathleen. 2021. "The Tone Police's Greatest Hits." *Composition Studies* 49 (2): 79–95.
Taylor, Leslie S. 2019. "Current-Traditional Rhetoric and the Hodges Harbrace Handbook: A Study in the Disconnect between Theory and Practice." PhD dissertation, Georgia State University, Athens.

PART III

The Long View

In our work with Coach B. on the practice fields and the film room, our attention was on the immediate: getting ready for a game, making sense of a game plan, unpacking what we had done the previous week so we could get a little better. But during (and outside of) this work, you could also see careful attention to a longer trajectory of personal and program development. For instance: offensive linemen, as you may or may not know, are rarely hyped for cardio. Legends are told of one or two who actively avoided it whenever possible. And it was the most possible to avoid cardio in the offseason. The problem, of course, was that if you came to camp out of shape, you spent your time trying to *get in shape* rather than trying to *be a better football player*.

Coach B. worked this problem with a long view in mind: he knew you didn't have to be ready to play a game in February. Why would you? The season starts in September. So, rather than pushing linemen to be ready for a game they weren't going to play in in February, he encouraged them to work themselves into some kind of shape: a slow, twenty-minute jog here, a few minutes of skipping rope there, and so on. This insistence resulted in linemen who were ready to get a little bit better (and in a little bit better game shape) in spring practices and then again when camp started in August.

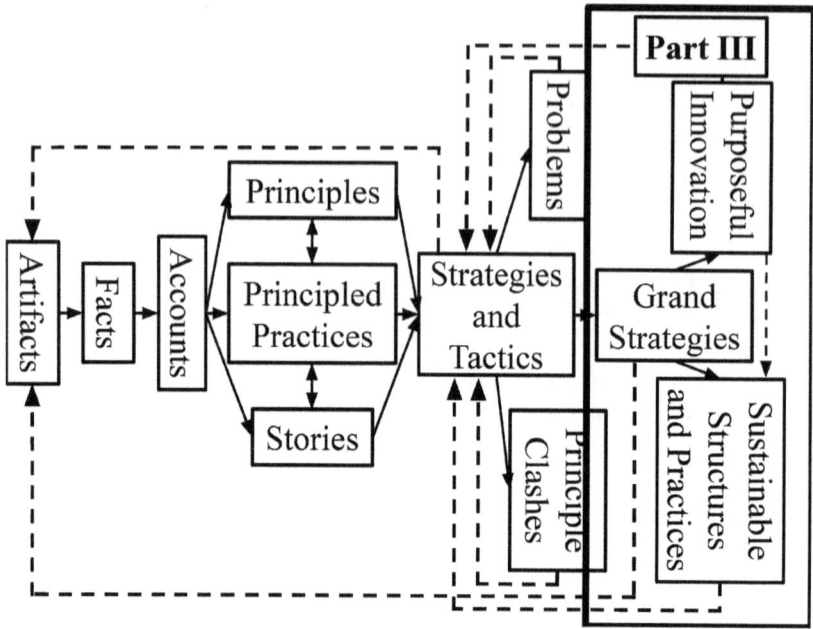

FIGURE 7.0. Part III's role in the work of this text

Coach B. also took the long view of a player's entire career. Some players come to college ready to start for their team; they can have a positive impact on their team's success from the moment they step on the field. Other players, though—probably most players—need time to learn the ins and outs of college football, to get a little stronger and faster, to get a sense of how they can best contribute to the team. Coach B. understood this, I think, better than most, and he certainly *communicated* it better than most. How could you use your time on the scout team, in drills, in the film room to make progress for the next year? Coach B. was constantly directing players to this kind of thinking, helping them see a larger picture of change over time. Much like Coach B. did, in part III we turn our attention to the long view. However, our "long view" is not tied to NCAA eligibility limits, so we can think in terms of a decade or more of change (figure 7.0).

The work you've articulated through parts I and II gives a sense of what your program can look like in a couple of years. It also gave you the chance to collect artifacts that show you (1) how your program works and (2) what your program needs to do differently, both now and in the future. With these as starting points, we can begin to figure out a viable set of long-term plans for growing your program.

You've likely heard about, seen, or participated in the enactment of five- and ten-year plans at institutions you've been part of. These plans guide fundraising, building construction, enrollment goals, and so on at a university. We did some version of this in part II of the text. But continually establishing such specific goals in the long term is difficult for writing program administrators (WPAs)—we don't have the kind of power a president or a dean might have at a university, and our options are informed at least in part by the initiatives on university campuses. So, we might have a great ten-year plan set up, only to find budget priorities changing, supportive administrators leaving, and so on.

To avoid this problem, chapter 7 guides you through the development of *grand strategies*: long-term goals that are both useful focusing agents for programmatic decision making and flexible enough that individual changes such as budget constraints, the loss of administrator support, and others will not impact the program's continued forward movement. Grand strategies help us communicate with our constituents and grow our program without constraining us or keeping us tied to particular initiatives or higher administrative personnel. They allow for the development of a wide vision, such as the one we see enacted in programs like Illinois State University's (Rose and Walker 2014).

Once we have some grand strategies in place, we use chapter 8 to begin *purposeful innovation* in the program. In other words, we use chapter 8 to tinker; we try out new things in specific, targeted ways and measure (in many ways) the successes of those innovations. Some of these attempts will succeed, and others will fail. Some will be responses to shifts in campus priorities, and others will be responses to perceived needs or the sense that a breakthrough in research might quickly be brought to bear on the program in a useful way. Chapter 8 is a guide through which we can implement programmatic changes in a small way without committing the entire program to a changing course of action.

But some of these innovations will gather strength and bring about a change in the program. And in chapter 9, we discuss how these changes can be rendered *sustainable*, integrated into the everyday life of the program. In that chapter I discuss *structures* and *practices*, which are the artifacts and actions we see our program through. Structures and practices are so deeply rooted in the program that we don't think twice about them. Consider, for instance, grades (at least in most institutions): we end our term by assigning student grades. We might think about doing away with grades, going to pass/fail, or something; but in the daily work of prepping and carrying out our courses, we think *through* the concept of grades. In chapter 9, we explore how we might take the successfully piloted innovations and work them into something as bone-deep as grades.

7
Growing a Program via Grand Strategies

The work of part II gave you a good sense of what a one- to three-year span of running your program might look like. In this chapter, we're going to think a good deal further into the future: from years to decades. Once we finish this chapter, you'll have a good sense of the directions you would like to move the program in over the course of several decades. The key concept of this chapter is *grand strategies*. I describe grand strategies below, but you can start by thinking of them as unattainable goals: things you work toward, for sure, but that you can never pin down as finished at any point.

The grand strategies you develop through the work of this chapter are going to underpin the work we do in chapters 8 and 9. Grand strategies help writing program administrators (WPAs) articulate how their attempted innovations in the program connect and the broader vision to which they contribute. Without grand strategies, the growth of your program as you articulate it in the final two chapters of the text will seem haphazard or emerging only as a response to particular changing circumstances. Grand strategies give your program a sense of direction, of a future it will be creating and participating in. The grand strategies are one of the many ways we make certain that your program *is* a program—that is, a coherent entity—rather than a collection of classes with the same title and outcomes.

https://doi.org/10.7330/9781646426416.c007

A note before we begin: some of you reading this text may find yourselves in the role of WPA on a limited basis. Maybe you're rotating into the role for a set amount of time, or you're stepping in as part of a broader change in departmental organization. Or perhaps you just don't plan on being in this role for the next few decades. None of this should dissuade you from taking up the work of developing grand strategies. A set of guiding strategies for resource allocation can be incredibly helpful for those who come after you. Perhaps you want to do this with a team of others or as part of a longer-term process that you set up but that stretches beyond your time as WPA. My point, though, is that you shouldn't feel concerned about jumping right in.

Why Grand Strategies?

Strategies and tactics (like the kind we developed in chapter 4) are certainly useful for developing a program. They help us determine how we—both individual WPAs and writing program personnel more broadly—are making use of our time, what we're paying attention to, and so on. But strategies and tactics have limits, particularly when it comes to longer spans of time. What happens when the work of a particular strategy wraps up? Where do we go from there? What logical next steps can we take in further developing the program we're a part of?

Grand strategies can help us answer these questions. Let's say I am enacting an outcomes assessment as part of a grand strategy of enhancing professional learning for the teachers in my program. The grand strategy gives me a way to mobilize what I've learned: now that we have the information, we can start to think about what our teachers know, what they need to know, and what support they need so we can revise the way we take on working with our students toward course outcomes.

You can see, in the examples above, how grand strategies pull together a number of what some people in your program might consider disconnected aspects of programmatic work. Grand strategies can give people in your program a sense that the program is *continuously becoming* something rather than just running on inertia. They can help people understand that particular initiatives and ideas are deliberate and targeted rather than simply reactions to outside events. This sense of movement is particularly crucial for programs that have a lot of teachers cycling through over time. Grand strategies provide a broader narrative to the work we're doing that these new teachers can pick up on and work within and that can give them a better sense of the bricolage (Reed 2020) they come to enact as they grow into their roles as teachers.

Defining Grand Strategies

I refer to a grand strategy as *grand* because of its scale: when we articulate grand strategies, we are going to be looking in the long term. So, you are going to want to think about not just a few years or even a decade but decades, plural. You want to imagine the kinds of worlds your program will both participate in building and then actively participate in, and you want to use grand strategies to guide that participation.

But both the world around you and your program can change in unexpected ways. Small innovations—such as in technology—can dramatically transform our options for teaching and learning (recent AI breakthroughs are a good example). There can also be large changes in public perception and education policy (see, for instance, Armstrong et al. 2020). You need to articulate strategies that can shape the ways you make sense of, respond to, and emerge from these unexpected transformations. For that reason, your grand strategies need to be tied to what you value in your program.

You now have criteria for deciding on effective grand strategies: they have to be long-term in nature, they have to be framed in ways that allow you to adjust for the unexpected, and they have to be tied to what you value. That is certainly a good start. But you have to also think about what a grand strategy *looks like*. You can use the criteria developed so far to create some problematic grand strategies. For instance, if I were to say that a grand strategy is to have 100 percent of our students pass English 101 over the next three decades, I would have a grand strategy that is long-term in its framing. It is tied to my valuing of student success. And it allows us to account for the unexpected; in the event of, say, a pandemic, we could adjust what counts as passing to help take into account the massive social and economic upheaval students are dealing with.

So, all of those criteria are met, but the grand strategy is still a deeply un-serious one. It has articulated "student success" as "passing the class," which is a thin description of student success, to say the least. It also pegs programmatic success to passing rates in the class—and, as we can see with the rampant problems in the No Child Left Behind Act, this decision leads to a flattening of learning in both the short and long run. When framing your grand strategies, then, you need not only your values but also your *expertise* as a WPA. You need to understand how organizations such as writing programs function, how particular choices about what to focus on shape student learning, and what that process looks like across a wide span of years. The hypothetical grand strategy I mention here fails to do that: by focusing on passing rates, I'm ignoring a great deal of what we know about how to support student success. This attention to our accumulated knowledge of our discipline can help you avoid grand strategies that lead in problematic directions.

You can support this criterion of expertise with another one, which will bring your vision of a grand strategy to a close: our grand strategies must create an umbrella for a wide variety of smaller, shorter strategies and tactics to fall under. This is also something the "100 percent pass rate" grand strategy fails to address. With a goal that focused, I can only create strategies and tactics that are tailored to that extremely focused target: study sessions, one-on-one support, and so on. Such outreach to students is helpful but again, in terms of the bigger picture, limited.

Let's compare this to one of my own grand strategies: collaborating with K–20 schools to support writing instruction and assessment across the state of Maine. This is something I want my program to be doing in a range of ways, from presenting at local teaching conferences to sitting on the boards of local English language arts– and K–12-focused organizations. It also shapes how I (and my program) interact with schools of education, both at UMaine and in other institutions of higher education across the state. This grand strategy offers a range of ways to move forward, programmatically: we can identify productive initiatives to jump into on campus, in the University of Maine System, and across Maine; we can start our own initiatives that recruit support from outside the program; and we can be receptive to changes in education at all levels and provide our support where and as needed. People in the program with interest and initiative can contribute to this grand strategy and can do so in a way that is less tightly constrained than "increasing passing rates."

These five criteria give us a good sense of what a grand strategy might look like. To sum up, a grand strategy must be

- Long-term in nature
- Framed to account for the unexpected
- Tied to our values
- Informed by WPA expertise
- A guide for smaller, shorter strategies and tactics.

Notice how these criteria come together in my "collaborating with K–20 schools to support writing instruction and assessment across the state of Maine" grand strategy to create what is, essentially, an unattainable (though still very useful) goal. At what point might I, as WPA, be able to say "okay, we've done all of the collaborating with K–20 schools. Mission accomplished"? Never. We are never going to be *finished* collaborating. The collaborating is always ongoing. And that is more than okay—it's ideal for thinking about the long term. We can start to articulate particular strategies and tactics that will let our program move forward coherently and bring about positive change.

Grand Strategies and Program Growth

The criteria for defining grand strategies are going to be helpful as you begin to articulate them in a couple of sections. Thinking about change, about program growth, on this scale is both necessary for the long-term planning of the program and difficult because of the wide variety of (often unseen) variables at work. Grand strategies help with this by mobilizing what your program currently is and what you and your program currently value for the future. And just as they provide a guide, an umbrella, for shorter-term decisions, they also help make clear—both to yourself and to the constituents in your program—that the innovation you engage in, the regular program revision you continually undertake, is purposeful, coordinated, and a good use of resources.

This kind of targeted, long-term planning with broader, value-informed strategies in mind is at odds with many of the kinds of things labeled as innovation that we see in action today in higher education. "Innovation" is often a result of opportunity: funding becomes available, a spot opens up in a particular administrative hierarchy, and the like. This opportunity, for good or for ill, often has an end point. The money might dry up, the administrator might move on, and so on. Grand strategies help you to both take advantage of opportunities *and* place what you get from those opportunities into a broader plan, one that can help the people involved in the program understand that programmatic change is *moving the program in a particular direction*. Such a broad understanding of the program can help interested parties see the value in innovation and not find themselves under the impression that the program is innovating for the sake of claiming innovation.

That said, however, grand strategies are only effective in this regard if they are anchored to the current work of the program, articulated in productive ways, and bought into by available (if ever-changing) interested parties both inside and outside the program. In the rest of this chapter, you will work up starting points for building grand strategies, articulate them with the above criteria in mind, and build a plan for recruiting interested parties to join in this long-term work.

Looking for Starting Points

If you now have a sense of what criteria are required for a grand strategy to be successful, you must also think about how to go about looking for grand strategies that you and your program would like to work with. So, where do you start? How can you go about finding the evidence you need to identify the grand strategies that can be used to direct this program into the future?

The short answer to these questions is "by looking at everything," which is, perhaps, not a helpful answer, short though it is. But thanks to the work of parts I and II, you've actually looked at a great deal already. This kind of deep and difficult investigation sets us up well to identify some useful starting points for the work of building up grand strategies. So, using the records, artifacts, facts, stories, principles, and other material that you've already collected, you can start to get a sense of what grand strategies might be (1) useful and (2) sensible to a wide audience of interested parties. You'll begin this work by looking for the low-hanging fruit: starting points for grand strategies that jump out at you from the information we have currently available.

You can find some low-hanging fruit by looking for repetition across the data you have. What seems to keep coming up as important for the people involved in the program? In particular, you want recurrences that are caught up in or resonant with the principles, principled practices, and strategies and tactics you've already articulated. You don't have to worry right now about articulating a grand strategy or anything else. You'll simply look through your data to see what keeps coming up.

For instance, when I was articulating a very early iteration of what became our program's grand strategies, I noticed a great deal of connection to the K–12 system. These connections were not coordinated in any way. Some of our adjunct instructors were also high school teachers; a fair number of our MA graduates over the years had gone on to teach high school in the state; some of our full-time, tenured faculty led workshops at area school districts; and one sat on the board of a local (and highly active) National Council of Teachers of English (NCTE) affiliate.

This recurrence seemed to suggest a bit of a current in the program that led toward K–12 teaching. With this as a starting point, then, I began to imagine how I might create structural pathways to help the people interested in that kind of work and, furthermore, guide people in K–12 systems to our program so they could see it as a resource. This was the seed of what became the K–20 grand strategy I articulated as an example earlier in the chapter.

In addition to looking at recurring phenomena, you might also look at recurring *need*. What, for instance, does your program seem to consistently need? This might be something the program is short of, but it might also be something that requires ongoing attention. At UMaine, one of our most frequent and ongoing challenges is professional learning for our English 101 instructors. Most of our graduate teaching assistants (GTAs) are gone in two years, and our turnover rate for adjunct faculty is also high (many of our GTAs stick around for a year or two after graduation before moving on). We might lose as many as half of our teachers in a single summer. So, keeping our attention on professional learning for our teachers is an ongoing concern: we are constantly trying to make sure we are offering them what they need (and what they need can vary). This constant attention served as a starting point for developing a grand strategy later on.

These two recurring issues—frequent interests of people in the program and ongoing needs of the program—offer some productive, low-hanging fruit to begin the work of articulating grand strategies. But you can take a deeper dive than this, and you can do so with the principled practices articulated in part I and the strategies and tactics developed in part II. Despite the readily available nature of the principles, strategies, and tactics, though, thinking through grand strategies in this manner is not as easy as looking for recurring phenomena. The principles, strategies, and tactics you've developed are abstracted from the data you analyzed throughout the first two parts of this book. And even though you took the time to confirm what you are finding with program constituents, you're doing yet another level of abstraction by trying to stitch together a broader arc from these findings. In short, it's harder than it looks.

Thankfully, developing grand strategies happens in a couple of different steps, so you've got space to work through the potential complications that arise from this approach. For now, you can start simply: look across your principles, strategies, and tactics for items that seem to relate to one another in some way. Perhaps you have a principle about promoting student-teacher

TABLE 7.1. A process for generating ideas for grand strategies

STARTING POINT 1: FREQUENT INTERESTS
What are the frequent interests of those in the program? How are these interests expressed and pursued? What facts, accounts, principles, and stories connect to those interests?
STARTING POINT 2: Recurring Needs
What recurring needs are there in the program? Who needs what, when, under what circumstances, from semester to semester? What facts, accounts, principles, and stories connect to these needs?

interactions, a strategy of articulating a theory of student-teacher interactions, and a particular tactic of a book group in a given semester. These all link up (as they should), but aside from student-teacher interactions, what else might you see when looking across these three items? Do you note, perhaps, how the knowledge of people in the program is prioritized? The theory mentioned in the long-term strategy is home-grown, one that is working from existing literature in the field through book groups. But the mediating influence is the people in the program. This isn't a recurrence as much as it is a point of convergence: the principle, the practice, and the tactic all work together to embrace local knowledge development. Such an aspect of the principles, strategies, and tactics might serve as a useful starting point for articulating grand strategies.

Once you have a range of starting points—both low-hanging fruit and the result of some abstract reasoning—you can begin to articulate grand strategies, which we discuss in the next section (table 7.1). A word of advice, though: you can easily end up, in this stage, with far more starting points than you probably want to work with in the next section. I suggest writing down all that you can see, for the moment.

Articulating Grand Strategies

Using the starting points as, well, starting points, you can begin to articulate some grand strategies. You already have a set of criteria to work through. A grand strategy should be

- Long-term in nature
- Framed to account for the unexpected
- Tied to our values

- Informed by WPA expertise
- A guide for smaller, shorter strategies and tactics.

You will want to return to these points after you've drafted your grand strategies, to make sure the grand strategies are going to work for you as you roll them out to your constituents (something covered in the next section). But this list doesn't tell you how to *write* the actual grand strategies. What should they look like? How long should they be? How much detail should they have?

Let's begin by trying to imagine a grand strategy that is announced as a single sentence. You might find yourself wanting to say more about your grand strategy than a single sentence, or you might find a short, persuasive phrase to stand in for it. And both of those are fine. But your grand strategies are going to go into reports to your chair and dean, be used in long-term planning documents, and be communicated to your colleagues in the program. A one-sentence announcement of a grand strategy fits most of those needs, and it is easy to add detail when needed and to shrink down the sentence into a phrase for those most closely involved in the day-to-day operation of the program.

For example, our program has been considering, from the ground up, what it means to be a program that makes policies with the needs of historically marginalized students at the center of attention. I could go into further detail on this, of course. I could discuss the particular marginalized communities on our campus that are most in need of our attention. And I could (and have) shorten(ed) what I mean here into two words, inspired by Cambridge and Stock's (2015) presence on my bookshelf: structural kindness. This short phrase, though perhaps unclear to those outside the program, has been tightly anchored to my emerging grand strategy of centering my program's policies on the needs of historically marginalized members of academia and has become a useful shorthand for bringing our attention back to it.

But the phrase "structural kindness" did not emerge first. It came only after we discussed why and how we could center our attention on historically marginalized communities. For developing grand strategies, the sentence is a useful focusing agent, one that leads to useful phrases but also that, in its production, creates the language that can later be used to articulate what is meant. We'll discuss how to articulate a grand strategy, then, in terms of a sentence.

I admit that I only have experience writing grand strategies for a single university (and a single, first-year composition program at that). So what I detail below might not be a perfect fit for your needs. You might find that the sentences you write, when compressed into this structure, leave out important parts of your intended grand strategies. If that's the case, revision might be in order, including revision that goes beyond what I have structured here. Listen to the feeling that something is missing, and revise accordingly. Remember the Lou Holtz reference from the introduction: if you have to, forget the game plan and do what you think is best.

Having said that, the grand strategies I have developed have several parts to them. First, they have an audience in mind. I don't mean the readers of the grand strategy (although you'll obviously want to account for those). Rather, I mean that the grand strategy aims to help a particular aspect of the program in its link to particular populations: other programs on campus, teachers in the program, students in the program, the field of writing studies, and others. A single grand strategy is focused on addressing a single (or small group of) audience(s).

Second, grand strategies do a particular thing for their targeted community. For instance, one of our grand strategies is to "raise awareness of UMaine in the writing studies community." Note that there's a particular audience (the field of writing studies, broadly construed) and a particular thing the grand strategy is doing (raising awareness). So, grand strategies do not simply aim for a targeted audience but aim to interact with that audience in particular ways.

Finally, grand strategies focus the contribution to an audience. Consider, for example, one of UMaine's principles referenced earlier, which aims to "collaborat[e] with K–20 schools to support writing instruction and assessment across the state of Maine." Note that there's an audience (K–20 schools) and a particular aim (collaborating), but there's also a *purpose* to that collaboration: writing instruction and assessment. This focus is broad enough to allow for the development of strategies and tactics in response to changing circumstances, but there's still a thread that leads the collaboration somewhere.

There are a number of ways to actually write a sentence that has these three parts—notice that I did not organize these parts along the lines of sentence structure or anything like that—but the goal, for you, is to look at your starting points and start to articulate sentences that encapsulate your program's long-term goals with an audience in mind, a particular contribution to that audience, and a specific purpose for that contribution. With these three points in mind, your next step is to start drafting some grand strategies. You can have as many or as few grand strategies as you need. Four has worked for me so far, although your circumstances and needs may be different. See four grand strategies as a point of information that you can work from.

TABLE 7.2. A process for articulating grand strategies

STEP 1: AUDIENCE: What particular segment of your community will be the focus of the strategy?
STEP 2: CONTRIBUTION: What will the strategy aim to provide for this community?
STEP 3: PURPOSE: Toward what end will this grand strategy will be working? Why will the contribution be meaningful?
STEP 4: DOUBLE-CHECK: Is the strategy long-term in nature?   Is the strategy framed to account for the unexpected?   Is the strategy tied to program values?   Is the strategy informed by WPA expertise?   Is the strategy a viable guide for smaller, shorter strategies and tactics?

After you have a few grand strategies that seem to work, run them through the five criteria developed above. Is the grand strategy long-term in nature, able to act as a focusing agent for decades of programmatic work to come? Is it framed to account for the unexpected, so you can use it to guide you through sudden and surprising shifts in the higher education landscape? Is it anchored to your values in some way? Does it link to WPA expertise, to what we know about writing and writing programs? Finally, does it offer a useful guide for the development of smaller, shorter strategies and tactics? (In particular—does it link to the strategies and tactics you've already developed?)

If you can get answers to these questions that you're happy with, then you have some grand strategies that may work for you. The question, of course, is whether they *will* work once they're out in the wild. You might find points of resistance, uncertainty, or confusion from some aspects of your program (or from interested parties outside your program). But these grand strategies need to have buy-in. To make sure they will work, that they have buy-in, you'll have to check in with those interested parties, getting feedback over a targeted period of time (table 7.2).

Recruiting Interested Parties

Articulating grand strategies can be useful for thinking through the use of program resources with interested parties (see Dippre 2023b for more information on how to do this with department chairs and other direct reports). But thinking through them presupposes that you have brought these interested parties onboard. Does your department chair like and agree with the time you've carved out for each of these strategies? Does your dean see these strategies as falling under your program's purview? Do the people *in* your program agree that the program should be spending time pursuing these strategies? These are all good questions (I wrote them myself). And they're ones we'll have to address as we go about getting feedback on and setting in motion these grand strategies.

Once you have the grand strategies ironed out (or at least a current draft of them), you can have a session with the teachers and administrators in your program to read, discuss, and provide feedback on them. You can also have an open window for feedback—so, send out the grand strategies on one day and have a session at a later date, with a closing date still later. This would work much like the principles (see chapter 3): the feedback you get from this session can inform the next stage of your revisions.

After you have received feedback from your team (and you may need more than one round of this), you can bring these grand strategies to your direct report and their direct report (often your department chair and your dean). Since these strategies will be guiding your attention and efforts in the coming years, these direct reports will want to have an idea of how your work fits in with the emerging initiatives and long-term planning of the department, the college, and the university. If all went well in the drafting stage of your work, your grand strategies should already account for the flow of life at your institution, including initiatives and long-term plans. Of course, there may be plans in the works that you don't know about, and your direct reports will give you that information if it's available.

There's a chance that a substantial revision of one or more grand strategies may be called for. Should that happen, you may have to conduct another feedback session with program constituents. This would add time to the rollout of the grand strategies, but it would also be exactly what the grand strategies are for: to make sure the long-term path the program is on is what all the interested parties want it to be.

With the above description in mind, then, you can set up a plan for how you might roll out your proposed grand strategies to your program's constituents. Who might want to see them first, and why? How much time might you give them to provide feedback and think through issues? How might you compose the document that has these grand strategies so your program's constituents can see the connections between the grand strategies and the strategies and tactics you've already set in motion (table 7.3)?

TABLE 7.3. A progression for recruiting interested parties

STAGE 1: Program constituents (teachers, administrators, students who were not involved in the drafting)
STAGE 2: Interested parties in connected communities (professional learning communities, connected community members linked to the grand strategies)
STAGE 3: Direct reports (e.g., department chair, dean)

Conclusion

Trying to articulate a path of growth for your program that will stretch across several decades is, to put it mildly, not easy. At this point, you've no doubt realized that. But it might help you to keep in mind that these grand strategies—like our principles, like our principled practices—are always subject to revision. The grand strategies you articulate now will be a useful starting point and will guide the innovation and program growth you undertake into the near future, particularly through the strategies and tactics you've articulated in part II. But in ten years, you (or your successor) might find that the language of your grand strategies needs an update. This is fine—it's always possible to revise your grand strategies, for your program to adapt to changing needs in effective ways. Articulating a long-term plan for your program is a reach, but it's *supposed* to be a reach; it's supposed to require painstaking care. And, obviously, there are supposed to be opportunities for course correction. So there's no reason not to be bold.

By the time you've finished the work of this chapter, you will have developed—from the facts, stories, principles, and principled practices of part I and the strategies and tactics of part II—a set of grand strategies your program can aim at as it moves into the future. But now that you know where you're going, how might you get there? What might you do to be sure the future changes you make to the program are moving forward those grand strategies you set up in this chapter and had confirmed by interested parties? You can answer this question in two stages, which we'll do in chapters 8 and 9. In chapter 8, you'll think about how to move toward your grand strategies in purposeful, structured innovations. In chapter 9, you'll build on successful innovations to create sustainable program revisions over time.

Resources

Below are resources to help you think through the grand strategies you're building from your principles, principled practices, stories, strategies, and tactics. "Building a WPA Life" has resources for thinking about these long-term plans with your own life (and the span of your career) in mind. "Context for Programmatic Work" offers insights about larger patterns of writing programs and writing program activity. Finally, "Thinking through Big Goals" offers resources for thinking through big goals in a variety of different writing program contexts.

BUILDING A WPA LIFE

Carter, Genesea M. 2023. "Is Resistance Futile? Struggling against Systemic Assimilation of Administrative Work." In *Systems Shift: Creating and Navigating Change in Rhetoric and Composition Administration*, edited by Genesea M. Carter and Aurora Matzke, 271–291. Fort Collins and Boulder: WAC Clearinghouse and University Press of Colorado.

Carter, Genesea M., and Aurora Matzke. 2023. "Conclusion: A Toolkit." In *Systems Shift: Creating and Navigating Change in Rhetoric and Composition Administration*, edited by Genesea M. Carter and Aurora Matzke, 345–355. Fort Collins and Boulder: WAC Clearinghouse and University Press of Colorado.

Cicchino, Amy, Sarah Elizabeth Snyder, and Natalie Szymanski. 2023. "We've Been Burned Out and Exhausted: GenAdmin WPA Labor Issues Exacerbated by the COVID-19 Pandemic." *WPA: Writing Program Administration* 47 (1): 102–116.

Costello, Kristi Murray. 2023. "The Quiet Revolution: How Newer WPAs Are Shifting the Profession." *WPA: Writing Program Administration* 47 (1): 133–147.

Costello, Kristi Murray, and Kate Navickas. 2023. "Naming What We Feel: Self-Dialogue as a Strategy for Negotiating Emotional Labor in WPA Work." In *Making Administrative Work Visible: Data-Driven Advocacy for Understanding the Labor of Writing Program Administration*, edited by Leigh Graziano, Kay Halasek, Remi Hudgins, Susan Miller-Cochran, Frank Napolitano, and Natalie Szymanski, 91–105. Logan: Utah State University Press.

Miller-Cochran, Susan. 2018. "Innovation through Intentional Administration: Or, How to Lead a Writing Program without Losing Your Soul." *WPA: Writing Program Administration* 42 (1): 107–122.

Moore, Cindy. 2018. "Mentoring WPAs for the Long Term: The Promise of Mindfulness." *WPA: Writing Program Administration* 42 (1): 89–106.

Pinkert, Laurie A., and Lauren M. Bowen. 2021. "Disciplinary Lifecycling: A Generative Framework for Career Trajectories in Rhetoric, Composition, and Writing Studies." *Composition Studies* 49 (1): 34–52.

Street, Nathaniel. 2020. "Affirming Difference: Inhabiting the WPA Otherwise." *Composition Studies* 48 (1): 53–70.

Vidali, Amy. 2015. "Disabling Writing Program Administration." *WPA: Writing Program Administration* 38 (2): 32–55.

Wenger, Christy I. 2023. "Approaching WPA Labor with *Ahimsa*: Mapping Emotional Geographies through Sustainable Leadership." In *Toward More Sustainable Metaphors* of *Writing Program Administration*, edited by Lydia Wilkes, Lilian Mina, and Patti Poblete, 123–144. Logan: Utah State University Press.

CONTEXT FOR PROGRAMMATIC WORK

Isaacs, Emily. 2018. *Writing at the State U: Instruction and Administration at 106 Comprehensive Universities*. Logan: Utah State University Press.

LaFrance, Michelle. 2016. "An Institutional Ethnography of Information Literacy Instruction: Key Terms, Local/Material Contexts, and Instructional Practice." *WPA: Writing Program Administration* 39 (2): 105–123.

National Census of Writing. 2017. University of San Diego. https://writingcensus.ucsd.edu/.

Thaiss, Chris, Gerd Brauer, Paula Carlino, Lisa Ganobcsik-Williams, and Aparna Sinha. 2012. *Writing Programs Worldwide: Profiles of Academic Writing in Many Places*. Fort Collins and Boulder: WAC Clearinghouse and University Press of Colorado.

THINKING THROUGH BIG GOALS

Clinnin, Kaitlin. 2023. "Practicing Equitable and Sustainable Trauma-Informed Writing Program Administration through Disability Justice." *WPA: Writing Program Administration* 47 (1): 117–132.

Dew, Debra Frank. 2004. "Conclusion: Ethical Options for Disciplinary Progress on the Issue of jWPA Appointments." In *Untenured Faculty as Writing Program Administrators: Institutional Practices and Politics*, edited by Debra Frank Dew and Alice Horning, 279–292. West Lafayette, IN: Parlor Press.

Fremo, Rebecca Taylor. 2007. "Redefining Our Rhetorical Situations: jWPAs in the Small College Contexts." In *Untenured Faculty as Writing Program Administrators: Institutional Practices and Politics*, edited by Debra Frank Dew and Alice Horning, 191–218. West Lafayette, IN: Parlor Press.

Morgan, Meg, Marsha Lee Baker, Wendy Sharer, and Tracy Ann Morse. 2020. "The Affiliate as Mentoring Network: The Lasting Work of the Carolinas WPA." *WPA: Writing Program Administration* 44 (1): 68–85.

Patton, Martha D., and Jo Ann Vogt. 2007. "The Center Will Not Hold: Redefining Professionalism in the Academy." In *Untenured Faculty as Writing Program Administrators: Institutional Practices and Politics*, edited by Debra Frank Dew and Alice Horning, 137–152. West Lafayette, IN: Parlor Press.

Perryman-Clark, Staci, and Collin Lamont Craig. 2023. "Introduction: Black Matters: Writing Program Administration in Twenty-First–Century Higher Education." In *Black Perspectives in Writing Program Administration*, edited by Staci Perryman-Clark and Collin Lamont Craig, 1–27. Urbana, IL: National Council of Teachers of English Books.

Yergeau, Melanie. 2016. "Saturday Plenary Address: Creating a Culture of Access in Writing Program Administration." *WPA: Writing Program Administration* 40 (1): 155–165.

8
Purposeful Innovation

In chapter 7, you spent time developing some grand strategies for the program. These strategies are aimed at growing the program in targeted and purposeful ways. In this chapter, you'll dive into the weeds of how you might bring those strategies to life through *purposeful innovation*. By purposeful innovation, I mean targeted transformations of the program that are studied, articulated, piloted, and (if all goes well) implemented. This kind of innovation is not the result of sudden changes to the broader institution or complex shifts in our social landscape; with purposeful innovation, you are thinking along the lines of your grand strategies, identifying an aspect of the program that you can change, and going about the work of testing and implementing said change.

The key word, at least to me, in this chapter's title is *purposeful*. I have spent much of my professional life rolling my eyes when I ran across innovations that seemed to happen for the sake of innovating. To be sure, programs *must* change over time. After all, society, people, technology, our larger institutions, and higher education generally speaking are always changing. If our programs are to remain responsive to the needs of our students, they must be attentive to those changes and willing to change themselves when necessary. But this is a far cry from changing for the sake of change, and this chapter focuses on the former rather than the latter.

When I talk about targeted innovation in this chapter, I am envisioning planned-in-advance activities that we aim to articulate, structure, pilot, reexamine, and (possibly) expand. But you can pilot just about anything, can't you? If I wanted to tweak a particular late policy with an elaborate pilot, I probably could. It might be a massive waste of time, but it could be done. I might also want to try new things in, say, my teaching practicum, such as situated performances (Finders and Rose 1998), but that wouldn't necessarily need a pilot. And that's the catch to piloting new ideas, to targeting innovation: you need to identify what you want to pilot, why you want to pilot it, and how such piloting is in line with your overall grand strategies. You need to aim, in other words, using the grand strategies themselves.

Identifying Potential Innovations

For me, innovation worth taking up is a convergence of several different forces. First and most obvious, the innovation needs to be aligned to the grand strategies that have been established. If the innovation is not going to forward grand strategies, if it isn't going to change the program for the better, why take on the work? Innovations, even small pilots of new approaches, are time-consuming. A potential innovation, then, should be in line with a grand strategy.

Furthermore, a potential innovation should also have the potential to solve problems, stumbling blocks to the program's pursuit of grand strategies. To be sure, we pilot something *because* we aren't sure it will work, so such innovations should not need to be a lock for improving the program. But by drawing on what we know of the program, of the recent and enduring knowledge of our field, and of our institution and local community, we should be able to identify a pilot that is reasonably worth pursuing.

Finally and most crucial, a potential innovation should not conflict with the program's principles or principled practices. When you plan out innovations, you need to be thinking through the values you have while looking toward your grand strategies. You may find that, unexpectedly, a potential innovation *does* clash with your principles, principled practice, or both—again, this is why you pilot—but, overall, you should go into any planned innovation with confidence that what you are trying is in line with your program's principles and principled practices.

So, what does it look like when our potential innovations solve problems, work to forward our grand strategies, and are organized according to our principles and principled practices? An ongoing example we are currently working with at UMaine might provide useful insights. Over the past several years, I've been working toward developing a UMaine-focused textbook about writing. This is hardly a unique innovation—many campuses use homegrown textbooks of some kind. But we have always used textbooks that were produced elsewhere—*Writing about Writing* (Downs and Wardle 2022) for instance, or the classroom edition of *Naming What We Know* (Adler-Kassner and Wardle 2016). So, developing a UMaine-focused text would be a new breakthrough at UMaine.

The textbook (in its current iteration) is web-based, so students can access it with the necessary login information. The textbook is also low-cost and thus does not impose a financial burden on students.[1] Finally, the textbook provides connections students can make between the world of UMaine and the demands made of them in English 101. Focusing on a homegrown textbook allows for those kinds of connections.

This textbook, as currently framed, solves several problems that stand in the way of two different grand strategies: supporting the professional learning of our teachers and growing connections with other programs on campus. Three problems stand in the way of pursuing these grand strategies effectively. First, UMaine recently received Carnegie R1 status. This means a shift to more research, particularly undergraduate research. So, students entering their programs will find themselves doing more hands-on work at the edge of their fields than they may have in years past.

This shift to R1 status creates a second problem, particularly for the College Composition program: we have few opportunities for our graduate teaching assistants (GTAs) to publish in writing studies in the time they are with us. Although this can and does happen, two years is often too short a time to get a publication out. But publications are important, particularly to a research university. The textbook solves that problem: our GTAs (and undergraduates, for that matter) can work their way to publishing a chapter or an inter-chapter that will be taken up by students in English 101. They will have real, live audiences to attend to their real, live publications.

Finally, the College Composition program has been and continues to be short on funds. This problem is not connected, really, to the more urgent matter of moving to R1 status but is instead an enduring issue for the program. Money tends to attract money, at least in higher education: if I have a small pot of money, I can, say, partner with another department on campus (that

---

1. I am interested in developing an entirely open-access resource for our students, but, as will soon be seen, the cost is currently solving one of our problems.

also has a small pot of money) to make some sort of workshop or other event happen. But if I have to go through departmental or college-level requests for funds, there is never a guarantee that I will get the money; even if I *do* get it, there's the chance that the moment for a particular collaboration with another unit on campus will pass by the time the funds become available. Having some money readily available for professional learning, for student celebrations of writing, and for other kinds of work with other units on campus and within our own program would create more opportunities for our students and teachers.

So, we have one innovation—a campus textbook—that is solving three problems (R1 status, graduate/undergraduate publications in writing studies, financial resources) to allow us to forward two grand strategies. This textbook also doesn't clash with our principled practices: in fact, it allows us to better respect student writing, not just what students do in a semester but what they produce for a longer-term publication. On the surface, according to the criteria I set out at the start of this section, the textbook sounds like a clear winner.

Now, *is* it a winner? Will it lead to productive growth of the program? Will our program, in the end, be better off for having it? I actually don't know; that's why we go about piloting these things. There may be issues we can't see until we try it out (e.g., Dean 2014), or perhaps there is a larger context at work that we need to figure out how to attend to first (e.g., Estrem et al. 2014). By having targeted rollouts of potential innovations, we can see what is working and what is not, what issues do and do not exist, and go from there. The next section discusses how to plan such an innovation—how to make sure it's a good use of the available time and resources regardless of whether it ends up a winner, and how to create the space you need to examine and interrogate what is and is not happening.

Planning Innovation

Planning innovation, as indicated above, is a matter of scheduling time and attention to issues worth innovating on in targeted ways. Again, not every change to your program is an innovation worth considerable time and attention. Furthermore, not every targeted innovation needs a complex pilot.

Consider, for example, my decision to move away from an attendance policy in the program. The early days of the pandemic eventually forced my hand on this—obviously, we couldn't have policies that would get people killed because they went to class—but my suspicions about our attendance policy reach back to 2018. I started to wonder what such a policy was actually doing for our students and teachers, but I did not have a good sense about how I might plan a pilot for going about doing that sort of thing—and even if I did, we were short on resources at the moment. In the end, I decided to delete the attendance policy from my syllabi in spring 2019 and see what happened.

This was not much of an innovation, really: I just deleted part of my syllabus and kept track of attendance, trying to get a sense of how attendance changed from the ways it typically flowed in a given semester. The result? Not much changed. Absences increased in the final weeks of the semester—normally, by that point, students had used up their available absences and so were more or less forced to attend class if they wanted to pass. But that was about it. Otherwise, the general flow of attendance throughout the semester changed little. And some students who may have been ineligible to submit a portfolio at semester's end because of absences were able to submit one, and they did, in fact, pass review.

This is a good example of a straightforward, low-cost approach to innovation: change one thing, see what happens, and keep track of the changes. It did not require additional funds, and it did not require a lot of setup on my part. I just did it and took note of the changes in student attendance. The information I got from this change was a solid return on the limited time and attention I gave it.

Other innovations might require more time and attention, smaller steps, and a bit more buy-in from various program constituents. These innovations involve more than just changing one thing. You might have to change several things—on occasion all at once—to make a particular kind of innovation happen. When you do so, you risk some destabilization. Planning for this destabilization ahead of time can be a useful way to make sure you're ready—and not demoralized—when it happens.

A good example of how *not* to do this is my decision to emphasize knowledge making in our program. This is an issue particularly close to my heart; as you've no doubt noted in the first two sections of this book, I think a great deal of knowledge about students is acquired in a writing program, and calling attention to (and working with) that knowledge is crucial for a writing program that is trying to tell new stories about writers and writing. But my initial attempt at knowledge making fell short. One of the reasons was that as a new writing program administrator (WPA), I did not recruit enthusiasm for the work—or, at the very least, not as much as I thought I did. When I first proposed having "knowledge making" be at the center of what we emphasize and do as a program, I was met with positive responses. But those positive responses were "hey, that sounds cool," not "hey, how can I get involved," and there is an important difference between the two.

A crucial step, then, in planning innovation is to persuade your program that it's an innovation worth trying. This can be done by tying the innovation to the problem it's trying to solve (as you saw above in "Identifying Potential Innovations"). At a strategically wise moment in time (say, a program-wide meeting), you can identify the problem, make the case that this particular innovation may help the program address that problem, and make the case that this innovation needs to be tried *now*, for whatever reason (e.g., urgency, temporarily available funding). You can invite participation in this innovation by identifying the particular tasks you are assigning to those who join, their compensation, and the length of the project.

Let's say, for instance, that you're looking to see what happens if you remove your attendance policy. This may be an issue of some urgency because the pandemic has made class attendance problematic to begin with, and you'd like to get a sense of how having no attendance policy may help or hinder the program. You might need several teachers who, for a small stipend, are willing to (1) meet several times throughout the semester, (2) keep track of attendance patterns, (3) keep records of conversations and discussions with students about attendance in class, and (4) earn a few hundred dollars for the extra meetings and work. This can all be presented at a mid-semester faculty meeting to give people time to consider joining and make revisions to their syllabi for the following semester.

In addition to rolling out a persuasive call to join an innovation, you'll also need a sense of what you'll do with the data you get from the innovation: what criteria you're focusing on, how you're analyzing the data, what conclusions you draw, and the impact the conclusions might have on the program. It is important that you retain the capacity to be surprised by your data. You shouldn't go in with particular assumptions that you want confirmed (although prior writing research can give you a sense of what might happen). But that's not the same as having no plan for collecting and analyzing data as they come in. How might you, say, code your interviews? How might you quantitatively analyze the patterns you're seeing in enrollment numbers? You need the right tool for the analytic job, of course, but having a sense of what you intend to do will shape the innovation you roll out.

Furthermore, you will need to have a sense of how your program will be shaped by what you find. To build on the example above: if you find that attendance is not negatively impacted by the lack of a policy, what do you do? As I've mentioned throughout the book, I prefer a collaborative approach to making decisions whenever possible, so the answer to this question might be "we'll discuss it as a group in a meeting the following semester." But what meeting? When will it happen? How might you be able to help your colleagues make sense of the flow of events from this pilot? In the next section, we walk through how we might create the conditions to discuss and consider the results.

Discussing and Considering Results

Once you've finished piloting, you will have to organize and articulate the results. But how do you do this? How might you go about framing what you've found in a way that can inform teaching and learning? There are several ways a pilot can go about influencing a program. Two are fairly straightforward: either the pilot goes well and it's a straight-to-series-order kind of thing, or the pilot goes badly and nearly the entire plan is trashed. But these are rather low-probability events: very often, pilots fall into a kind of middle area, where the results are in need of discussion, retooling, and sometimes expanded piloting.

A good example of this is UMaine's decision to switch from *Writing about Writing* (Downs and Wardle 2022) as its major textbook to *Naming What We Know*, classroom edition (Adler-Kassner and Wardle 2016). This switch happened over the course of about three years. The work began with some teachers who were interested in using threshold concepts from *Naming What We Know* in their English 101 courses: Mitchell Herring, Kelly Hartwell, Claire Jackson, Peter Lowe, and Samantha O'Shea. This small group of teachers tested out the idea over the course of about a year. Associate Director of Assessment and Program Research Dylan Dryer looked at the portfolio assessment results of these sections and noted a moderate improvement in results between the scores in the *Naming What We Know* section over the *Writing about Writing* sections.

Despite this improvement, we were slow to adopt the text. There were a number of reasons for this. First, although there was a positive, moderate improvement in outcomes, this may have occurred for a range of reasons. The teachers of those sections were highly capable, deeply interested in English 101 curriculum and pedagogy, and motivated by their curricular innovation. These facts alone might have boosted the assessment results in those sections.

Second, we weren't sure what the impact would be of losing *Writing about Writing* as a text for teachers, particularly struggling teachers. Sure, we could still use longer texts from the school library, but as one of our teachers, Katelyn Connolly, pointed out at an end-of-year meeting, one of the reasons we used *Writing about Writing* was the extensive framing Doug Downs and Elizabeth Wardle (2022) provide for the use of materials. This is often helpful for both students and teachers, and we were not sure what the impact would be if we lost that.

These causes for concern led us to expand the pilot in a highly targeted way. The pilot happened in the 2016–2017 academic year. In 2017–2018, we took on four new adjunct instructors who would teach about 20 percent of our English 101 courses that year. We provided them with a course curriculum that used *Naming What We Know*, classroom edition, and we took a look at how that went. Once again, students did well in the end-of-term assessment. At this point, we were confident that using *Naming What We Know* would provide students with a text at a lower cost that would lead to at least equal outcomes as those of our previous textbook. We decided to roll it out to the first-year GTAs in the 2018–2019 academic year. This larger rollout also went smoothly; a year later, nearly all of our teachers were using *Naming What We Know* in their courses.

So, we can see from this example how it is possible to get some results, consider what those results might mean, and take steps to move further ahead with more piloting. The slow ramp-up from our most capable teachers to our newest teachers over the course of three years illustrates how you can keep forward movement going on a project but also, and at the same time, create opportunities for dialogue and revision. Eventually, the small steps we took led to a course text that is considerably less expensive than *Writing about Writing* and that gives about the same results in terms of our portfolio assessment. We have saved students money without compromising our course outcomes.

In considering and discussing results, we can think about the kinds of information people in our program need to have. In the piloting of *Naming What We Know*, we made time at our end-of-year meeting to discuss the pilot and its impact on learning and outcomes in our courses. This invited the entire program to the table for the discussion, which was important, as eventually such a text could be sitting at the core of the program. But there were other discussions that did not require everyone's attention: what threshold concepts seemed to work, what order of concepts seemed to work best, how to pair threshold concepts with more complex texts, and similar issues. These kinds of details were important for people doing the work of the piloting but not so much for those who were still using *Writing about Writing*. Giving space for both program-wide and innovation-specific conversations helped the pilot move along.

So, how might you go about discussing and considering the results of a pilot? How might you bring in the constituents in the pilot (that is, the teachers and perhaps students involved), the constituents in the program, and the interested parties outside the program to consider next steps?

You can begin this work by thinking about a rollout of the results. How can you present your results to the group? When? Through what means? Do you need a presentation, or would a short report work just as well? Or perhaps you need both: a short report to help people prepare for a meeting, followed by a presentation and a discussion? It's essentially up to you how this information might best be reported out, but the goal is the same for all of us: to help create a productive discussion about what was found in the pilot.

Once people have the data, they'll need some time to work through them together. Perhaps this happens over a few faculty meetings or maybe in small groups throughout the semester. Or maybe it can happen asynchronously, over email or in a Google Doc. Whatever the approach, what matters is that the program constituents can mull over the idea together: to think about how these data shape their sense of the program and what it's doing and what the data might mean to their own work as teachers.

A helpful way to "wrap up" a period of discussing and considering results is to create a venue for submitting final comments on the discussion, through a survey or a Google Form. This can help you identify the common themes running through the thinking of people in the program and can help you start to do the difficult work of deciding whether another (revised) pilot is necessary or if your program is ready to scale the innovation in some way.

Scaling Innovation

John Hattie's *Visible Learning* (2009) provides an extensive meta-synthesis of ongoing meta-analyses in K–12 education and discusses the cost of an innovation (or intervention) in an effective and usable way and in a way that is particularly useful for us in this chapter. He uses the concept of *effect size* as a way to measure the impact of a particular intervention on student learning. The larger an effect size, the larger the size of the effect an intervention has on student learning. An effect size of, say, 0.06 might not impact learning that much, but an effect size of 0.8 would have a considerable (and rather obvious) impact on student learning.

Hattie's book is full of effect sizes and considerations of what they tell us, but he makes a particularly compelling argument about how to frame effect sizes within a broader context of education. Just because an effect size is small, he argues, does not mean that pursuing the particular intervention is not worth it. To know whether an intervention is worthwhile, we have to consider not just the effect of the intervention but also the cost of its implementation. An effect size of, say, 0.06 might be negligible in a lot of ways, but it also might be incredibly cheap and easy to implement and therefore may be worth the trouble. Likewise, an intervention with a large effect size might cost too much to implement, and just the gain in learning would not be the return on investment interested parties might want.

This idea of the cost of implementation applies to my early pilot of a new attendance policy I mentioned above: it was something that gave us useful information without much trouble and that we were able to work with rather effectively (and quickly). It was a low-cost approach to pilot, and it remained a low-cost approach to implement. We did not need professional learning events or any particular kind of training at all, really. Teachers needed the information on what changes might emerge as a result of the new approach, and we were all set. New teachers did not need anything: they hadn't taught in our program before, so having no attendance policy was, for them, not very different from having one. It was just one more element in the newness their roles as teaching assistants entailed.

But it's possible to imagine a different kind of innovation, one that might take more effort and energy to get off the ground. Let's say, for instance, that you were to run with the Institute of Race, Rhetoric, and Literacy's (IRRL) goals for first-year composition in your program. The IRRL's goals might be a challenge to implement (in a good way) in your program, given your program's (or your larger institution's) history and practices. Let's say you followed the steps from earlier in this chapter and, in doing so, managed to develop and pilot a curriculum that works through the IRRL's goals. This is a difficult (and, in this hypothetical, compensated) task to undertake, one that requires some risk on behalf of the teachers doing the work.

How do you expand this task, then? Do you, as WPA, announce a new curricular change? Do you mandate its use in particular parts of the program? To go back to our discussion in chapter 6, this might be something that needs doing if it reduces harm. Again, though, it's difficult to mandate a change in curriculum or pedagogy that *actually* reduces harm, if only because a teacher resistant to change might do worse work with an unfamiliar curriculum or pedagogical approach than if they had carried on with their original approach. You might, then, think about how such an approach might be scaled over time, with interested teachers developing experience, resources, and results to share with more reluctant teachers. The program can grow its new stories about curriculum and pedagogy until its strength wins over those less inclined to jump in during the early days of the innovation. This is something that can come about as you generate discussions about the pilot, as you collect final thoughts from your colleagues during the discussion period, and as you start to plan out subsequent semesters of teaching.

Recruiting Interested Parties

I'll begin this section with a caveat: not all interested parties need to be involved (or even onboard with) any particular innovation. By its nature, a pilot is just something you're trying out in a targeted way. Pilots often lack the room for all constituents to get involved, so leaving some out (or letting some leave themselves out) is not much of an issue. Consider, for instance, a bit of a renovation I did with what we called "extended mentoring" for our first-year GTAs. All first-year GTAs are assigned a mentor, an experienced teacher who can help them think through issues like responding to student writing and planning class meetings during their first year. By the end of first semester, though, we've usually identified a handful of GTAs who are struggling with particular aspects of their teaching. In the past, we had identified a very few (usually two or three) and provided "extended mentoring" to them, which included extra one-on-one mentoring with another mentor in the program.

This process pre-dated my arrival at UMaine, but it was supported by the rest of the WPA team and the department chair. Any opportunity to mentor new teachers is a good one, so I stuck with it. But eventually, I got the sense that this idea of "extended mentoring" was problematic. First, it gave the GTAs who were selected the sense that they had failed in some way, which wasn't true. Having something you need to work on is just a fact of life as a teacher, but these teachers felt they had done something wrong to be assigned extended mentoring. Second, it gave GTAs who were not selected the idea that they *didn't* have anything to work on. But, as I said, we all have something to work on. So eventually, I decided to expand the "extended mentoring" to *all* new GTAs in their second semester. At the end of the term, we identified an aspect of teaching that each new GTA could work on, paired them with a mentor, and set them to work on a schedule that worked for them (and the mentor, of course).

This wasn't much of an innovation. Mentoring was still happening; I was just extending the extended aspect. The WPA team didn't need to be convinced; they served as mentors, but they would have done that anyway. So, the only thing that was strange was that *all* of the new GTAs were being mentored.

I happened to try this in spring 2020, so it worked out quite well; each teacher needed all the support they could get just to make it through the term and the start of the pandemic, so the extra support was a win. But this is an example of an innovation that not everyone had to be onboard with: it was a straightforward shift that had a big return on time and attention when it finally rolled out (not that I had planned for the pandemic). We still engage in what I've named our "individual professional learning" this way, and it seems to have improved GTA morale and led to productive discussions about teaching—although I still take heat for the terrible new name.

Bringing in interested parties for particular innovations, then, is a tactical choice. If you have someone who is dead set against a particular curricular change, you might want to leave them out of the pilot until you can demonstrate that such a change can be successful. Contrariwise, you might want to bring them in early to allow their concerns to be assuaged through the piloting process. The particular choice is up to you, but keep in mind that involving particular parties *is a choice*, and how you go about it can inform the success or failure of both the pilot and the pilot's uptake over time.

Conclusion

Targeted innovation—particularly the kinds of targeted innovation discussed throughout this chapter—is a great way to test out particular ways to successfully grow your program. You can learn a great deal about your program without having to go through the trouble of making substantial, program-wide changes that may or may not have a positive effect on student outcomes. The grand strategies developed in chapter 7 provide useful guideposts to make sure the pilots and targeted innovations are not haphazard or sporadic in nature. Yet even with the grand strategies, the pilots and other innovations bring a bit of risk, since there's no guarantee that a successful pilot can or will be expanded into the program. If you want to make program innovation stick, that innovation must be sustainable in nature. In chapter 9, we discuss how we can leverage successful innovation to build sustainable structures and practices in your program.

Resources

Below are resources that may guide your work in innovating through pilot studies. "Program Pilot Resources" offers insights for developing within-program pilots. The section "Outward-Facing Pilot Resources" offers useful tips for looking beyond the program and to pilots that happen with units outside the program.

PROGRAM PILOT RESOURCES

Burrows, Cedric D. 2016. "The Yardstick of Whiteness in Composition Textbooks." *WPA: Writing Program Administration* 39 (2): 42–46.

Chemishanova, Polina, and Robin Snead. 2017. "Reconfiguring the Writing Studio Model: Examining the Impact of the *PlusOne* Program on Student Performance and Retention." In *Retention, Persistence, and Writing Programs*, edited by Todd Ruecker, Dawn Shepherd, Heidi Estrem, and Beth Brunk-Chavez, 167–184. Logan: Utah State University Press.

Cicchino, Amy. 2020. "A Broader View: How Doctoral Programs in Rhetoric and Composition Prepare Their Graduate Students to Teach Composition." *WPA: Writing Program Administration* 44 (1): 86–106.

Cox, Anicca. 2023. "(Re)viewing Faculty Observation and Evaluation Beyond the 'Means Well' Paradigm." In *Institutional Ethnography as Writing Studies Practice*, edited by Michelle LaFrance and Melissa Nicolas, 35–46. Fort Collins and Boulder: WAC Clearinghouse and University Press of Colorado.

Fedukovich, Casie, and Tracy Ann Morse. 2017. "Failures to Accommodate: GTA Preparation as a Site for a Transformative Culture of Access." *WPA: Writing Program Administration* 40 (3): 39–60.

Harris, Sarah E. 2017. "The *Kairotic* Classroom: Retention Discourse and Supplemental Instruction in the First Year." In *Retention, Persistence, and Writing Programs*, edited by Todd Ruecker, Dawn Shepherd, Heidi Estrem, and Beth Brunk-Chavez, 204–218. Logan: Utah State University Press.

Hitt, Allison Harper. 2023. *Rhetorics of Overcoming*. Logan: Utah State University Press.

Messuri, Kristin, and Elizabeth A. Sharp. 2021. "Dedicating Time and Space for Women to Succeed in the Academy: A Case Analysis of a Women Faculty Writing Program at a Research 1 Institution." *WPA: Writing Program Administration* 45 (1): 50–70.

Moxley, Joseph M., and David Eubanks. 2016. "On Keeping Score: Instructors' vs. Students' Rubric Ratings of 46,689 Essays." *WPA: Writing Program Administration* 39 (2): 53–80.

Ray, Brian, Jacob Babb, and Courtney Adams Wooten. 2018. "Rethinking SETs: Retuning Student Evaluations of Teaching for Student Agency." *Composition Studies* 46 (1): 34–56.

Santana, Christina, Shirley K. Rose, and Robert LaBarge. 2018. "A Hybrid Mega-Course with Optional Studio: Responding Responsibly to an Administrative Mandate." In *The Writing Studio Sampler: Stories about Change*, edited by Mark Sutton and Sally Chandler, 97–114. Fort Collins and Boulder: WAC Clearinghouse and University Press of Colorado.

Snyder, Sarah Elizabeth. 2017. "Retention Rates of Second Language Writers and Basic Writers: A Comparison within the Stretch Program Model." In *Retention, Persistence, and Writing Programs*, edited by Todd Ruecker, Dawn Shepherd, Heidi Estrem, and Beth Brunk-Chavez, 185–203. Logan: Utah State University Press.

Wolfe, Joanna, Ryan Roderick, and Andrea Francioni Rooney. 2019. "Improving Instructor Ethos through Document Design." *Composition Studies* 47 (2): 146–166.

OUTWARD-FACING PILOT RESOURCES

Burdick, Melanie, and Jane Greer. 2017. "Paths to Productive Partnerships: Surveying High School Teachers about Professional Development Opportunities and 'College-Level' Writing." *WPA: Writing Program Administration* 41 (1): 82–101.

Holmes, Ashley J., and Christine Busser. 2017. "Beyond Coordination: Building Collaborative Partnerships to Support Institutional-Level Retention Initiatives in Writing Programs." In *Retention, Persistence, and Writing Programs*, edited by Todd Ruecker, Dawn Shepherd, Heidi Estrem, and Beth Brunk-Chavez, 38–55. Logan: Utah State University Press.

Teagarden, Alexis, and Michael Carlozzi. 2017. "Time Enough? Experimental Findings on Embedded Librarianship." *WPA: Writing Program Administration* 41 (1): 12–32.

Tremain, Lisa. 2023. "Heavy Lifting: How WPAs Broker Knowledge Transfer for Faculty." In *Making Administrative Work Visible: Data-Driven Advocacy for Understanding the Labor of Writing Program Administration*, edited by Leigh Graziano, Kay Halasek, Remi Hudgins, Susan Miller-Cochran, Frank Napolitano, and Natalie Szymanski, 240–252. Logan: Utah State University Press.

9
Building Sustainable Structures and Practices

Chapter 8 traced how you can engage in the work of targeted innovation over time and in line with your grand strategies. But now that you have a plan for taking on change to the program, you need to make sure you render those changes *sustainable*. I refer to sustainable *structures* and *practices* in this chapter, which work together to help you continue to grow your program over time. I mentioned at the start of this text that I am interested in helping people create programs that gain their own momentum, that grow beyond a single person and a single career. In this chapter, I get into the nuts and bolts of how you might go about making the change you bring to your program sustainable over the long term.

As always, you'll be working through these sustainable structures and practices toward your grand strategies. In fact, the structures and practices you develop are ways of solidifying the gains in your grand strategies. *Structures*, for the purposes of this chapter, will refer to positions, budgetary allotments, space on campus, and others. A structure is something built into the functioning of the program at a material or financial level, or both. You might, for instance, get short-term funding for an in-program assessment of one or more of your outcomes. This would be a temporary structure but a structure nonetheless. Now, if you were to acquire a regular addition to your budget or an assessment specialist in the program, you would have a structure that's sustainable; it's something you can build the program with or on over time.

Practices are a bit different from structures. A *practice* is a recurring component of the program that people come to understand *as* the program; it is seen as "the way things are done around here." The setting up of the schedule before a semester, for instance, is a programmatic practice: teachers expect to be assigned sections according to a certain process, and that process happens at roughly the same time(s) every year. When we are looking at a program in action, we see practices. When we look at how a program is supported by a larger institution, we see structures.

I've separated these two to help you highlight what is and what is not helping your program be sustainable over time. You might have helpful *structures* in place but lack the *practices* needed to move your grand strategies forward. But (and this is probably more likely) you might also have some helpful *practices* in place but without the necessary *structures* to perpetuate that kind of work over time. The ability to separate these two as you discuss how to move forward according to your grand strategies (and, for that matter, move your grand strategies themselves forward) will allow you to think more flexibly about the ways your program is changing.

Forwarding Principles and Principled Practices

Moving forward through your grand strategies in principled ways will allow you to highlight—for both yourself and others—the principles and principled practices that shape the work you do in your program. The targeted innovations in chapter 8 are one of many ways to bring your program further into conversation with other programs in your university and in your field, and doing so highlights that which you value, as well as why you value it. So, pursuing grand strategies allows you to also forward your principles and principled practices.

But you might realize, as you take on this work, that your principles and principled practices are not doing all you hoped they might. You might have more to say about a particular practice or more to examine about a particular principle you have articulated. So, how can you go about revising these principles?

Thanks to the work of part I, you have principles that shape the work your program does. These principles have been articulated over a particular period of time and have the approval of all (or most) folks in the program. Over time, you and your colleagues may come to realize that they need revising. To do that, you can develop a committee to revise the program's statement of principles. Depending on the degree of change, this might be a short- or long-term committee. Again, if it's a transformation that's far outside the bounds of the usual work of the program, doing this might take some time. If it's a matter of updating language or adding an already largely popular principle to the list, it won't take long at all.

This revision of programmatic principles can also be something that is done on a regular basis, much like a program review. Perhaps you could schedule the revision to happen a year before a programmatic review so the review can be informed by the newly revised principles. Such regularity can be baked into commonly held understandings of how the program operates ("We do this every X number of years") so procedures for collecting and analyzing records that can inform the principles can be established.

Such a revision of principles might not produce extensive changes every time. That is, some years there might be considerable revision of what the program values and why. Other years, there might simply be clarifications of the program's values or perhaps more detailed language in particular places throughout the statement of principles. But ongoing attention to what the program values and why could be a useful and effective way of keeping the program up-to-date on why it does what it does and how it does it.

Regardless of whether a revision of program principles is a regular occurrence or emerges as circumstances warrant, a few key components would be useful for you to keep an eye on. First, of course, is compensation. If you are going to have a committee of people engage with and revise the principles, it's going to take time and energy. So, they should be compensated—adequately—for that time and energy. Where, then, might you get that money? Does the department have it? Your college? Is there some sort of professional development initiative you can tap into?

Once you have funding set up to compensate the people on the committee, you can identify some targets for the members. What is it you want them to do, in what time frame, for the work they're being compensated for? How often should they meet? Over what time span? With what outcome in mind? Will they be engaging in a tinkering with the principles or doing a wholesale revision (which would take more time and energy and thus demand more compensation)? This will help you make sure you know what you are getting for the resources you are putting into the committee.

Finally, you want to think about how the rest of your program members will get a say in the revisions. If you have a committee of five people, how might the other thirty or forty people in your program be able to comment on their work? Will there be a review period? Will the program members be surveyed before or during the committee's work? Will the final product be voted on? These steps slow down the process of finalizing new principles, but it's also important, as I mentioned earlier, that the voices of those in the program be baked into the operations of the program itself.

Engaging in regular revisions of principles and principled practices offers a program a continual renewal and allows it to adapt, over time, to what we learn about our students, our teaching, and ourselves. This is just one way, however, of stabilizing the work of the program. In the rest of this chapter, I discuss how we might make programmatic change sustainable through established structures and practices.

Making Programmatic Change Sustainable

Sustainability is a key factor in making programmatic change last. Many fantastic writing programs out there are held together by the ceaseless efforts of a single person (or a few people). To make programmatic change sustainable, we need things in place that make the work that is going on in the program be supported by people, time, resources, and money. Note that I've separated *resources* and *money*. Money is a resource, sure, but it's important enough to stand on its own. It is far too easy for higher-level administrators to make unfunded asks of faculty, thus increasing the long-term strain on everyone (and shortchanging the possibilities of further developing the program).

But before I go further, I should specify what I mean by *sustainability*. Specifically, how much time counts as sustainability. Most writing programs in the country are not funded by some kind of perpetual endowment and cannot count on a steady stream of money year in and year out, immune to the influence of changes in the currents of higher education. Writing program administrators (WPAs), then, as well as the chairs and deans who support them, will always find themselves fighting for the resources they need to get the job done.

So, when I talk about "sustainability" in this chapter, I'm going to be discussing how we can go about creating resources for the program that are seen by people both inside and outside it as required for the ongoing work, as unquestioned (or mostly unquestioned) tools the program needs to do the work it needs to do. I've placed this chapter in part III because you want to think long-term about these kinds of resources, beyond individual initiatives and particular, immediate needs. But you need to keep in mind that some of the battles you will engage in to maintain this funding will be recurring (if sporadic) over the course of decades.

Let's consider, for instance, the hiring of an assistant director of the writing program at your campus (if you already have one, imagine a new assistant director taking on a new kind of role). Once the job search has been approved, things will roll onward until someone is hired. Then you'll have an assistant director of the writing program, someone who is, perhaps, tenure stream and has to spend the next six years or so working to be promoted. Through all of this, the notion that the program *needs* an assistant director will, slowly but surely, one report and activity at a time, become taken for granted. This would be creating a stable structure: a slot for someone to handle a particular kind of work that is compensated appropriately and visible within the broader hierarchy of the program and the university.

But let's say that, in an excellent turn of events, this assistant director is picked up by another program and receives a promotion to director. That's great news for the assistant director and for the program, too—it helps make the ongoing work of the program more visible in the field and underscores how visible the people doing that work are disciplinarily. In the short term, for you, the news might not be great; you have to make a case for hiring a *new* assistant director. The job search must be proposed, approved up the chain, and conducted successfully.

At any of these stages, the question "do you really need a new assistant director" can easily be asked—particularly if the tenure line is in competition with other programs and departments on campus. This is not unexpected and is difficult to avoid. Even if you make the need for an assistant director explicit and compelling, someone in another department might want another hire badly enough to ignore how compelling your argument is and ask the question anyway.

All of this does not mean the program is not sustainable but rather that it's caught up in larger machinations of higher education from which it cannot pull free, even if it wanted to. When we think about sustainability, then, we need to think about the kinds of changes that improve the program and render that improvement relatively stable over time, even if unexpected outside forces can sometimes prove disruptive.

Building Sustainable Practices

With this notion of sustainability in mind, then, we can turn our attention to building sustainable *practices* and *structures*. As I mentioned above, a *practice* is a function of the program. It's how the program operates in one way or another. This practice becomes *sustainable* when it is seen as a way the program operates. A good example from UMaine is our end-of-semester assessment. All English 101 students submit portfolios to be read by two teachers other than their own instructor, according to our *Portfolio Assessment Rubric*. The portfolio review runs three days in the final week of the semester, and all English 101 teachers are expected to participate the entire three days, except when other classes they are taking or teaching conflict.

The portfolio review began in the early 2000s, and over time it grew into a three-day event. At this point, after several decades, it is an expected part of being an English 101 teacher: those who are teaching 101 *know* that they will be submitting portfolios at the end of the semester, they will do three days of portfolio review, and the results will shape student passing rates.

This is what I mean by a *sustainable practice*: it's sustainable because people expect to participate in it. In fact, if they *didn't* participate in it, they'd be at a loss for what to do—who passes the class, how grades are decided, and so on. The mental effort of deciding that such a practice is worthwhile or crucial to the function of the program no longer occurs. Instead, it's assumed. It has become "the way things work around here."

Now, you'll note that the language I just used echoes that of the theoretical framing in chapter 1 and the discovery of facts in chapter 2. A sustainable practice is not *necessarily* a good thing—it can hinder program development as easily as it can spur it. So, you have to be careful in how you go about creating sustainable practices and what practices your program comes to see as sustainable. This is where the grand strategies come in: by tying the practices you make sustainable to the goals you are working toward in the longer arc of the program, you can start to be sure your sustainable practices are what you need them to be.

Of course, you do not need to live on grand strategy alone; you also have the principles and principled practices that are informing what you do and why you do it. Creating sustainable practices happens at the intersection of grand strategy, principles, and principled practice. When a practice is at the center of grand strategy, principles, and principled practice, then that strategy is *also* at the center of how the program operates. And when the program constituents come to see the program as operating through a particular practice, the need to keep such a practice going becomes readily apparent.

For practices to become sustainable, they have to become woven into the fabric of the program, something people think *through* rather than something they just think *about*. I discuss this with an image I tried (and failed) to use through the language of Actor-Network Theory, as something that needs to be *sedimented* into the ongoing functioning of a program (Dippre 2021).

Below are questions to help you think through whether an emerging practice is (or can become) sustainable:

1. Is the practice compensated?
2. Does the practice inform other practices?
3. Can the practice become part of the regular labor of those in the program?

If the answer to any of these questions is "no," what might you change to move the answer to "yes?"

Building Sustainable Structures

You may have noticed that creating a sustainable practice can easily become something that doesn't stand on its own very well. For instance, you might struggle to find the personnel, year in and year out, to operate a particular (and, in terms of grand strategy, important) aspect of the program. To support sustainable practices, then, you need to also turn to sustainable *structures*: the resources, time, personnel, and money that can help you to make sure these crucial aspects of your program can continue, year after year.

Making structures sustainable, as I discussed above, can be tricky business; after all, we can't guarantee that a dean or a provost will approve a particular line item in perpetuity. That said, though, we can at least put ourselves and our program in a position where certain things can be counted on, materially and financially, over longer stretches of time. A tenure line set aside for an assessment expert, for instance, might not be something that's guaranteed to be renewed if the person leaves. But having a full-time position in place for that sort of thing at least creates the conditions for people to expect the position to be filled. While the assessment expert is there, at least, the position *will* be filled.

So, how do you go about drawing on your expanded innovations to create sustainable structures in your programs? Once again, we find ourselves back at issues of fact and the stories we tell about writers and writing. You need to draw on artifacts—both those already existing and those you construct through new kinds of record collection—to create facts, things people can take for granted in the program and small, stubborn facts people will struggle to overcome in their arguments against your ideas.

An example may be in order here to walk you through what these steps might look like. Let's say that in the work of piloting some innovations in the program, you and your teachers have developed a plan for a program-wide textbook for students. This would allow you to capture the expertise of your teachers and your students as they talk about (and with) language in different ways and can also allow you to make sure the program is tailored to the needs of the people in it and is resonant with their interests. Through piloted studies, you've worked on some chapters and integrated them into some sections. These sections have gone smoothly, and you would like to ramp this up into a full, program-wide textbook.

But there's a problem: you have some chapters written—and it is hoped that this was done by people in the program through some form of compensation—but you don't have a full book finished. And you don't own a printing press in your basement, not even a broken one as a conversation piece. So there are no further texts to round out the book, and there is no way to print the book. You'd like to include student voices, but there's no way to get those voices into the unfinished, unprinted book. And since undergraduates cycle through the program at quite a clip, you have no means of paying someone to continually update your unfinished, unprinted book with no undergraduate voices in it. So, what is one to do?

There are a few ways to go about this. As we can see from the above details, you have some *practices* that are, at least in part, ready to go: teachers and students who want to write, and a program that is (or seems to be) expecting a program-wide text to work from. But you need to make such work *sustainable* over time. You need to make sure that the people doing this work are compensated for continually doing it, that there's a process for handing off that work as people graduate or otherwise leave the program, and that the means of support available to this work is not patchwork but an ongoing occurrence.

Unfortunately, patchwork might be what you have to start with, and that can be a starting point toward something more sustainable over time. Now, this doesn't always happen; there is always a tendency to stick with what seems to work, not just in education but in nearly every industry. In other words, if you have a particular compensation plan set up that is intended to be temporary but things go smoothly, it can easily become permanent, at least in the minds of future department chairs and deans. The challenge in terms of patchwork compensation is to move from the patchwork to more enduring forms of compensation as quickly as possible.

So, how do you do that? How do you create, from patchwork solutions, the kinds of sustainable structures in terms of both pots of money and sustained employment that allow your program to continue to grow? That's a good question, and I wish I could answer it in a more straightforward way. Solidarity helps: having the weight of the department behind big requests can be immensely helpful in making the need for particular financial commitments visible.

In the absence of such solidarity—or, more accurately, as a way of building such solidarity—you could start to build a coherent sense of what the patchwork solutions are doing in yearly (or quarterly or semesterly) reports to upper-level administrators. If it can become visually apparent to those higher ranking than you and your program exactly what problems are being solved with patchwork solutions, it can lay the groundwork for proposing more permanent solutions to those problems. This approach does bring the chance that an administrator might want to stick with the patchwork approach under the "if it ain't broke" rule, but using recent successes of patchwork issues as a launching point for imagining how a more permanent solution could lead to *more* and *better* solutions might allow you to work around that.

Much as in the previous section, a few key questions can help you think through whether an emerging structure is (or can become) sustainable over time:

1. Is the structure supporting multiple practices in the program?
2. Is the structure supported financially, in the short or long term?
3. Can the structure become embedded in long-standing budgetary decisions?

And, similar to the previous section, if the answer to any of these questions is "no," what might you change to move the answer to "yes?"

Building the Program in Principled Ways

At this point—nine chapters into the journey through building a principled writing program—you've worked your way through investigating a program (part I), solving particular, pressing problems in the program (part II), and thinking about the long-term future of the program (part III). I close this chapter by returning more centrally to the issue of principles and how they can powerfully shape the programs we direct.

As you further your grand strategies by developing sustainable structures and practices, you'll find yourself realizing that your principles and principled practices might be falling short of helping you do this work. Remember that the principles you have articulated are only the tip of the iceberg of your values: there is a lot that you don't realize is shaping the way you see the world and how you decide what you value in it.

You might also find yourself running into the issue of old principles no longer applying well. For instance, you might have had running principles about diversity and inclusion in your program. But in the past decade, a great deal of work has been done on anti-racist approaches to writing instruction. This new work may have led you to recast your principles, to help you see things differently. Your sense of how to go about implementing diversity and inclusion in your program may have changed a lot, and the language in your earlier statements might not be a good fit in helping you move that change forward.

Your principles will also be different because by the time you're applying this chapter, your *program* is different. You're not the same WPA you were when you took on the work of tracing the facts, principles, and stories in your program that you did in chapter 1. You've grown, and your program has grown with you. Your principles, by extension, will have to grow as well. They'll have to account for the transformations of your thought, of what you and your program have experienced in the time that has elapsed, and they will have to change so they can be helpful when you and your program go through more changes in the future.

For that reason, this book is recursive in nature. You can always begin collecting and analyzing artifacts anew, starting with what you've learned about the program—where it was, where it is, and where it's going—in the work you've done throughout these chapters. Principle-driven writing programs get built, but they don't *stay* built unless we continually attend to them. The principles, principled practices, strategies and tactics, grand strategies, sustainable structures and practices, and so on that you've developed can be a useful starting point for continuing that work into the future.

Resources

The resources below can help you develop sustainable structures and practices in your program. "Crafting Sustainable Programs" offers resources for thinking about how to deal with the various forces shaping your program so the changes you make can be sustainable. "Sustainable Institutional Connections" looks outward, at the ways writing programs can be sustainably connected to other institutions or a larger bureaucracy. "Sustainable Program Mechanics" drills down into particular aspects of program life (e.g., Student Evaluations of Teaching [SETs], assessment) to imagine sustainable change in more focused ways.

CRAFTING SUSTAINABLE PROGRAMS

Del Principe, Annie. 2020. "Cultivating a Sustainable TYC Writing Program: Collaboration, Disciplinarity, and Faculty Governance." *WPA: Writing Program Administration* 43 (3): 54–72.

Malenczyk, Rita. 2016. "Opening Plenary Address: Locations of Administration; or, WPAs in Space." *WPA: Writing Program Administrators* 40 (1): 114–133.

McCrary, Jennifer, and Ashley J. Holmes. 2022. "Toward Sustainable Writing Programs in the Quality Enhancement Plan Era." *College English* 85 (1): 37–63.

Welch, Nancy. 2018. "'Everyone Should Have a Plan': A Neoliberal Primer for Writing Program Directors." *WPA: Writing Program Administration* 41 (2): 104–112.

SUSTAINABLE INSTITUTIONAL CONNECTIONS

Murphy, Susan Wolff, and Mark G. Hartlaub. 2017. "Enhancing Alliances and Joining Initiatives to Help Students: The Story of How We Created Developmental Learning Communities at Texas A&M University–Corpus Christi." In *Retention, Persistence, and Writing Programs*, edited by Todd Ruecker, Dawn Shepherd, Heidi Estrem, and Beth Brunk-Chavez, 219–236. Logan: Utah State University Press.

Schoen, Megan. 2019. "Your Mission, Should You Choose to Accept It: A Survey on Writing Programs and Institutional Mission." *WPA: Writing Program Administration* 42 (2): 37–57.

Wess, Holly. 2015. "Partnerships for College Readiness: A Qualitative Multi-Site Case Study of Secondary/Post-Secondary Instructors' Collaboration." PhD dissertation, Northeastern University, Boston, MA.

SUSTAINABLE PROGRAM MECHANICS

Brueggemann, Brenda Jo, Linda Feldmeier White, Patricia A. Dunn, Barbara A. Heifferon, and Johnson Cheu. 2001. "Becoming Visible: Lessons in Disability." *College Composition and Communication* 52 (3): 368–398.

Graphenreed, Tieanna, and Mya Poe. 2022. "Antiracist Genre Systems: Creating Nonviolent Writing Classroom Spaces." *Composition Studies* 50 (2): 53–76.

Martin, Caitlin A. 2021. "Facilitating Institutional Change through Writing-Related Faculty Development." PhD dissertation, Miami University of Ohio, Miami, OH.

Scott, Marc. 2017. "Big Data and Writing Program Retention Assessment: What We Need to Know." In *Retention, Persistence, and Writing Programs*, edited by Todd Ruecker, Dawn Shepherd, Heidi Estrem, and Beth Brunk-Chavez, 56–73. Logan: Utah State University Press.

White, Edward M., Norbert Elliot, and Irvin Peckham. 2015. *Very Like a Whale: The Assessment of Writing Programs*. Logan: Utah State University Press.

Wooten, Courtney Adams, Brian Ray, and Jacob Babb. 2016. "WPAs Reading SETs: Toward an Ethical and Effective Use of Teaching Evaluations." *WPA: Writing Program Administration* 40 (1): 50–66.

CONCLUSION

Writing Programs for Human Beings

One of the many takeaways I have from my time working with Coach B. is his ongoing work to help not the *player* on the team but the *human being*. This is an important difference: Coach B. didn't only care about what you could bring to the team, how you could make the team better, but he cared about how you were doing, generally speaking. The bulk of our conversations might have been about football (because most of our interactions happened in practice and meetings), but that always seemed, at least to me, to be just another way for Coach B. to make sure you, the human being, were hanging in there, doing well. I think Coach B. knew intuitively what many sports psychologists have come to realize: athletes who have their other needs met (e.g., psychological, social) are in a better position to be successful in their sport.

Coach B.'s emphasis on helping human beings resonates with one of my earliest meetings with my graduate adviser. I was in a meeting with Charles Bazerman and a fellow graduate student, Charlyne, and we were discussing some of the theoretical and empirical approaches Chuck took over the years. He mentioned, in an offhand manner, that "some people think activity is primary, but I think people are primary." He said that in late 2011, and ever since then, it's been one of the guiding lights of my own research, teaching, and administrative work. At the core of what we do, as teachers, researchers,

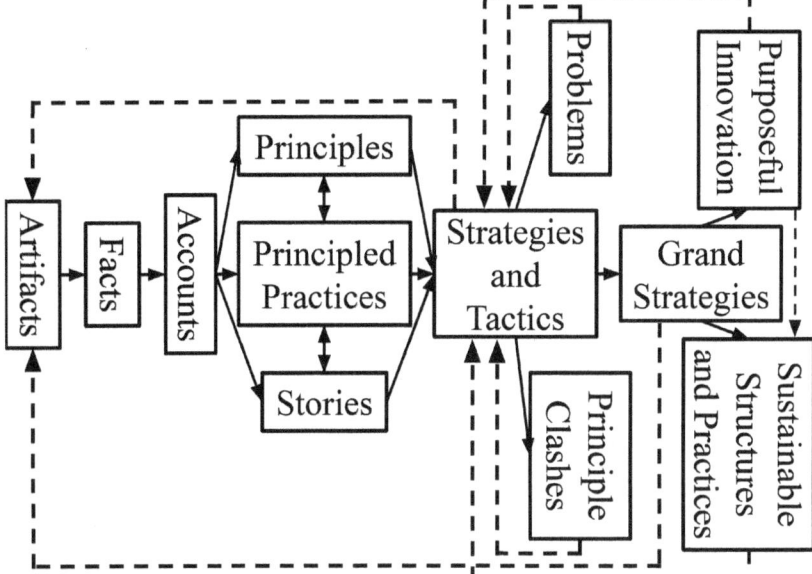

FIGURE 10.1. The work of this text

and administrators, is working with human beings, trying to help them live the lives they want to live. It's with this core in mind that I close this text: by bringing together the threads that have run through this text to highlight the potential for action those threads offer us for growing our programs with human beings in mind.

Now, at the close of this text, you've worked your way through the model in figure 10.1—generating principles, principled practices, and stories about writers and writing; finding new strategies and tactics, resolving problems, and moving past clashes of principle; generating grand strategies, developing pilots informed by those grand strategies, and building toward sustainable change. This work, however, doesn't *stay* finished once it's done. Principle-driven writing programs need regular and ongoing attention from their members, with frequent checks on how the program is working, its sustainability, and its ability to meet its members' needs. This means that you (or those who take the reins of the program after you) will be returning to the work you've done throughout this book again and again in the coming years: collecting new artifacts, finding new facts and accounts and stories, and using that information to steer the program. Building a principle-driven writing program from the ground up means routinely returning to what's happening on the ground, in the lived experience of students, teachers, staff, and administrators.

Interaction and What It Means to Be Human

Throughout this text, I have tried to drive home the idea that we are all responsible to one another in the work we do. From the interactional framing I provide in chapter 1 to the development of grand strategies and long-term planning that emerges in part III of this text, I have tried to emphasize how, to a greater and lesser extent, we as writing program administrators (WPAs) and teachers of writing are responsible—to our colleagues, our students, and our community members—for helping people live the lives they want to live.

This responsibility is deeply tied to interaction, and it is through interaction that we are, and become, most human. In aligning with one another to produce facts, we are sharing with one another, working together with one another to make social reality happen, yet again and for another first time. The combination of trust and responsibility that emerges in these constantly unfolding moments builds and deepens our humanity, allows us to understand who we are and what we are doing in the world. In many ways, interaction is the most profound and fundamental aspect of our lived experience.

And yet, at the same time that interaction is where we are most human, interaction is also where we do so much of our work to dehumanize one another—where we do things, for whatever reason, that make people feel less than, like they don't belong, like they are not part of whatever is happening. The power of interaction is also, and by extension, the danger of interaction. Thinking about WPA work, about program operation, through an interactional frame highlights for us, as I mentioned in chapter 1, where we commit the sins of our shared pasts anew—co-creating bias, discrimination, and systemic injustice for another first time. This is not to say that we should be laying structural issues at the feet of individuals but rather that part of the work of combatting structural issues, of rebuilding and renovating our social structures to be equitable and just, emerges from and contributes to the interactional worlds we build together.

Helping People Live the Lives They Want to Live

I mentioned at the start of this text that if the work of a writing program administrator wasn't going to help people live the kind of lives they want to live, what's the point? I hope the connection between making lives better—creating structurally kind programs that support students, teachers, and administrators alike—and the long-term plans we might make for the programs we are part of is evident to the reader. In case I have managed to somehow underwhelm on this point, I would like to take some time now to make the argument for how—building from an interactional framework as articulated both above and in part I—we help our students, our teachers, and our fellow administrators live the lives they want to live through the ongoing work we do across our WPA careers.

In chapter 1, as a preface to the interactional framing I develop later in the chapter, I quoted at some length the work of Viktor Frankl (2020). Frankl saw life as a series of possibilities—potentials for action—that emerged from the choices we make, day in and day out, in the daily work of being human. In this ongoing, day-to-day work, Frankl saw that we had, in each new moment, a chance to realize potential for action, to make real some possibilities and to consign others forever to the ash heap of history. And, once the moment had passed, the possibilities we chose would be frozen in history—unalterable, untouchable, for better or for worse. The weight of such responsibility clearly bore down on Frankl in his writings and in what he was trying to convey as he made sense of the unwavering brutality he had suffered through. And it's the responsibility of each moment that I called attention to in the framing of chapter 1: we have the responsibility to understand how our work of building a program shapes each moment for our students, our teachers, and our administrators in the program.

But as I've articulated the individual responsibility of WPAs to attend to these moments, to understand how they shape the broader stories about writers and writing that we tell, I have also come to realize that I would be remiss if I did not emphasize the attention in this book to the *structural* ways we've gone about attending to and building from these moments. There is no scenario anywhere in society—not in voting rights, not in education, and certainly not in writing programs—in which individual initiative can, on its own, solve structural issues.

The field of writing program administration, both in disciplinary work and in daily practice, has seen mixed results on realizing this, for both students and teachers. It isn't difficult to find people on social media calling out particular teaching practices as moral and ethical issues without attending to the larger structural issues that gave rise to them. Throughout this text, I have tried to direct the reader's attention back to structural issues. The structure of the organization and the ethics of the choices we can make within them are not separable: there are times when we need to make the best bad decision we can while simultaneously pushing for the kinds of structural change that will keep us from having to be in such a position in the future.

As we go about attempting to help people live lives of their own choosing through our administrative work, then, we need to keep our attention on how our programs are structurally supporting the work we are doing. Making a program that helps the people in it means making a program that is sustainable, that emerges from collaborative work done well over time.

The Ongoing Work of Principles

I have also tried to suggest throughout this text that the work of developing, supporting, and thinking through our principles is something that we not only have to pay close attention to but that we have to pay *ongoing* attention to. Our principles never rest easy: as the most visible part of our complex arrangement of thoughts, values, beliefs, and intuitions, our principles are always both *shaping* the moments we participate in and *being shaped by* those moments as we engage with them. Each new social situation, each new interaction, is the chance to see something new about ourselves and our principles, something we had missed earlier, and something we might be able to glean new insights from.

Our work with principles, then, needs to be an ongoing and recursive process, one that is never quite "finished" in the sense of "we know all we can about what we value and why." To assume that we can be "finished" with our principles (and the programs that emerge by living them) is to assume that society is itself static, that it is not in a constant state of flux in one way or another. I am certain that I am not the only WPA who has recently learned a great deal more about social injustice and, particularly, anti-Black racism in the US and how it impacts my work as a WPA. But this learning did not happen as a result of a single event—not the split of the Institute of Race, Rhetoric, and Literacy (IRRL) from the Council of Writing Program Administrators (CWPA) (see Inoue 2021; Poblete 2021 for details), or the recent publication of a particular book, or any similar single event. Rather, this learning, this challenge to the principles that were informing my work as WPA, came as a wave of awareness of the racial complexities of society swept the many institutions I participate in and act through. The IRRL split, the recent publication of many books, and other events worked together to bring to my awareness of widespread social injustice.

These changes in the field of WPA work resonate with larger social change, some of which shapes the institutions I am part of. But if I were simply to label my principles as "finished" and walk away from them, then I cannot use these changes as an opportunity to think anew about what I value and how I value it (and, by extension, I cannot think about those things for my program). Social change would then seem less like an opportunity to learn than it would a threat, and it is difficult to learn—and to change—when one feels threatened.

We need, then, to be constantly seeing new circumstances as an opportunity to develop a more complex and nuanced understanding of our values and to revise those values as well. I recall that Pat Burnes, the longtime director of composition at UMaine, would often greet unexpected circumstances on a positive note. I heard her say more than once, when talking to a teaching assistant, that by engaging with this or that surprising issue, "we can learn a lot about our teaching." If we are to take up the potential for action continuing to unfold before us, we need to be responsible to the world and the people around us and use them to further develop a sense of our principles and—through those revised principles—revisions of our strategies, tactics, and grand strategies.

The Singular and the Programmatic: Embracing the Irreconcilability of the Irreconcilable

Drawing on Jonathan Alexander's (2017) language of the *irreconcilability* of tensions (and the potential inherent in such tensions), I have been working across two very different—and, in the end, irreconcilable—orientations. On the one hand, there is the *programmatic* vision: the development of a course (or set of courses) that helps a broad population move forward toward particular outcomes in particular ways. This programmatic vision is at the heart of much WPA work: we are administrators of writing *programs*, after all. But I've also discussed the individuated actions of particular people: the needs of particular students, faculty, administrators, community members, and other interested parties.

I see these two—that is, the program on the one hand and the singular human being on the other—as fundamentally irreconcilable. We can develop writing programs that account for many of students' needs, but we cannot assume (and we *must not* assume) that we know all of the needs students have, let alone that we can meet all of those needs. If we assume we know everything about our students, we begin to think about things like normative paths of development, particular markers we can expect all students to meet at certain times throughout a course, sequence of courses, or undergraduate career. And it is in that assumption that we begin to lose sight of an inclusive and accessible program.

Throughout this text, I've been trying to identify (and lead you through) the kinds of structures that can help you build a coherent writing program that creates the kinds of space needed for the singular interactions of student and teacher. The focus has been on principles, principled practices, stories, strategies, tactics, and grand strategies. By paying careful attention to these concepts, we can avoid unnecessary bureaucratic structure while also maintaining an ongoing, socially sensitive, and ever-innovating program. Students and faculty can carefully engage with one another with attention to the singular while also contributing to the ongoing flow of the programmatic.

But, like any other aspect of human life, the framing I suggest is not a *guarantee* of balancing the singular and the programmatic. The two are, as I say in the header of this section, fundamentally irreconcilable: we always need to create a balance between the two, which means that local decisions—the work of continuing to build social facts—contribute to how well that balance is maintained. The work you accomplished throughout this book provides the *possibility* of productively engaging with that irreconcilability, but it's a possibility that must always be engaged, day in and day out, for another first time.

"Burnin' Daylight": Taking Action amid Uncertainty

Coach B hasn't been my coach in nearly two decades, but *burnin' daylight* still echoes throughout my life. The call to get up, get moving, get things into gear before I burn too much daylight has been helpful to me as I try to overcome what can be the breathtaking scope of demands that come with running a writing program. The questions and uncertainty can easily get to a WPA: there's always, at minimum, a small fire or four to put out, a few emails to respond to, a schedule to prep, a class to plan for, a meeting to organize, and so on. In the ongoing rush of things to do, we can lose sight of the bigger picture, the broader transformations we're trying to bring about in our program. The competing pressures are enough to freeze one into indecision. But hey, we're *burnin' daylight* here, I tell myself, so I better get to it. And it's important that I do, because the ongoing work of developing our programs, of making them more principled, more inclusive, more sustainable, is how we can go about transforming our world for the better.

Our programs can be a force for good, a place from which sustained and sustainable structural transformations can occur. This kind of change is often (if not always) slower than we'd like, and change needs not only merely to occur but to *endure*, which is yet another kind of work we and our programs need to undertake. But we can only do that in communities, both inside and outside our disciplines, our programs, and our larger institutions. It is my hope that the guide laid out in this text can help interested readers engage with their communities and bring about (and sustain) the kinds of change we hope to see around us.

As I think back on the people—like Coach B., like Linda Adler-Kassner, like Chuck Bazerman—who have shaped my growth throughout my life, I see a constant thread of attending to community. These people had goals, but they worked toward those goals by building up the people around them, by making stronger the ties that held us all together through whatever purposes we had come together for. Communities—both large and small—were not an addition to the work they were doing but a deeply ingrained aspect of it. The raising of social consciousness to the issues of equity and social justice that have emerged so powerfully in these past years calls us to look at our communities anew, to see the harms that we, purposefully or accidentally, inflict on those around us. A long, careful look at what good and ill our communities do and how they do it is the only way to build more just and equitable writing programs, institutions of higher learning, and societies in general. I hope the work you've done as you've moved through these pages has led you to envision a program that does that kind of deep, demanding work—work that can give way to a better program, a better institution, and eventually (I hope) a better world.

References

Accardi, Steven, Nicholas Behm, and Peter Vandenberg. 2022. "Assembling Multi-Institutional Writing Programs: Reimagining the English Major While Expanding Writing Studies." *WPA: Writing Program Administration* 46 (1): 16–36.

Adler-Kassner, Linda. 2008. *The Activist WPA: Changing Stories about Writing and Writers*. Logan: Utah State University Press.

Adler-Kassner, Linda. 2012. "The Companies We Keep, or the Companies We Would Like to Try to Keep: Strategies and Tactics in Challenging Times." *WPA: Writing Program Administration* 36 (1): 119–140.

Adler-Kassner, Linda. 2016. "What Is Principle?" In *A Rhetoric for Writing Program Administrators*, second edition, edited by Rita Malenczyk, 460–474. West Lafayette, IN: Parlor Press.

Adler-Kassner, Linda. 2018. "Taking Action in the Age of Reaction: Constructing Architectures of Participation." In *Writing for Engagement: Responsive Practice for Social Action*, edited by Mary P. Sheridan, Megan J. Bardolph, Megan Faver Hartline, and Drew Holladay, 3–13. New York: Lexington Books.

Adler-Kassner, Linda, and Susanmarie Harrington. 2010. "Responsibility and Composition's Future in the Twenty-First Century: Reframing Accountability." *College Composition and Communication* 62 (1): 73–99.

Adler-Kassner, Linda, and Elizabeth Wardle, eds. 2016. *Naming What We Know: Threshold Concepts of Writing Studies*, classroom edition. Logan: Utah State University Press.

Adler-Kassner, Linda, and Elizabeth Wardle. 2022. *Writing Expertise: A Research-Based Approach to Writing and Learning across Disciplines*. Fort Collins and Boulder: WAC Clearinghouse and University Press of Colorado.

Alexander, Jonathan. 2017. "Queer Ways of Knowing." *WPA: Writing Program Administration*, 41 (1): 137–149.

Ansley, Jennifer. 2020. "Queering Ethos: Interrogating Archives in the First Year Writing Classroom." *Composition Studies* 48 (3): 16–34.

Applebee, Arthur N. 1986. "Musings . . . Principled Practice." *Research in the Teaching of English* 20: 5–7.

Armstrong, Erik, Megan Baptista Geist, and Joshua Geist. 2020. "Withstanding the Backlash: Conceptualizing and Preparing for Coercive Reactions to Placement Reform and Corequisite Support Models in California." *Composition Studies* 48 (2): 74–92.

Asmuth, Charlotte. 2022. "Re-Localizing Writing Assessment: Sites of Knowledge." PhD dissertation, University of Louisville, Louisville, KY.

Assembly for the Teaching of English Grammar (ATEG). 2002. *Some Questions and Answers about Grammar*. https://ncte.org/statement/qandaaboutgrammar/.

Babb, Jacob. 2023. "Seeing the Forest and the Trees: A Rhizomatic Metaphor for Writing Program Administration." In *Toward More Sustainable Metaphors of Writing Program Administration*, edited by Lydia Wilkes, Lilian Mina, and Patti Poblete, 35–48. Logan: Utah State University Press.

Baca, Isabela. 2021. "Hispanic-Serving or Not: La Lucha Sigue in Academia; the Struggle Continues in Academia." *Composition Studies* 49 (2): 70–78.

Baez, Elizabeth, and Rosanne Carlo. 2021. "Encouraging Student Voices: Toward a Voice-Based and Antiracist Culture from the MA Program to Basic Writing." *Journal of Basic Writing* 40 (1): 99–126.

Baker-Bell, April, Bonnie J. Williams-Farrier, Davena Jackson, Lamar Johnson, Carmen Kynard, and Teaira McMurtry. 2020. *This Ain't Another Statement! This Is a demand for Black Linguistic Justice*. Conference on College Composition and Communication. https://cccc.ncte.org/cccc/demand-for-black-linguistic-justice.

Banks, William P., Michael J. Faris, Collie Fulford, Timothy Oleksiak, GPat Patterson, and Trixie G. Smith. 2020. "Writing Program Administration: A Queer Symposium." *Writing Program Administration* 43 (2): 11–44.

Bastian, Heather. 2019. "The F-Word: Failure in WPA Work." *WPA: Writing Program Administration* 43 (1): 94–110.

Beavers, Melvin, Beth L. Brunk-Chavez, Neisha-Anne Greene, Asao B. Inoue, Iris Ruiz, Tanita Saenkhum, and Vershawn Ashanti Young. 2021. *Toward Anti-Racist First-Year Composition Goals*. https://tinyurl.com/FYCGoalsStatement.

Beckett, Jessica Marie. 2017. "Negotiating Expertise: The Strategies Writing Program Administrators Use to Mediate Disciplinary and Institutional Values." PhD dissertation, Virginia Tech University, Blacksburg.

Belanger, Kelly, and Sibylle Gruber. 2005. "Unraveling Generative Tensions in the Composition Practicum." In *Don't Call It That: The Composition Practicum*, edited by Sidney I. Dobrin, 113–140. Urbana: National Council of Teachers of English.

Benander, Ruth, and Brenda Refaei. 2021. "Access, Outcomes, and Diversity: Opportunities and Challenges in Basic Writing." In *Improving Outcomes: Disciplinary Writing, Local Assessment, and the Aim of Fairness*, edited by Diane Kelly-Riley and Norbert Elliot, 67–78. New York: Modern Language Association.

Bishop, Wendy, and Gay Lynn Crossley. 1996. "How to Tell a Story of Stopping: The Complexities of Narrating a WPA's Experience." *WPA: Writing Program Administration* 19 (3): 70–79.

Blank, Susan, and Beth Greenberg. 1981. "Living at the Bottom." *WPA: Writing Program Administration* 5 (1): 9–12.

Blankenship, Lisa. 2019. *Changing the Subject: A Theory of Rhetorical Empathy*. Logan: Utah State University Press.

Bloom, Lynn Z. 2002. "Are We Having Fun Yet? Necessity, Creativity, and Writing Program Administration." *WPA: Writing Program Administration* 26 (1–2): 57–70.

Brandt, Deborah. 2016. "Studying Writing Sociologically." Paper and workshop on the 50th Anniversary of the Dartmouth Research Institute. Hanover, NH, August 1–8.

Broad, Bob. 2003. *What We Really Value: Beyond Rubrics in Teaching and Assessing Writing*. Logan: Utah State University Press.

Broad, Bob, Linda Adler-Kassner, Barry Alford, Jane Detweiler, Heidi Estrem, Susanmarie Harrington, Maureen McBride, Eric Stalions, and Scott Weeden. 2009. *Organic Writing Assessment: Dynamic Criteria Mapping in Action*. Logan: Utah State University Press.

Brueggemann, Brenda Jo, Linda Feldmeier White, Patricia A. Dunn, Barbara A. Heifferon, and Johnson Cheu. 2001. "Becoming Visible: Lessons in Disability." *College Composition and Communication* 52 (3): 368–398.

Burdick, Melanie, and Jane Greer. 2017. "Paths to Productive Partnerships: Surveying High School Teachers about Professional Development Opportunities and 'College-Level' Writing." *WPA: Writing Program Administration* 41 (1): 82–101.

Burns, Michael Sterling, Randall Cream, and Timothy R. Dougherty. 2018. "Fired Up: Institutional Critique, Lesson Study, and the Future of Antiracist Writing Assessment." In *Writing Assessment, Social Justice, and the Advancement of Opportunity*, edited by Mya Poe, Asao B. Inoue, and Norbert Elliot, 257–292. Fort Collins and Boulder: WAC Clearinghouse and University Press of Colorado.

Burrows, Cedric D. 2016. "The Yardstick of Whiteness in Composition Textbooks." *WPA: Writing Program Administration* 39 (2): 42–46.

Buyserie, Beth, Tialitha Macklin, Matt Frye, and Patricia Freitag Ericsson. 2021. "Opening an Assessment Dialogue: Formative Evaluation of a Writing Studies Program." In *Improving Outcomes: Disciplinary Writing, Local Assessment, and the Aim of Fairness*, edited by Diane Kelly-Riley and Norbert Elliot, 133–146. New York: Modern Language Association.

Buyserie, Beth, Anna Plemons, and Patricia Freitag Ericsson. 2017. "Retention, Critical Pedagogy, and Students as Agents: Eschewing the Deficit Model." In *Retention, Persistence, and Writing Programs*, edited by Todd Ruecker, Dawn Shepherd, Heidi Estrem, and Beth Brunk-Chavez, 151–166. Logan: Utah State University Press.

Cambridge, Darren, and Patricia A. Stock. 2015. *Structural Kindness: Essays on Literacy Education in Honor of Kent D. Williamson*. Urbana, IL: NCTE Books.

Carter, Genesea M., and Aurora Matzke. 2023. "Conclusion: A Toolkit." In *Systems Shift: Creating and Navigating Change in Rhetoric and Composition Administration*, edited by Genesea M. Carter and Aurora Matzke, 345–355. Fort Collins and Boulder: WAC Clearinghouse and University Press of Colorado.

Carter-Tod, Sheila. 2020. "The Importance of Documenting Oft-Unspoken Narratives." *WPA: Writing Program Administration* 44 (1): 148–156.

Carter-Tod, Sheila. 2023. "Nothing New: Systemic Invisibility, Epistemological Exclusion, and Faculty and Administrators of Color." In *Making Administrative Work Visible: Data-Driven Advocacy for Understanding the Labor of Writing Program Administration*, edited by Leigh Graziano, Kay Halasek, Remi Hudgins, Susan Miller-Cochran, Frank Napolitano, and Natalie Szymanski, 27–38. Logan: Utah State University Press.

Cavazos, Alyssa. 2019. "Encouraging Languages Other than English in First-Year Writing Courses: Experiences from Linguistically Diverse Writers." *Composition Studies* 47 (1): 38–56.

Champoux-Crowley, Alexander J. 2022. "Negotiation and Translation in First Year Composition WPA Work: Transformative Professional Knowledge to Composition Practice." PhD dissertation, University of Minnesota, Minneapolis.

Charlton, Colin, Jonnika Charlton, Tarez Samra Graben, Kathleen J. Ryan, and Amy Ferdinand Stolley. 2011. *GenAdmin: Theorizing WPA Identities in the Twenty-First Century*. West Lafayette, IN: Parlor Press.

Charmaz, Kathy. 2014. *Constructing Grounded Theory*, second edition. Thousand Oaks, CA: Sage.

Chemishanova, Polina, and Robin Snead. 2017. "Reconfiguring the Writing Studio Model: Examining the Impact of the *PlusOne* Program on Student Performance and Retention." In *Retention, Persistence, and Writing Programs*, edited by Todd Ruecker, Dawn Shepherd, Heidi Estrem, and Beth Brunk-Chavez, 167–184. Logan: Utah State University Press.

Cheramie, Deany M. 2004. "Sifting through Fifty Years of Change: Writing Program Administration at an Historically Black University." In *Historical Studies of Writing Program Administration: Individuals, Communities, and the Formation of a Discipline*, edited by Barbara L'Eplattenier and Lisa Mastrangelo, 145–165. West Lafayette, IN: Parlor Press.

Cicchino, Amy. 2020. "A Broader View: How Doctoral Programs in Rhetoric and Composition Prepare Their Graduate Students to Teach Composition." *WPA: Writing Program Administration* 44 (1): 86–106.

Cicchino, Amy, Sarah Elizabeth Snyder, and Natalie Szymanski. 2023. "We've Been Burned Out and Exhausted: GenAdmin WPA Labor Issues Exacerbated by the COVID-19 Pandemic." *WPA: Writing Program Administration* 47 (1): 102–116.

Clinnin, Kaitlin. 2021. "In the Event of an Emergency: Crisis Management for WPAs." *Writing Program Administration* 45 (1): 9–31.

Clinnin, Kaitlin. 2023. "Practicing Equitable and Sustainable Trauma-Informed Writing Program Administration through Disability Justice." *WPA: Writing Program Administration* 47 (1): 117–132.

Committee on CCCC Language Statement. 1974. "Students' Right to Their Own Language." Conference on College Composition and Communication. https://prod-ncte-cdn.azureedge.net/nctefiles/groups/cccc/newsrtol.pdf.

Conference on College Composition and Communication. 2020. *CCCC Statement on Second Language Writing and Multilingual Learners*. https://cccc.ncte.org/cccc/resources/positions/secondlangwriting.

Condon, Frankie, and Vershawn Ashanti Young. 2016. *Performing Antiracist Pedagogy in Rhetoric, Writing, and Communication*. Fort Collins and Boulder: WAC Clearinghouse and University Press of Colorado.

Conti, Maria, Rachel LaMance, and Susan Miller-Cochran. 2017. "Cultivating Change from the Ground Up: Developing a Grassroots Programmatic Assessment." *Composition Forum* 37. https://compositionforum.org/issue/37/arizona.php.

Cook, Justin H., and Jackie Hoermann-Elliot. 2022. "Standing Outside Success: A Reevaluation of WPA Failure during the Covid-19 Pandemic." *WPA: Writing Program Administration* 46 (1): 60–76.

Costello, Kristi Murray. 2023. "The Quiet Revolution: How Newer WPAs Are Shifting the Profession." *WPA: Writing Program Administration* 47 (1): 133–147.

Costello, Kristi Murray, and Kate Navickas. 2023. "Naming What We Feel: Self-Dialogue as a Strategy for Negotiating Emotional Labor in WPA Work." In *Making Administrative Work Visible: Data-Driven Advocacy for Understanding the Labor of Writing Program Administration*, edited by Leigh Graziano, Kay Halasek, Remi Hudgins, Susan Miller-Cochran, Frank Napolitano, and Natalie Szymanski, 91–105. Logan: Utah State University Press.

Council of Writing Program Administrators, National Council of Teachers of English, and the National Writing Project. 2011. *The Framework for Success in Postsecondary Writing*. https://wpacouncil.org/aws/CWPA/asset_manager/get_file/350201?ver=7548.

Cox, Anicca. 2023. "(Re)viewing Faculty Observation and Evaluation Beyond the 'Means Well' Paradigm." In *Institutional Ethnography as Writing Studies Practice*, edited by Michelle LaFrance and Melissa Nicolas, 35–46. Fort Collins and Boulder: WAC Clearinghouse and University Press of Colorado.

Cox, Michelle, Jeffrey Galin, and Dan Melzer. 2018. "Building Sustainable WAC Programs: A Whole Systems Approach." *WAC Journal* 29: 64–87.

Craig, Collin Lamont, and Staci M. Perryman-Clark. 2016. "Troubling the Boundaries Revisited: Moving towards Change as Things Stay the Same." *WPA: Writing Program Administration* 39 (2): 20–27.

Craig, Sherri. 2016. "A Story-less Generation: Emergent WPAs of Color and the Loss of Identity through Absent Narratives." *WPA: Writing Program Administration* 39 (2): 16–20.

currie, sarah madoka, and Ada Hubrig. 2022. "Care Work through Course Design: Shifting the Labor of Resilience." *Composition Studies* 50 (2): 132–153.

Danielewicz, Jane, and Peter Elbow. 2009. "A Unilateral Grading Contract to Improve Learning and Teaching." *College Composition and Communication* 61 (2): 244–268.

Davies, Laura J. 2013. "Taking the Long View: Investigating the History of a Writing Program's Teacher Evaluation System." *WPA: Writing Program Administration* 37 (1): 81–111.

Davies, Laura J. 2017. "Grief and the New WPA." *WPA: Writing Program Administration* 40 (2): 40–51.

Davila, Bethany. 2016. "The Inevitability of 'Standard' English: Discursive Constructions of Standard Language Ideologies." *Written Communication* 33 (2): 127–148.

Davila, Bethany. 2017. "Standard English and Colorblindness in Composition Studies: Rhetorical Constructions of Racial and Linguistic Neutrality." *WPA: Writing Program Administration* 40 (2): 154–173.

Dean, Ann C. 2014. "Understanding Why Linked Courses Can Succeed with Students but Fail with Institutions." *WPA: Writing Program Administration* 38 (1): 65–87.

de Mueller, Genevieve Garcia. 2016. "WPA and the New Civil Rights Movement." *WPA: Writing Program Administration* 39 (2): 36–41.

de Mueller, Genevieve Garcia, and Ana Cortes Lagos. 2023. "Building an Antiracist WAC Program." In *Making Administrative Work Visible: Data-Driven Advocacy for Understanding the Labor of Writing Program Administration*, edited by Leigh Graziano, Kay Halasek, Remi Hudgins, Susan Miller-Cochran, Frank Napolitano, and Natalie Szymanski, 253–263. Logan: Utah State University Press.

de Mueller, Genevieve Garcia, and Iris Ruiz. 2017. "Race, Silence, and Writing Program Administration: A Qualitative Study of US College Writing Programs." *WPA: Writing Program Administration* 40 (2): 19–39.

Del Principe, Annie. 2020. "Cultivating a Sustainable TYC Writing Program: Collaboration, Disciplinarity, and Faculty Governance." *WPA: Writing Program Administration* 43 (3): 54–72.

Del Principe, Annie, and Jacqueline Brady. 2018. "Academic Freedom and the Idea of a Writing Program." *Teaching English in the Two-Year College* 45 (4): 351–360.

Dew, Debra Frank. 2004. "Conclusion: Ethical Options for Disciplinary Progress on the Issue of jWPA Appointments." In *Untenured Faculty as Writing Program Administrators: Institutional Practices and Politics*, edited by Debra Frank Dew and Alice Horning, 279–292. West Lafayette, IN: Parlor Press.

Dibrell, Denae, Andrew Hollinger, and Maggie Shelledy. 2023. "Fugitive Administrative Rhetorics." *WPA: Writing Program Administration* 47 (1): 148–162.

Ding, Huiling. 2019. "Development of Technical Communication in China: Program Building and Field Convergence." *Technical Communication Quarterly* 28 (3): 223–237.

Dippre, Ryan J. 2021. "Visualizing the Role of Small, Stubborn Facts: Changing Stories of Writers and Writing." In *Radiant Figures: Visual Rhetorics in Everyday Administrative Contexts*, edited by Rachel Gramer, Logan Bearden, and Derek Mueller. Logan: Computers and Composition Digital Press / Utah State University Press.

Dippre, Ryan J. 2023a. "Grounding WPA Work: A Phenomenology of Program Development as a Liminal WPA." In *Toward More Sustainable Metaphors of Writing Program*

Administration, edited by Lydia Wilkes, Lilian Mina, and Patti Poblete, 66–80. Logan: Utah State University Press.

Dippre, Ryan J. 2023b. "Trading Time: Communicating Grand Strategy to Administration through Hour-Tracking." In *Making Administrative Work Visible: Data-Driven Advocacy for Understanding the Labor of Writing Program Administration*, edited by Leigh Graziano, Kay Halasek, Remi Hudgins, Susan Miller-Cochran, Frank Napolitano, and Natalie Szymanski, 109–120. Logan: Utah State University Press.

Dorfeld, Natalie, ed. 2022. *The Invisible Professor: The Precarious Lives of the New Faculty Majority*. Fort Collins and Boulder: WAC Clearinghouse and University Press of Colorado.

Downs, Doug, and Elizabeth Wardle, eds. 2022. *Writing about Writing*, 5th ed. New York: Bedford/St. Martin's.

Dryer, Dylan, and Irvin Peckham. 2014. "Social Contexts of Writing Assessment: Toward an Ecological Construct of the Rater." *WPA: Writing Program Administration* 38 (1): 12–41.

Elder, Cristyn L. 2023. "From a Faculty Standpoint: Assessing with IE a Sustainable Commitment to WAC at a Minority-Serving Institution." In *Institutional Ethnography as Writing Studies Practice*, edited by Michelle LaFrance and Melissa Nicolas, 113–128. Fort Collins and Boulder: WAC Clearinghouse and University Press of Colorado.

Elder, Christyn L., and Bethany Davila. 2019. "Responding to Bullying in the WPA Workplace." *WPA: Writing Program Administration* 43 (1): 73–94.

Estrem, Heidi, Dawn Shepherd, and Lloyd Duncan. 2014. "Relentless Engagement with State Education Policy Reform: Collaborating to Change the Writing Placement Conversation." *WPA: Writing Program Administration* 38 (1): 88–128.

Eubanks, David, and Sarah Vanovac. 2020. "Divergent Writer Development in College." *Journal of Writing Analytics* 4 (1): 15–54.

Farris, Christine. 2021. "Reclaiming English's Disciplinary Responsibility in the Transition from High School to College." In *Improving Outcomes: Disciplinary Writing, Local Assessment, and the Aim of Fairness*, edited by Diane Kelly-Riley and Norbert Elliot, 121–132. New York: Modern Language Association.

Faye, Sarah, Erika I-Tremblay, Dan Melzer, D. J. Quinn, and Lisa Sperber. 2023. "The Adoption of Contract Grading in a University Writing Program: Navigating Disruptions to Assessment Ecologies." *WPA: Writing Program Administration* 46 (2): 62–84.

Fedukovich, Casie. 2013. "WPA as Tempered Radical: Lessons from Occupy Wall Street." *WPA: Writing Program Administration* 37 (1): 112–133.

Fedukovich, Casie, and Sue Doe. 2018. "Beyond Management: The Potential for Writing Program Leadership during Turbulent Times." *Reflections* 18 (2): 87–115.

Fedukovich, Casie, and Tracy Ann Morse. 2017. "Failures to Accommodate: GTA Preparation as a Site for a Transformative Culture of Access." *WPA: Writing Program Administration* 40 (3): 39–60.

Ferris, Dana, and John Hedgcock. 2013. *Teaching L2 Composition: Purpose, Process, and Practice*. New York: Routledge.

Finders, Margaret J., and Shirley K. Rose. 1998. "Learning from Experience: Using Situated Performances in Writing Teacher Development." *WPA: Writing Program Administration* 22 (1–2): 33–52.

Fodrey, Crystal N., Meg Mikovits, Chris Hassay, and Erica Yozell. 2019. "Activity Theory as Tool for WAC Program Development: Organizing First-Year Writing and Writing-Enriched Curriculum Systems." *Composition Forum* 42. https://compositionforum.org/issue/42/moravian.php.

Foley-Schramm, Ashton, Bridget Fullerton, Eileen M. James, and Jenna Morton-Aiken. 2018. "Preparing Graduate Students for the Field: A Graduate Student Praxis Heuristic for WPA Professionalization and Institutional Politics." *WPA: Writing Program Administration* 41 (2): 89–103.

Frankl, Viktor E. 2020. *Yes to Life: in Spite of Everything*. New York: Beacon.

Franklin, Joseph. 2021. "Transnational Writing Program Administration: Mobility, Entanglement, Work." PhD dissertation, University of Louisville, Louisville, KY.

Fremo, Rebecca Taylor. 2007. "Redefining Our Rhetorical Situations: jWPAs in the Small College Contexts." In *Untenured Faculty as Writing Program Administrators: Institutional Practices and Politics*, edited by Debra Frank Dew and Alice Horning, 191–218. West Lafayette, IN: Parlor Press.

Friedman, Sandie, and Robert Miller. 2018. "'Give All Thoughts a Chance': Writing about Writing and the ACRL Framework for Information Literacy." *WPA: Writing Program Administration* 42 (1): 72–88.

Garfinkel, Harold. 1967. *Studies in Ethnomethodology*. Malden, MA: Blackwell.

Garfinkel, Harold. 2002. *Ethnomethodology's Program: Working out Durkheim's Aphorism*. New York: Rowman and Littlefield.

Garfinkel, Harold. 2019. *Parsons' Primer*, edited by Anne Warfield Rawls. London: J. B. Metzler.

Garrett, Nathan, Matthew Bridgewater, and Bruce Feinstein. 2017. "How Student Performance in First-Year Composition Predicts Retention and Overall Student Success." In *Retention, Persistence, and Writing Programs*, edited by Todd Ruecker, Dawn Shepherd, Heidi Estrem, and Beth Brunk-Chavez, 93–113. Logan: Utah State University Press.

George, Barbara, and Ana Marie Wetzl. 2020. "Addressing Erasure: Networking Language Justice Advocacy for Multilingual Students in the Rustbelt." *Composition Forum* 44. https://compositionforum.org/issue/44/addressing-erasure.php.

Ghimire, Asmita, and Elizabethada Wright. 2021. "FYC's Unrealized NNEST Egg: Why Non-Native English Speaking Teachers Belong in the First-Year Composition Classroom." *Academic Labor* 5: 88–106.

Gindlesparger, Kathryn Johnson. 2020. "Trust on Display: The Epideictic Potential of Institutional Governance." *College English* 83 (2): 127–146.

Giordano, Joanne, Holly Hassel, Jennifer Heinert, and Cassandra Phillips. 2017. "The Imperative of Pedagogical and Professional Development to Support the Retention of Underprepared Students at Open-Access Institutions." In *Retention, Persistence, and Writing Programs*, edited by Todd Ruecker, Dawn Shepherd, Heidi Estrem, and Beth Brunk-Chavez, 74–92. Logan: Utah State University Press.

Gladstein, Jill M., and Dara Rossman Regaignon. 2012. *Writing Program Administration at Small Liberal Arts Colleges*. West Lafayette, IN: Parlor Press.

Glaser, Barney G. 1992. *Emergence vs. Forcing: The Basics of Grounded Theory Analysis*. Thousand Oaks, CA: Sociology Press.

Glaser, Barney G., and Anselm L. Strauss. 1967. *Discovery of Grounded Theory: Strategies for Qualitative Research*. Piscataway, NJ: Transaction.

Glotfelter, Angela, Ann Updike, and Elizabeth Wardle. 2020. "'Something Invisible . . . Has Been Made Visible for Me': An Expertise-Based WAC Seminar Model Grounded in Theory and (Cross)Disciplinary Dialogue." In *Diverse Approaches to Teaching, Learning, and Writing across the Curriculum: IWAC at 25*, edited by Lesley Bartlett, Sandra L. Tarabochia, Andrea R. Olinger, and Margaret J. Marshall, 167–192. Fort Collins, CO: WAC Clearinghouse.

Gomes, Matthew, and Wenjuan Ma. 2019. "Student Expectation Auditing and Mapping: A Method for Eliciting Student Input in Writing Program Assessment." *Writing Program Administration* 43 (1): 111–139.

Gonzales, Laura, and Janine Butler. 2020. "Walking toward Social Justice through Multilingualism, Multimodality, and Accessibility in Writing Classrooms." *Composition Forum* 44. https://compositionforum.org/issue/44/multilingualism.php.

Graham, Margaret Baker, Elizabeth Birmingham, and Zachry Mark. 1997. "Reinventing First-Year Composition at the First Land-Grant University: A Cautionary Tale." *WPA: Writing Program Administration* 21 (1): 19–30.

Graham, Steve, and Dolores Perin. 2007. "A Meta-Analysis of Writing Instruction for Adolescent Students." *Journal of Educational Psychology* 99 (3): 445–476.

Graphenreed, Tieanna, and Mya Poe. 2022. "Antiracist Genre Systems: Creating Nonviolent Writing Classroom Spaces." *Composition Studies* 50 (2): 53–76.

Grayson, Mara Lee. 2023. "Working within the Rhetorical Constraints: Renovation and Resistance in a First-Year Writing Program." In *Systems Shift: Creating and Navigating Change in Rhetoric and Composition Administration*, edited by Genesea M. Carter and Aurora Matzke, 165–187. Fort Collins and Boulder: WAC Clearinghouse and University Press of Colorado.

Graziano, Leigh, Kay Halasek, Susan Miller-Cochran, Frank Napolitano, and Natalie Szymanski. 2020. "A Return to Portland: Making Work Visible through the Ecologies of Writing Program Administration." *WPA: Writing Program Administration* 43 (2): 131–151.

Graziano, Leigh, Kay Halasek, Remi Hudgins, Susan Miller-Cochran, Frank Napolitano, and Natalie Szymanski. 2023a. "Introduction: Making Work Visible Work through Data-Informed Advocacy." In *Making Administrative Work Visible: Data-Driven Advocacy for Understanding the Labor of Writing Program Administration*, edited by Leigh Graziano, Kay Halasek, Remi Hudgins, Susan Miller-Cochran, Frank Napolitano, and Natalie Szymanski, 3–23. Logan: Utah State University Press.

Graziano, Leigh, Kay Halasek, Remi Hudgins, Susan Miller-Cochran, Frank Napolitano, and Natalie Szymanski, eds. 2023b. *Making Administrative Work Visible: Data-Driven Advocacy for Understanding the Labor of Writing Program Administration*. Logan: Utah State University Press.

Greer, Murphy, and Troy Mikanovich. 2023. "Labor and Loneliness of the Multilingual WPA." In *Making Administrative Work Visible: Data-Driven Advocacy for Understanding the Labor of Writing Program Administration*, edited by Leigh Graziano, Kay Halasek, Remi Hudgins, Susan Miller-Cochran, Frank Napolitano, and Natalie Szymanski, 203–216. Logan: Utah State University Press.

Grijalva, Regina McManigell. 2016. "Sustaining Balance: Writing Program Administration and the Mentorship of Minority College Students." *WPA: Writing Program Administration* 39 (2): 31–35.

Grouling, Jennifer. 2022. *Adapting VALUEs: Tracing the Life of a Rubric through Institutional Ethnography*. Fort Collins and Boulder: WAC Clearinghouse and University Press of Colorado.

Gunner, Jeanne. 1999. "Identity and Location: A Study of WPA Models, Memberships, and Agendas." *WPA: Writing Program Administration* 22 (3): 31–54.

Gunter, Kim. 2023. "I'm Just Playin': Directing Writing Programs as Improv." In *Toward More Sustainable Metaphors of Writing Program Administration*, edited by Lydia Wilkes, Lilian Mina, and Patti Poblete, 215–234. Logan: Utah State University Press.

Harris, Sarah E. 2017. "The *Kairotic* Classroom: Retention Discourse and Supplemental Instruction in the First Year." In *Retention, Persistence, and Writing Programs*, edited by Todd Ruecker, Dawn Shepherd, Heidi Estrem, and Beth Brunk-Chavez, 204–218. Logan: Utah State University Press.

Haswell, Richard, and Min-Zhan Lu, eds. 2000. *Comp Tales: An Introduction to College Composition through Its Stories*. London: Longman.

Hattie, John. 2009. *Visible Learning: A Synthesis of Over 800 Meta-Analyses Relating to Achievement*. London: Routledge.

Heckathorn, Amy. 2004. "Moving toward a Group Identity: WPA Professionalization from the 1940s to the 1970s." In *Historical Studies of Writing Program Administration: Individuals, Communities, and the Formation of a Discipline*, edited by Barbara L'Eplattenier and Lisa Mastrangelo, 191–220. West Lafayette, IN: Parlor Press.

Heckathorn, Amy. 2019. "The Professional Is Personal: Institutional Bullying and the WPA." In *Defining, Locating, and Addressing Bullying in the WPA Workplace*, edited by Chris L. Elder and Bethany Davila, 151–171. Logan: Utah State University Press.

Hillin, Sara. 2017. "We Are All Needed: Feminist Rhetorical Strategies for Building Trust among Colleagues." In *Surviving Sexism in Academia*, edited by Kirsti Cole and Holly Hassel, 287–295. New York: Routledge.

Hillocks, George. 1986. *Research on Written Composition*. Urbana, IL: National Council of Teachers of English Books.

Hillocks, George. 2009. "A Response to Peter Smagorinsky: Some Practices and Approaches Are Clearly Better than Others and We Had Better Not Ignore the Differences." *English Journal* 98 (6): 23–29.

Hitt, Allison Harper. 2023. *Rhetorics of Overcoming*. Logan: Utah State University Press.

Holmes, Ashley J., and Christine Busser. 2017. "Beyond Coordination: Building Collaborative Partnerships to Support Institutional-Level Retention Initiatives in Writing Programs." In *Retention, Persistence, and Writing Programs*, edited by Todd Ruecker,

Dawn Shepherd, Heidi Estrem, and Beth Brunk-Chavez, 38–55. Logan: Utah State University Press.

Horning, Alice. 2007. "The Definitive Article on Class Size." *WPA: Writing Program Administration* 31 (1–2): 11–34.

Huot, Brian. 2003. *Rearticulating Writing Assessment for Teaching and Learning*. Logan: Utah State University Press.

Inoue, Asao B. 2015. *Antiracist Writing Assessment Ecologies: Teaching and Assessing Writing for a Socially Just Future*. Fort Collins and Boulder: WAC Clearinghouse and University Press of Colorado.

Inoue, Asao B. 2016. "Friday Plenary Address: Racism in Writing Programs and the CWPA." *WPA: Writing Program Administration* 40 (1): 134–155.

Inoue, Asao B. 2019. *Labor-Based Grading Contracts: Building Equity and Inclusion in the Compassionate Writing Classroom*. Fort Collins and Boulder: WAC Clearinghouse and University Press of Colorado.

Inoue, Asao B. 2021. "Why I Left the CWPA (Council of Writing Program Administrators)." *Asao B. Inoue's Infrequent Words*. April 18. https://asaobinoue.blogspot.com/2021/04/why-i-left-cwpa-council-of-writing.html.

Isaacs, Emily. 2018. *Writing at the State U: Instruction and Administration at 106 Comprehensive Universities*. Logan: Utah State University Press.

Isabella, Marcy, and Heather McGovern. 2018. "Identity, Values, and Reflection: Shaping (and Being Shaped) through Assessment." *New Directions for Teaching and Learning* 155: 89–96.

Jack, Jordynn. 2022. "The Cognitive Vernacular as Normative Mandate in Habits of Mind." *College English* 84 (4): 335–355.

Jackson, N. Claire. 2021. "Writing Program Administration at Public Liberal Arts Colleges." PhD dissertation, University of Louisville, Louisville, KY.

Jaxon, Kim, Laura Sparks, and Chris Fosen. 2020. "Epic Learning in a 'Jumbo' Writing Course." *Composition Studies* 48 (2): 116–127.

Jensen, Darin, and Emily Suh. 2020. "Introducing Lived Interventions: Located Agency and Teacher-Scholar-Activism as Responses to Neoliberalism." *Basic Writing e-Journal* 16 (1): 1–11.

Johnston, Emily R. 2023. "Negotiating Dominance in Writing Program Administration: A Case Study." In *Systems Shift: Creating and Navigating Change in Rhetoric and Composition Administration*, edited by Genesea M. Carter and Aurora Matzke, 189–202. Fort Collins and Boulder: WAC Clearinghouse and University Press of Colorado.

Jones, Natasha, Gerald Savage, and Han Yu. 2014. "Tracking Our Progress." *Programmatic Perspectives* 6 (1): 132–152.

Kahn, Seth. 2017. "The Problem of Speaking for Adjuncts." In *Contingency, Exploitation, and Solidarity: Labor and Action in English Composition*, edited by Seth Kahn, William B. Lalicker, and Amy Lynch-Biniek, 259–270. Fort Collins and Boulder: WAC Clearinghouse and University Press of Colorado.

Kinney, Kelly. 2009. "Fellowship for the Ring: A Defense of Critical Administration in the Corporate University." *WPA: Writing Program Administration* 32 (3): 37–48.

Konrad, Annika M. 2021. "Access Fatigue: The Rhetorical Work of Disability in Everyday Life." *College English* 83 (3): 179–199.

Kopelson, Karen. 2013. "Queering the Writing Program: Why Now? How? And Other Contentious Questions." *WPA: Writing Program Administration* 37 (1): 199–213.

Kynard, Carmen. 2022. "Fakers and Takers: Disrespect, Crisis, and Inherited Whiteness in Rhetoric-Composition Studies." *Composition Studies* 50 (3): 131–136.

Kynard, Carmen. 2023. "Administering While Black: Black Women's Labor in the Academy and the 'Position of the Unthought.'" In *Black Perspectives in Writing Program Administration*, edited by Staci Perryman-Clark and Collin Lamont Craig, 28–50. Urbana, IL: National Council of Teachers of English Books.

LaFrance, Michelle. 2016. "An Institutional Ethnography of Information Literacy Instruction: Key Terms, Local/Material Contexts, and Instructional Practice." *WPA: Writing Program Administration* 39 (2): 105–123.

LaFrance, Michelle. 2019. *Institutional Ethnography: A Theory of Practice for Writing Studies Researchers*. Logan: Utah State University Press.

LaFrance, Michelle. 2023. "Practice, Work, and Further Possibilities for IE." In *Institutional Ethnography as Writing Studies Practice*, edited by Michelle LaFrance and Melissa Nicolas, 17–31. Fort Collins and Boulder: WAC Clearinghouse and University Press of Colorado.

LaFrance, Michelle, and Anicca Cox. 2017. "Brutal(ist) Meditations: Space and Labor-Movement in a Writing Program." In *Contingency, Exploitation, and Solidarity: Labor and Action in English Composition*, edited by Seth Kahn, William B. Lalicker, and Amy Lynch-Biniek, 279–301. Fort Collins, CO: WAC Clearinghouse.

Lang, Susan M. 2016. "Taming Big Data through Agile Approaches to Instructor Training and Assessment: Managing Ongoing Professional Development in Large First-Year Writing Programs." *WPA: Writing Program Administration* 39 (2): 81–104.

Lehn, Jeanette. 2019. "A Renewed Critical Pedagogy: Rethinking Activism within Writing Program Administration." PhD dissertation, Florida State University, Tallahassee.

Leon, Kendall, and Tom Sura. 2013. "'We Don't Need Any More Brochures': Rethinking Deliverables in Service-Learning Curricula." *WPA: Writing Program Administration* 36 (2): 59–74.

Leverenz, Carrie S. 2016. "Redesigning Writing Outcomes." *WPA: Writing Program Administration* 40 (1): 33–49.

Liberman, Kenneth. 2007. *Husserl's Criticism of Reason: With Ethnomethodological Specifications*. Blue Ridge Summit, PA: Lexington Books.

Liberman, Kenneth. 2013. *More Studies in Ethnomethodology*. Albany: SUNY Press.

Liebman, Glenn. 1997. *Football Shorts: 1,001 of the Game's Funniest One-Liners*. Lincolnwood, IL: Contemporary Books.

Lindenmann, Erika. 1979. "Evaluating Writing Programs: What an Outside Evaluator Looks For." *WPA: Writing Program Administration* 3 (1): 17–24.

Livingston, Eric. 1987. *Making Sense of Ethnomethodology*. New York: Routledge.

Malenczyk, Rita, ed. 2013. *A Rhetoric for Writing Program Administrators*, second edition. Logan: Utah State University Press.

Malenczyk, Rita. 2016. "Opening Plenary Address: Locations of Administration; or, WPAs in Space." *WPA: Writing Program Administrators* 40 (1): 114–133.

Malenczyk, Rita. 2017. "Retention≠ PanoPticon: What WPAs Should Bring to the Table in Discussions of Student Success." In *Retention, Persistence, and Writing Programs*, edited by Todd Ruecker, Dawn Shepherd, Heidi Estrem, and Beth Brunk-Chavez, 21–37. Logan: Utah State University Press.

Maraj, Louis. 2022. "Unlike Conventional Form(s) Of: Beyond Reparative Antiracism." *Composition Studies* 50 (3): 40–58.

Martin, Caitlin A. 2021. "Facilitating Institutional Change through Writing-Related Faculty Development." PhD dissertation, Miami University of Ohio, Miami, OH.

McClure, Randall. 2008. "An Army of One: The Possibilities and Pitfalls of WPA Work for the Lone Compositionist." In *The Promise and Perils of Writing Program Administration*, edited by Theresa Enos and Shane Borrowman, 102–108. West Lafayette, IN: Parlor Press.

McCrary, Jennifer, and Ashely J. Holmes. 2022. "Toward Sustainable Writing Programs in the Quality Enhancement Plan Era." *College English* 85 (1): 37–63.

McGlaun, Sandee K. 2007. "Administering Writing Programs in the 'Betweens': A jWPA Narrative." In *Untenured Faculty as Writing Program Administrators: Institutional Practices and Politics*, edited by Debra Frank Dew and Alice Horning, 219–248. West Lafayette, IN: Parlor Press.

McLeod, Susan H. 2007. *Writing Program Administration*. West Lafayette, IN: Parlor Press.

McLeod, Susan H., David Stock, and Bradley T. Hughes, eds. 2017. *Two WPA Pioneers: Ednah Shepherd Thomas and Joyce Steward*. Fort Collins and Boulder: WAC Clearinghouse and University Press of Colorado.

McNabb, Richard. 2008. "Rocking the Boat: Asserting Authority and Change in a Writing Program." In *The Promise and Perils of Writing Program Administration*, edited by Theresa Enos and Shane Borrowman, 64–71. West Lafayette, IN: Parlor Press.

Messuri, Kristin, and Elizabeth A. Sharp. 2021. "Dedicating Time and Space for Women to Succeed in the Academy: A Case Analysis of a Women Faculty Writing Program at a Research 1 Institution." *WPA: Writing Program Administration* 45 (1): 50–70.

Miles, Libby. 2000. "Constructing Composition: Reproduction and WPA Agency in Textbook Publishing." *WPA: Writing Program Administration* 24 (1–2): 27–52.

Miller-Cochran, Susan. 2018. "Innovation through Intentional Administration: or, How to Lead a Writing Program without Losing Your Soul." *WPA: Writing Program Administration* 42 (1): 107–122.

Mills, Charles W. 1997. *The Racial Contract*. Ithaca, NY: Cornell University Press.

Moore, Cindy. 2018. "Mentoring WPAs for the Long Term: The Promise of Mindfulness." *WPA: Writing Program Administration* 42 (1): 89–106.

Morgan, Meg, Marsha Lee Baker, Wendy Sharer, and Tracy Ann Morse. 2020. "The Affiliate as Mentoring Network: The Lasting Work of the Carolinas WPA." *WPA: Writing Program Administration* 44 (1): 68–85.

Morton-Aiken, Jenna. 2023. "Flexible Framing, Open Spaces, and Adaptive Resources: A Networked Approach to Writing Program Administration." In *Systems Shift:*

Creating and Navigating Change in Rhetoric and Composition Administration, edited by Genesea M. Carter and Aurora Matzke, 321–344. Fort Collins and Boulder: WAC Clearinghouse and University Press of Colorado.

Moxley, Joseph M., and David Eubanks. 2016. "On Keeping Score: Instructors' vs. Students' Rubric Ratings of 46,689 Essays." *WPA: Writing Program Administration* 39 (2): 53–80.

Murphy, Susan Wolff, and Mark G. Hartlaub. 2017. "Enhancing Alliances and Joining Initiatives to Help Students: The Story of How We Created Developmental Learning Communities at Texas A&M University–Corpus Christi." In *Retention, Persistence, and Writing Programs*, edited by Todd Ruecker, Dawn Shepherd, Heidi Estrem, and Beth Brunk-Chavez, 219–236. Logan: Utah State University Press.

Nathaniel, Alvita. 2011. "An Integrated Philosophical Framework That Fits Grounded Theory." In *Grounded Theory: The Philosophy, Method, and Work of Barney Glaser*, edited by Vivian B. Martin and Astrid Gynnild, 187–200. Boca Raton: BrownWalker.

National Census of Writing. 2017. University of San Diego. https://writingcensus.ucsd.edu/.

Nicolas, Melissa. 2017. "Ma(r)king a Difference: Challenging Ableist Assumptions in Writing Program Policies." *WPA: Writing Program Administration* 40 (3): 10–22.

Nicolay, Theresa Freda. 2002. "Placement and Instruction in Context: Situating Writing within a First-Year Program." *WPA: Writing Program Administration* 25 (3): 61–78.

Norgaard, Rolf. 2017. "The Uncertain Future of Past Success: Memory, Narrative, and the Dynamics of Institutional Change." In *Contingency, Exploitation, and Solidarity: Labor and Action in English Composition*, edited by Seth Kahn, William B. Lalicker, and Amy Lynch-Biniek, 133–149. Fort Collins and Boulder: WAC Clearinghouse and University Press of Colorado.

Norris, Christine. 2008. "Exploitation, Opportunity, and Writing Program Administration." In *The Promise and Perils of Writing Program Administration*, edited by Theresa Enos and Shane Borrowman, 250–254. West Lafayette, IN: Parlor Press.

O'Meara, Katherine Daily. 2023. "Learning, Representing, and Endorsing the Landscape: WPA as Cartographer." In *Toward More Sustainable Metaphors of Writing Program Administration*, edited by Lydia Wilkes, Lilian Mina, and Patti Poblete, 97–122. Logan: Utah State University Press.

O'Neill, Erin. 2008. "Irreconcilable Differences: One Former WPD's Cautionary Tale." In *The Promise and Perils of Writing Program Administration*, edited by Theresa Enos and Shane Borrowman, 72–78. West Lafayette, IN: Parlor Press.

Odasso, A. J. 2022. "Everything Is Connected: A Review of Institutional Ethnography." *WPA: Writing Program Administration* 46 (1): 137–141.

Oddo, John, and Jamie Parmelee. 2008. "Competing Interpretations of 'Textual Objects' in an Activity System: A Study of the Requirements Document in the _Writing Program." *WPA: Writing Program Administration* 31 (3): 63–88.

Olds, Barbara. 1990. "Does a Writing Program Make a Difference? A Ten-Year Comparison of Faculty Attitudes about Writing." *WPA: Writing Program Administration* 14 (1–2): 27–40.

Olejnik, Mandy. 2019. "Changing Conceptions of Writing: An Interview with Elizabeth Wardle." *WPA: Writing Program Administration* 42 (3): 59–64.

Osorio, Ruth. 2021. "A Disability-as-Insight Approach to Multimodal Assessment." In *Improving Outcomes: Disciplinary Writing, Local Assessment, and the Aim of Fairness*, edited by Diane Kelly-Riley and Norbert Elliot, 26–36. New York: Modern Language Association.

Osorio, Ruth, Allison Hutchison, Sarah Primeau, Molly E. Ubbesen, and Alexander Champoux-Crowley. 2021. "The Laborious Reality vs. the Imagined Ideal of Graduate Student Instructors of Writing." *WPA: Writing Program Administration* 45 (1): 131–152.

Oswal, Sushil K., and Lisa Meloncon. 2017. "Saying No to the Checklist: Shifting from an Ideology of Normalcy to an Ideology of Inclusion in Online Writing Instruction." *WPA: Writing Program Administration* 40 (3): 61–77.

Overstreet, Matthew. 2019. "First Year Writing as *the* Critical Thinking Course: An Interactionist Approach." *Double Helix* 7: 2–12.

Parsons, Talcott. 1937. *The Structure of Social Action*. New York: Free Press.

Patton, Martha D., and Jo Ann Vogt. 2007. "The Center Will Not Hold: Redefining Professionalism in the Academy." In *Untenured Faculty as Writing Program Administrators: Institutional Practices and Politics*, edited by Debra Frank Dew and Alice Horning, 137–152. West Lafayette, IN: Parlor Press.

Perryman-Clark, Staci, and Collin Lamont Craig. 2023. "Introduction: Black Matters: Writing Program Administration in Twenty-First–Century Higher Education." In *Black Perspectives in Writing Program Administration*, edited by Staci Perryman-Clark and Collin Lamont Craig, 1–27. Urbana, IL: National Council of Teachers of English Books.

Phelps, Louise Wetherbee, Sheila Carter-Tod, Jessie L. Moore, Patti Poblete, Casey Reid, and Sarah Elizabeth Snyder. 2019. "Sustainable Becomings: Women's Career Trajectories in Writing Program Administration." *WPA: Writing Program Administration* 43 (1): 12–32.

Phillips, Talinn, Paul Shovlin, and Megan L. Titus. 2016. "(Re)identifying the gWPA Experience." *WPA: Writing Program Administration* 40 (1): 67–89.

Pinkert, Laurie A., and Lauren M. Bowen. 2021. "Disciplinary Lifecycling: A Generative Framework for Career Trajectories in Rhetoric, Composition, and Writing Studies." *Composition Studies* 49 (1): 34–52.

Pinkert, Laurie A., and Kristen R. Moore. 2021. "Programmatic Mapping as a Problem-Solving Tool for WPAs." *WPA: Writing Program Administration* 44 (2): 58–80.

Poblete, Patti. 2021. "How to Respond When You're BIPOC and Your Organization Is Called Out for Racism." *WPA: Writing Program Administration* 44 (3): 181–184.

Poe, Mya, and John A. Cogan Jr. 2016. "Civil Rights and Writing Assessment: Using the Disparate Impact Approach as a Fairness Methodology to Evaluate Social Impact." *Journal of Writing Assessment* 9 (1): 1–24.

Potts, Maureen, and David Schwalm. 1983. "A Training Program for Teaching Assistants in Freshman English." *WPA: Writing Program Administration* 7 (1–2): 47–54.

Powell, Pegeen Reichert. 2017. "Absolute Hospitality in the Writing Program." In *Retention, Persistence, and Writing Programs*, edited by Todd Ruecker, Dawn Shepherd, Heidi Estrem, and Beth Brunk-Chavez, 135–150. Logan: Utah State University Press.

Ranieri, Paul, and Jackie Grutsch McKinney. 2004. "Fitness for the Occasion: How Context Matters for jWPAs." In *Untenured Faculty as Writing Program Administrators: Institutional Practices and Politics*, edited by Debra Frank Dew and Alice Horning, 249–278. West Lafayette, IN: Parlor Press.

Rawls, Anne Warfield, and Waverly Duck. 2020. *Tacit Racism*. Chicago: University of Chicago Press.

Ray, Brian, Jacob Babb, and Courtney Adams Wooten. 2018. "Rethinking SETs: Retuning Student Evaluations of Teaching for Student Agency." *Composition Studies* 46 (1): 34–56.

Reed, Meredith. 2020. "Enacting Bricolage: Theorizing the Teaching Practices of Graduate Writing Instructors." *WPA: Writing Program Administration* 44 (1): 107–128.

Reese, Stephen D. 2001. "Prologue: Framing Public Life, a Bridging Model for Media Research." In *Framing Public Life Perspectives on Media and Our Understanding of the Social World*, edited by Stephen D. Reese, Oscar H. Gandy, and August E. Grant, 7–31. Mahwah, NJ: Lawrence Erlbaum.

Reid, E. Shelley. 2018. "Beyond Satisfaction: Assessing the Goals and Impacts of Faculty Development." *WPA: Writing Program Administration* 41 (2): 122–135.

Restaino, Jessica. 2012. *First Semester: Graduate Students, Teaching Writing, and the Challenge of Middle Ground*. Carbondale: Southern Illinois University Press.

Ritter, Kelly. 2018. "Making (Collective) Memory Public: WPA Histories in Dialogue." *WPA: Writing Program Administration* 41 (2): 35–64.

Rose, Jeanne Marie. 2005. "Coming of Age as a WPA: From Personal and to Personnel." *WPA: Writing Program Administration* 28 (3): 73–88.

Rose, Shirley K., and Joyce Walker. 2014. "Flat and Fertile: A Conversation about the Writing Program at Illinois State University." *WPA: Writing Program Administration* 37 (2): 141–156.

Rudy, Jill Terry. 2004. "Building a Career by Directing Composition: Harvard, Professionalism, and Sith Thompson at Indiana University." In *Historical Studies of Writing Program Administration: Individuals, Communities, and the Formation of a Discipline*, edited by Barbara L'Eplattenier and Lisa Mastrangelo, 71–88. West Lafayette, IN: Parlor Press.

Rutz, Carol. 2006. "Recovering the Conversation: A Response to 'Responding to Student Writing' via 'Across the Drafts.'" *College Composition and Communication* 58 (2): 257–262.

Ryan, Kathleen J. 2012. "Thinking Ecologically: Rhetorical Ecological Feminist Agency and Writing Program Administration." *WPA: Writing Program Administration* 36 (1): 74–94.

Rylander, Jonathan J., and Travis Webster. 2020. "Embracing the 'Always-Already': Toward Queer Assemblages for Writing across the Curriculum Administration." *College Composition and Communication* 72 (2): 198–223.

Saldana, Johnny. 2009. *The Coding Manual for Qualitative Researchers*. Thousand Oaks, CA: Sage.

Salem, Lori, and Peter Jones. 2010. "Undaunted, Self-Critical, and Resentful: Investigating Faculty Attitudes toward Teaching Writing in a Large University Writing-Intensive Course Program." *WPA: Writing Program Administration* 34 (1): 60–83.

Samuels, Robert. 2023. *A Working Model for Contingent Faculty*. Fort Collins, CO: WAC Clearinghouse.

Sanchez, Fernando. 2013. "Creating Accessible Spaces for ESL Students Online." *WPA: Writing Program Administration* 37 (1): 161–185.

Sanchez, James Chase, and Tyler S. Branson. 2016. "The Role of Composition Programs in De-normalizing Whiteness in the University: Programmatic Approaches to Anti-Racist Pedagogies." *WPA: Writing Program Administration* 39 (2): 47–53.

Sanchez, Raul. 2015. "Theory Building for Writing Studies." *WPA: Writing Program Administration* 39 (1): 141–157.

Santana, Christina, Shirley K. Rose, and Robert LaBarge. 2018. "A Hybrid Mega-Course with Optional Studio: Responding Responsibly to an Administrative Mandate." In *The Writing Studio Sampler: Stories about Change*, edited by Mark Sutton and Sally Chandler, 97–114. Fort Collins and Boulder: WAC Clearinghouse and University Press of Colorado.

Scafe, Robert, and Michele Eodice. 2021. "Finding Writing Where It Lives: Departmental Relationships and Relationships with Departments." In *Writing-Enriched Curricula: Models of Faculty-Driven and Departmental Transformation*, edited by Chris Anson and Pamela Flash, 235–251. Fort Collins and Boulder: WAC Clearinghouse and University Press of Colorado.

Schell, Eileen. 1998. "Who's the Boss: The Possibilities and Pitfalls of Collaborative Administration for Untenured WPAs." *WPA: Writing Program Administration* 21 (2–3): 65–80.

Schoen, Megan. 2019. "Your Mission, Should You Choose to Accept It: A Survey on Writing Programs and Institutional Mission." *WPA: Writing Program Administration* 42 (2): 37–57.

Scott, Marc. 2017. "Big Data and Writing Program Retention Assessment: What We Need to Know." In *Retention, Persistence, and Writing Programs*, edited by Todd Ruecker, Dawn Shepherd, Heidi Estrem, and Beth Brunk-Chavez, 56–73. Logan: Utah State University Press.

Serfling, Nathan A. 2019. "Crafting a Pedagogical Identity: A Multiple-Method Examination of an English Department's Writing Pedagogy." PhD dissertation, Old Dominion University, Norfolk, VA.

Shea, Kelly A. 2017. "Kindness in the Writing Classroom: Accommodations for All Students." *WPA: Writing Program Administration* 40 (3): 78–93.

Sicari, Anne. 2020. "Complaint as 'Sticky Data' for the Woman WPA: The Intellectual Work of a WPA's Emotional and Embodied Labor." *Journal of the Assembly for Expanded Perspectives on Learning* 25 (1): 99–117.

Smagorinsky, Peter. 2002. *Teaching English through Principled Practice*. Upper Saddle River, NJ: Merrill Prentice-Hall.

Smagorinsky, Peter. 2009. "EJ Extra: Is It Time to Abandon the Idea of 'Best Practices' in the Teaching of English?" *English Journal* 98 (6): 15–22.

Smith, Nicole Boudreau. 2017. "A Principled Revolution in the Teaching of Writing." *English Journal* 106 (5): 70–75.

Snyder, Sarah Elizabeth. 2017. "Retention Rates of Second Language Writers and Basic Writers: A Comparison within the Stretch Program Model." In *Retention, Persistence, and Writing Programs*, edited by Todd Ruecker, Dawn Shepherd, Heidi Estrem, and Beth Brunk-Chavez, 185–203. Logan: Utah State University Press.

Sommers, Nancy. 1982. "Responding to Student Writing." *College Composition and Communication* 33 (2): 148–156.

Spiegel, Cheri Lemieux, Darin Jensen, and Sara Z. Johnson. 2020. "Don't Call It a Comeback: Two-Year College WPA, Tactics, Collaboration, Flexibility, Sustainability." *WPA: Writing Program Administration* 43 (3): 7–19.

Stolley, Amy Ferdinand. 2015. "Narratives, Administrative Identity, and the Early Career WPA." *WPA: Writing Program Administration* 39 (1): 18–31.

Street, Nathaniel. 2020. "Affirming Difference: Inhabiting the WPA Otherwise." *Composition Studies* 48 (1): 53–70.

Tang, Jasmine Kar, and Noro Andriamanalina. 2016. "'Rhonda Left Early to Go to Black Lives Matter': Programmatic Support for Graduate Writers of Color." *WPA: Writing Program Administration* 39 (2): 10–15.

Tarr, Kathleen. 2021. "The Tone Police's Greatest Hits." *Composition Studies* 49 (2): 79–95.

Taylor, Leslie S. 2019. "Current-Traditional Rhetoric and the Hodges Harbrace Handbook: A Study in the Disconnect between Theory and Practice." PhD dissertation, Georgia State University, Athens.

Teagarden, Alexis. 2023. "Representing the Basement." In *Toward More Sustainable Metaphors of Writing Program Administration*, edited by Lydia Wilkes, Lilian Mina, and Patti Poblete, 145–156. Logan: Utah State University Press.

Teagarden, Alexis, and Michael Carlozzi. 2017. "Time Enough? Experimental Findings on Embedded Librarianship." *WPA: Writing Program Administration* 41 (1): 12–32.

Thaiss, Chris, Gerd Brauer, Paula Carlino, Lisa Ganobcsik-Williams, and Aparna Sinha. 2012. *Writing Programs Worldwide: Profiles of Academic Writing in Many Places*. Fort Collins and Boulder: WAC Clearinghouse and University Press of Colorado.

Townsend, Martha A. 2007. "Negotiating the Risks and Reaping the Rewards: Reflections and Advice from a Former jWPA." In *Untenured Faculty as Writing Program Administrators: Institutional Practices and Politics*, edited by Debra Frank Dew and Alice Horning, 72–96. West Lafayette, IN: Parlor Press.

Tremain, Lisa. 2023. "Heavy Lifting: How WPAs Broker Knowledge Transfer for Faculty." In *Making Administrative Work Visible: Data-Driven Advocacy for Understanding the Labor of Writing Program Administration*, edited by Leigh Graziano, Kay Halasek, Remi Hudgins, Susan Miller-Cochran, Frank Napolitano, and Natalie Szymanski, 240–252. Logan: Utah State University Press.

Vidali, Amy. 2015. "Disabling Writing Program Administration." *WPA: Writing Program Administration* 38 (2): 32–55.

Voss, Julia, and Kathryn Bruchmann. 2023. "'It's Complicated': Scheduling as an Intellectual, Networked Social Justice Issue for WPAs." In *Systems Shift: Creating and Navigating Change in Rhetoric and Composition Administration*, edited by Genesea M. Carter and Aurora Matzke, 293–320. Fort Collins and Boulder: WAC Clearinghouse and University Press of Colorado.

Welch, Nancy. 2018. "'Everyone Should Have a Plan': A Neoliberal Primer for Writing Program Directors." *WPA: Writing Program Administration* 41 (2): 104–112.

Wenger, Christy I. 2014. "Feminism, Mindfulness, and the Small University jWPA." *WPA: Writing Program Administration* 37 (2): 117–140.

Wenger, Christy I. 2023. "Approaching WPA Labor with *Ahimsa*: Mapping Emotional Geographies through Sustainable Leadership." In *Toward More Sustainable Metaphors of Writing Program Administration*, edited by Lydia Wilkes, Lilian Mina, and Patti Poblete, 123–144. Logan: Utah State University Press.

Wess, Holly. 2015. "Partnerships for College Readiness: A Qualitative Multi-Site Case Study of Secondary/Post-Secondary Instructors' Collaboration." PhD dissertation, Northeastern University, Boston, MA.

White, Edward M., Norbert Elliot, and Irvin Peckham. 2015. *Very Like a Whale: The Assessment of Writing Programs*. Logan: Utah State University Press.

Wible, Scott. 2023. "Forfeiting Privilege for the Cause of Social Justice: Listening to Black WPAs and WPAs of Color Define the Work of White Allyship." In *Black Perspectives in Writing Program Administration*, edited by Staci Perryman-Clark and Collin Lamont Craig, 74–100. Urbana, IL: National Council of Teachers of English Books.

Wilkes, Lydia. 2023. "From Putting Out Fires to Managing Fires: Lessons for WPAs from Indigenous Fire Managers." In *Toward More Sustainable Metaphors of Writing Program Administration*, edited by Lydia Wilkes, Lilian Mina, and Patti Poblete, 19–34. Logan: Utah State University Press.

Wilkes, Lydia, Lilian Mina, and Patti Poblete, eds. 2023. *Toward More Sustainable Metaphors of Writing Program Administration*. Logan: Utah State University Press.

Wittstock, Stacy. 2022. "Gatekeeping by Design: The Use of an Exit Exam as a 'Boss Text' in a Basic Writing Course." *Journal of Basic Writing* 41 (1–2): 40–75.

Wolfe, Joanna, Ryan Roderick, and Andrea Francioni Rooney. 2019. "Improving Instructor Ethos through Document Design." *Composition Studies* 47 (2): 146–166.

Wood, Shane Alden. 2018. "Intersections of Genre and Assessment: Systems, Uptakes, and Ideologies." PhD dissertation, University of Kansas, Lawrence.

Wood, Tara. 2021. "Writing Program Administration and the Title IX Controversy: Disability Theory, Agency, and Mandatory Reporting." *WPA: Writing Program Administration* 44 (2): 40–57.

Wooten, Courtney Adams, Jacob Babb, Kristi Murray Costello, Kate Navickas, and Laura Micciche, eds. 2020. *The Things We Carry: Strategies for Recognizing and Negotiating Emotional Labor in Writing Program Administration*. Logan: Utah State University Press.

Wooten, Courtney Adams, Brian Ray, and Jacob Babb. 2016. "WPAs Reading SETs: Toward an Ethical and Effective Use of Teaching Evaluations." *WPA: Writing Program Administration* 40 (1): 50–66.

Workman, Erin, Madeline Crozier, and Peter Vandenberg. 2023. "Writing Standpoint(s): Institution, Discourse, and Method." In *Institutional Ethnography as Writing Studies Practice*, edited by Michelle LaFrance and Melissa Nicolas, 81–96. Fort Collins and Boulder: WAC Clearinghouse and University Press of Colorado.

Yergeau, Melanie. 2016. "Saturday Plenary Address: Creating a Culture of Access in Writing Program Administration." *WPA: Writing Program Administration* 40 (1): 155–165.

Young, Vershawn Ashanti. 2023. "Foreword: A Forenote from an Angry Black Man: Blackness Should Always Be Center." In *Black Perspectives in Writing Program Administration*, edited by Staci Perryman-Clark and Collin Lamont Craig, vii–xiv. Urbana, IL: National Council of Teachers of English Books.

Zenger, Amy A. 2016. "Notes on Race in Transnational Writing Program Administration." *WPA: Writing Program Administration* 39 (2): 26–32.

Zhou, Quan. 2014. "'That Usability Course': What Technical Communication Programs Get Wrong about Usability and How to Fix It." *Communication Design Quarterly* 2 (3): 25–27.

Index

accommodations, 11, 58–59
account, 47–48, 54–57, 63–69, 87–88, 121–122, 146
accreditation, 69, 84, 106, 109
adjunct, 74–75, 88–92, 124–127, 144–145, 161
Adler-Kassner, Linda, 13–14, 23–24, 35, 63, 71, 84–87
Applebee, Arthur, 13–14
artifacts, 32, 40, 43–45, 49–51, 52–54
attendance, 96, 157–160, 163

Barbieri, Bob. *See* Coach B.
Bazerman, Charles, 180, 187
burnin' daylight, 31, 43, 186–187
Buzbee, Heather, 8

clashes of principle, 119–122, 131–132
Coach B., 3–4, 27, 31, 79, 135–136, 180, 187
codebook, 51
contingent. *See* adjunct
compensation, 159, 163, 170, 174–176
constituents, 19, 49, 107–109, 121–122, 150–151, 162
context, 14–15, 22–24, 67–69, 89, 124, 130–131, 152–153
contract, 35–40, 48, 63

contradiction, 40, 49, 64, 72–74
cost, 91–92, 94, 103, 115, 162–163

direct report, 149–151
disciplinary knowledge, 110, 113, 115–116, 122, 127, 131
Duck, Waverly, 37–38
DFW rates, 50, 57–58

equitable, 182, 187
ethnomethodology. 11, 34–35, 37, 50

facts, 9–12, 32–35, 38, 47–49, 53–54, 62–63
first-generation students, 69
Frankl, Viktor, 32–34, 183

Garfinkel, Harold, 34–36, 39, 55–56
Glaser and Strauss, 45, 49
grand strategies, 137, 139–140
grounded theory, 45, 49–51

Holtz, Lou, 8, 148

innovation, 20, 137, 143–144, 154–155, 157–160, 165–166
interaction, 34–38, 48–49, 182

interested parties, 70–74, 93–94, 108–109, 124–127, 149–151, 164–165
intersectional, interdependent framework, 38

labor, 69, 70, 95–96, 104–105, 174
labor-based grading contracts, 65–69
literal, 55–56
little picture, 19, 79–81
live the lives they want to live, 9, 181–183
long view, 81, 135–138

mapping, 59, 84, 87–88
Mills, Charles W., 37

Naming What We Know, 156, 160–161

open coding, 51–52
outcome, 65, 72–73, 160–161

perpetuating writing programs, 39
perspicuous sites, 39
Portfolio Assessment Rubric, 71, 74, 173
position statement, 110–112, 115, 127–130
positionality, 5–6, 23–25
principle, 13, 62–67, 184–185
principle-driven, 4–5, 177, 181
principled practice, 9, 12–18, 23–24, 67–71, 169–171
pulverizing artifacts, 49–51
purposeful, 154–155

racial contract, 35, 37–38
rationality, 27, 45, 48–49, 50, 59

Rawls, Anne Warfield, 37
recur, 52–53, 62–63, 102–103, 115, 144–146, 169
recruiting, 72–75, 93–94, 108–109, 124–127, 150–151, 164–165
render, 47–48, 55–57
recent and germinal research, 110–113, 127–131
resolution, 110–112, 115, 128–130
responsible, 4, 8, 32–35, 182–183, 185
results, 160–162

Saldana, Johnny, 51
scale, 5, 162–164
singular, 185–186
Smagorinsky, Peter, 13–14, 24
small, stubborn facts, 9–12, 175
social facts, 34–36, 55, 63, 186
spaced practice, 65–69
strategies, 14, 19, 85–87, 88–91, 106, 114–115
structural kindness, 147
student labor, 69–70, 104–105, 120
sustainable structures, 20, 168–169, 174–176
sustainable practices, 173–174

tactics, 14, 87, 88–93
telling stories, 69–72
textbook, 93, 114, 132, 156–157, 175

uncertainty, 72, 149, 186
unexpected, 45, 94–98, 141–142, 146, 149, 185

values, 13–18, 27–29, 63–71, 120–124, 141–143, 184–185

About the Author

Ryan J. Dippre is associate professor of English and the director of the College Composition program at the University of Maine, where he teaches undergraduate and graduate courses in writing and writing pedagogy. In addition to studying writing program administration, he also studies writing through the lifespan and the teaching of writing. He is the author of *Talk, Tools, and Texts: A Logic-in-Use for Studying Lifespan Literate Action Development* (WAC Clearinghouse, 2019) and the co-editor (with Talinn Phillips of Ohio University) of *Approaches to Lifespan Writing Research: Generating an Actionable Coherence* (WAC Clearinghouse, 2020). With Talinn Phillips, he serves as co-chair of the Writing through the Lifespan Collaboration (lifespanwriting.org) and co-editor of the Lifespan Writing Research book series at the WAC Clearinghouse (wac.colostate.edu/books/lwr). He lives in Maine with his wife and son.

www.ingramcontent.com/pod-product-compliance
Lightning Source LLC
Chambersburg PA
CBHW060600080526
44585CB00013B/634